C000092552

The Biblical Seminar

12

Series Editor
David E. Orton

NARRATIVE ART IN GENESIS

Also available in this series:

1. Anthropology and the Old Testament
   John W. Rogerson

2. The Israelite Woman
   Athalya Brenner

3. Kingship and the Psalms
   John H. Eaton

4. Colossians as Pseudepigraphy
   Mark Kiley

5. Ancient Israel
   Niels-Peter Lemche

6. Problems and Prospects of Old Testament Theology
   J. Høgenhaven

7. Judaism in Antiquity
   Benedikt Otzen

8. God in Strength
   Bruce D. Chilton

9. Essays on Old Testament History and Religion
   Albrecht Alt

10. Ruth
    Jack M. Sasson

11. Tradition and Theology in the Old Testament
    Douglas A. Knight (ed.)

Narrative Art in Genesis

Specimens of Stylistic and Structural Analysis

Second Edition

J. P. Fokkelman

Wipf & Stock
PUBLISHERS
Eugene, Oregon

Wipf and Stock Publishers
199 West 8th Avenue, Suite 3
Eugene, Oregon 97401

Narrative Art in Genesis
Specimens of Stylistic and Structural Analysis
By Fokkelman, J.P.
Copyright©1991 by Fokkelman, J.P.
ISBN: 1-59244-691-4
Publication date 5/14/2004
Previously published by JSOT Press, 1991

CONTENTS

PREFACE TO THE SECOND EDITION

This book was written twenty years ago, and the research that it relies on is therefore work from the sixties. At the time, I was traveling a lonely path of discovery. There seemed to be no one around who was willing to believe that a synchronic reading made sense, or prepared to expend a sustained effort on exploring new paradigms. When I came forward to defend my book in front of my academic community, the reception it got from my university and the biblical scholars of my country was hesitant and evasive, if not decidedly hostile. Most of my colleagues were too deeply obsessed by the diachronic issues of historical critical scholarship and caught in the intentional fallacy or the referential illusion to be able to discern and sympathize with the very special turn of mind requisite to the study of literature as art. My students, however, were more perceptive and a source of encouragement to me. They felt that the study of Hebrew prose and poetry could greatly benefit from a new set of more appropriate questions and that an 'ergocentric' approach would be a more congenial way of close reading. Every year a couple of students developed into independent and creative readers.

The text of the Bible itself was my source of inspiration. In my analysis of this text I departed from a dual impulse. My intuition told me that the narratives from the Hebrew Bible which I knew were more than a patchwork resulting from traditionary and redactional meddling. And second, it was my firm conviction that I would need to trust myself to and surrender to the guidance and manipulation of biblical narrative, which in due course would lead me to discover and appreciate the rules and conventions of its art; the better I was equipped as a reader, the better the text would be able to speak to me. Half of the interpreter's work consists in constantly scrutinizing his or her own presuppositions, unspoken criteria as regards ideas about textual unity and coherence, its functions and nature, and its relation to the audience, and it should also entail an awareness of the extent to which interpretation relies on the reader's contribution. During the time that I received a thorough training in Semitic languages, history and philology, I was shocked to find, on the part of the historical-critical school, a persistent unwillingness or inability to engage with the text as a living entity. By raising its own ideal of objectivity to the status of an idol, this method of 'higher' criticism had stubbornly ignored the intersubjective truth that meaning and sense are constituted on the ground where text and reader meet in a process of profound communication with one another that has a mutual effect on both parties. Historical-critical scholars, by contrast, do not tire of passing negative value judgments on the stories or the poems they interpret, without even bothering to account for the presuppositions or the criteria on which their evaluative comments are based. How often do we hear that there is contradiction in the text, or that there is a tension that must be a trace of a complex genetical process, or that there is too much repetition, another sure sign that more than one writer has worked on the text? And as soon as one encounters a textual seam, a doubling, or a locus of tension, one is supposed to stop listening and to forge hypotheses about the background of the text, the intention of the author, and especially about its origins, growth and redactional reworkings. In this way scholarly energy becomes deflected from the text itself and, abandoning a dialogue with it, disappears into a black hole of diachronic reifications.

What is one to do in such circumstances? I had to listen patiently. For many years my research kept shuttling between trial and error. It often seemed as if I were busy inventing the wheel. That is nothing to feel ashamed or guilty about. It was indeed an endeavor full of surprise and excitement. I finally saw the wheel would have to be perfectly round and to notice this come about after having measured and provided the spokes was a thrilling experience. In the seventies I decided to extend my field and to engage in an interpretation of the books of Samuel. Now that I am writing the final volume of a tetralogy, I see more clearly than twenty years ago that my real purpose is no longer merely to offer a full interpretation but—a greater challenge—to explore in detail the ways in which meaning is engendered and to establish the laws and conventions of biblical style and structure. Interpretation is a field on which one exchanges a variety of different viewpoints; it will always be pluriform. In interpreting the texts of Genesis or Samuel, my overriding concern is really with the poetics of classical Hebrew literature. In this discipline one can find the same dynamic tension of playfulness and rigor of method that I encounter in many stories and poems of the Bible and whose dialectic often fails to be understood by scholars. The method that I use, structural analysis, is, to my mind, a most adequate response to the life and coherence of the text as our engaging interlocutor.

These days the field of biblical studies is changing. It is not necessary any more for a student of the Bible to feel isolated if he or she wants to stay face to face with the text and refuses to run away from its handed-down form. When the first edition of this book came out, I soon noticed that there were some kindred souls after all, and I was very happy to meet those authors and to appreciate their work. At the end of the seventies books offering a comprehensive approach to Hebrew narration began to appear. I mention *The Art of Biblical Narrative* (1981) by Robert Alter, and Shimon Bar-Efrat, *Narrative Art in the Bible* (first in Hebrew 1979, but now in English and available from Almond Press in Sheffield, 1989). Since 1985, moreover, the insights and sophistication of Meir Sternberg are accessible in *The Poetics of Biblical Narrative*—a profound exploration of the powerful triangle formed by narrative art, historiography and ideology. Works such as these have provided the creative study of biblical texts with a firm foundation in literary theory. They equip us with tools that were not yet available when I studied the Jacob cycle. There was then no actantial model, and we had no monographs studying plot or dialogue, or time and space. At that time I had not yet fully developed the model which I would present later, in my Samuel studies—a model that covers the hierarchy of all the textual and compositional levels of the text.

Looking back now I recognize that my strategy of immersing myself in the narrative at certain junctures prevented me from keeping the text at arm's length, which would have enabled me to try out both the close and the distant view and to be flexible in shuttling between the one and the other. Nevertheless, I still stand by the interpretation offered in this book.

I have deleted some twenty printing errors, mostly of minor significance, and wish to correct my view on the verb *ng'*, the verb that is used in the nocturnal scene of Jacob wrestling at the Jabbok river. I now assume that it denotes a blow rather than a touch, administered by the mysterious opponent that is often too quickly identified with an angel. Finally I want to point out to my readers that I have developed my views on Genesis in two more recent studies. I present an overall perspective on the book of Genesis in R. Alter and Frank Kermode (eds.), *The Literary Guide to the Bible* (Cambridge, MA: Harvard University Press, 1987), and I undertook an analysis of time that leads me to defend the coherence of the Abraham cycle; the article is called 'Time and the Structure of the Abraham Cycle' and appeared in 1989 in *Oudtestamentische Studiën* 25. This work can be regarded as an extension of my study of the Jacob cycle, which I am now offering to my readers in its pristine form.

Jan P. Fokkelman
March 1991
National Humanities Center
Research Triangle Park
North Carolina

FOREWORD

Jan Fokkelman's *Narrative Art in Genesis* was an inspiration for many of us in the late seventies, and it is a curious experience to revisit it. It is still more curious that the novelty and strangeness have not left it, that it has dated in only superficial ways.

I met Jan Fokkelman first, together with his wife Margriet, at the Jewish–Christian Bible Week in Bendorf, Germany, in 1980. Jan spoke of his childhood in internment camps in Indonesia, about gestalt therapy in relation to the text, about his Sufi practice; we spoke of how the text had the uncanny knack of taking over our lives; we decided to have a special session about this, quarrelled, I think, for the sake of quarrelling, and for the pleasure of making up and embracing. We met at the same Bible Week the following year, which was less dramatic, in Israel at the time of the Kahan report, and then not for several years before I spent a delightful afternoon in their garden in Leiden. In the meantime, *Narrative Art and Poetry in the Books of Samuel* was unfolding volume by volume, with a long hiatus in the middle.

Narrative Art in Genesis was remarkable for its uncompromising insistence on the analysis of the 'final form' of the text, and for the attempt at a total description of every level of organization, from the phoneme up. Literary-criticism, the immanent, synchronic analysis of the text, has become commonplace, and hence frequently banal; for Fokkelman, however, this was still a comparatively neglected enterprise, as he notes on the first page, fraught with academic unrespectability, difficult to publish, and self-financed, as he informs us on the last. The effect of adventure into entirely unexplored terrain is combined, however, with an astonishingly deep absorption in European literary theory and in the work of his few precursors in biblical studies. Alonso Schökel intersects oddly with the Israeli school, represented especially by Meir Weiss; the footnotes abound in quotations in Spanish and Hebrew, as well as German. The total interpretation, based on New Critical principles and the somewhat moralistic approach advocated by Weiss is interleaved with the lyric insight of Alonso Schökel. No one writing at that time—with the exception perhaps of Jonathan Magonet—had quite that range; and even today literary-critical studies of the Bible often impress with the shallowness of their reading and their limitation to one language and hence one literary tradition.

Narrative Art in Genesis has no agenda, except to demonstrate that the narrative is a 'literary work of art' (p. 6). The commitment to the intricacy of structure is unrelated to religious preconceptions. This was refreshing indeed in 1975! The result is a freedom from context that allows us to follow the hero on his quest without haloes or historical reconstruction. But this results also in a certain vacuum. As Fokkelman says, 'the work...is a world-in-words' (p. 6). He is expert at communicating the rhythms and symmetries of that world; the intensity of structuration persuades us both of its integration and its tension. It is not just that there is nothing outside the structure, that the denotated world is relegated to a few fascinating footnotes, but that the absence of the usual conceptual freight introduces us to an imaginary world whose meaning is left open. The hero returns home, after his encounter with various doubles, to bring healing to his ruptured family and to enable his father to die (p. 236). His adventure reverses the story of the Tower of Babel, with which the book opens; the scattering of humanity, in search of a name, comes to rest in the return of the wandering hero and the gift of a divine name. Chapter 2, on Jacob's dream, corresponds particularly closely with the first, as the insistent but inverted plays on the words *šem/šām/šāmayim* indicate. These connections remain for the most part implicit; Fokkelman does not draw attention to his own artistry. Similarly, the patterning does not yield any overt or obvious meaning, apart from the insistent law of *talio*, which ensures that Jacob suffers that which he inflicts, which matches Babel with Bethel. We do not know what Jacob discovers at the end of his quest. But this is the point: Jacob defines himself by founding places. There is no essential Jacob, no single consistent character. There are as many Jacobs as situations; it is this that makes him a rich and elusive personality, or, as his name suggests, 'wily'. He is defined only by his 'singleness of purpose', as Fokkelman explicates his description as *tam* (p. 91); but this purpose is only fulfilled through its renunciation. At the end of the book, when all conflicts have been resolved, Jacob disappears as a character, fades into the completed narrative pattern.

This brings us to a third characteristic of Fokkelman's approach, that it is intensely dialogic. Characters can only be perceived in relation to others, so that we might speak of dyads, such as Jacob–Rachel or Jacob–Laban. Each encounter evokes a different response, and involves varying degrees of projection. This approach Fokkelman owes not only to Buber and Rosenzweig, whom he cites frequently, but to gestalt psychology. His book acquires thereby a sensitivity to drama.

It is remarkable, then, how little space is accorded the actual encounters between the participants, compared to their thoughts and anxieties about each other. We know much about their passions, but not of the quality of the relationship of, for example, Jacob and Rachel. This contributes to the intense isolation that marks Jacob in particular. Fokkelman manages to focus on this solitude without needing to state it explicitly, simply through patient exegesis of each speech and act, in the light of Jacob's self-consciousness. But this is also through insistence on what cannot be known, unrevealed by or to the narrator and certainly the reader. For example, in his discussion of the prelude to Jacob's struggle with the 'man' at the Jabbok (Gen. 32.23-33), Fokkelman quotes Auerbach's famous description of biblical narrative as *hintergründig* and *deutungsbedürftig* (the switch into German compounds, I think, the sense of romantic and abstract mystery), senses, apologizing for the cliché, that our text is only the 'tip of the iceberg', wonders why Jacob could not sleep, reflects on his bad conscience—that he is no longer *tam* in his own eyes—considers whether he intended to be alone, decides that probably he did not, and crosses a minor Jabbok of the critic's own in tentatively suggesting that Jacob wishes to make amends (pp. 209-213). This is all very sensitive and focuses our attention wonderfully on Jacob's fraught state of mind, but what really makes it interesting are Fokkelman's continual asides on the dangers that beset the exegete of this passage, how one must proceed from the known to the unknown, the care needed not to succumb to romantic speculation, 'to be tortured for ever by chimeras' (p. 210). It is not that Fokkelman is a particularly modest critic, but his self-reflection on the impossibility of understanding the text, on his limitations, distances the hero and narrator, makes them yet more unfathomable, and himself their counterpart. Jacob's experience of the '*mysterium tremendum ac fascinans*' (p. 220) is then accompanied by the critic's withdrawal in the face of Jacob's own fascinating mystery.

Fokkelman makes things difficult for historical critics, though he grants them the validity of their own enterprise (p. 2). If the 'final form' of the text is a perfect literary work of art, intricately structured, then one of the principal criteria for its dissection disappears. Especially in 1975, when classical documentary theory was widely unchallenged, this would have been disturbing. Indeed, the growth of the literary study of the Bible has been largely responsible for the disintegration of documentary theory and the rethinking of the task of the biblical historian as the study of power and ideology in relatively late interpretative communities. All this is far beyond the horizon for Fokkelman. His summary of the underlying theme of the Jacob narrative is rather dated, for example in its stress on the history of salvation. Implicit in his work there is, nevertheless, a conflict with historical thinking. On the first page he tells us that diachronic analysis has approached its conclusion with the publication of Wolfgang Richter's *Exegese als Literaturwissenschaft*; by the second we learn that diachronic analysis is not only not necessary for the understanding of texts, but also impossible, though still valid; thereafter the synchrony is so comprehensive that diachrony would have difficulty in finding a foothold (perhaps in the discussion of ch. 35?). A similar tension pervades the almost contemporaneous works of Lévi-Strauss. The ahistoricism, with its stress on the infinite recreation of texts by their readers (p. 4) and the transformation of received material, since nothing is ever new, by the biblical authors, accounts for the aforementioned sense of a vacuum, one met by silence, both by traditional biblical critics, among whom the name of Fokkelman is rarely mentioned, and their sociologically oriented cousins.

The ahistoricism combines with an existentialism. What matters is where a person is at a particular moment, and how he or she responds to its demands. The past dogs Jacob especially, but in the narrative he becomes free of it. Fokkelman is extremely resistant to psychoanalytic reading that might in fact be compatible with his own; psychoanalysis also sees itself as a way of liberation from the thrall of the past. I think the resistance is attributable to distrust of the concept of a person as an enclosed being, programmed by the unconscious and history, homologous to that of literature as the product of the political unconscious. The existentialism, however, is always existence-in-society, and as such differs from the western and romantic myth of individual salvation.

If there is a theology in the book, it derives from Buber and Rosenzweig; God is the God of the encounter, who brings a person from the world of things and facts, from contingency, to the duality of relationship. But this theology cannot be expressed in abstractions. It emerges, perhaps, through those encounters and their patient analysis, through the exhausting and irrepressibly vivid attempts to find adequate translations and exegesis—of which Buber and Rosenzweig's translation, often cited, is itself a model. The impossibility, together with the looseness of Fokkelman's theological loyalties, can, however, lapse into moralism, though this trait is much more marked in his volumes on the books of Samuel.

Fokkelman is often criticized for predictability; it is held that once one has learned his methodology, his work can be duplicated. In particular, his capacity to detect concentric patterns everywhere lends itself to the suspicion of selective vision. Only those who have not tried to imitate Fokkelman can think that it is easy. The colometrics, the search for mirroring, intertwining structures, is a control that provides some anchorage for his genius, that constantly surprises with its depth of insight, that analyses prose with the same concentration and sensitivity as poetry, and combines this with an intimate sense of the overall shape and rhythm of the text.

Fokkelman's weak point is his failure to recognize ambiguity except as a local and passing phenomenon, that can be resolved in the final interpretation. In his analysis of the story of the Tower of Babel, for example, two complementary structures converge on the principle of *ius talionis*. Although he does recognize indeterminacy, as in his discussion of Jacob's consciousness at the river-crossing, he cannot resist the temptation to try to explicate it. Likewise, the pervasiveness of structure makes us wonder what is excluded from it, to look for disruptive, incoherent elements. *Narrative Art in Genesis* in this respect, as in many others, suggests possibilities not developed in Fokkelman's *magnum opus*. For example, one notes instances when chiastic pairs are acknowledged not to be entirely convincing, as on p. 93.

I wonder where Fokkelman's work will take him. He could engage more closely with psychoanalysis and deconstruction, seeking points of inner conflict in the text, determining the play of narrative voices. Where, for example, in the Jacob story does the voice of the father, with its indissoluble gift of blessing and guilt, interact with the absent, cursed, mother, in the construction of Jacob's narcissism? I find, incidentally, Fokkelman to be extraordinarily hard on Rebekah. I look forward to Fokkelman's reentry into history, to take up the questions left on the first page of this book. He is a very restless person, but one also developing a centre of quietness. That was my impression when we last saw each other. The mystical element, wherewith the annihilation of personality coincides with its absorption into the rhythms and completion of the text, will be crucial in determining any new direction. For Fokkelman, every discovery in the text is also a self-discovery.

Narrative Art in Genesis is a pleasure, because of the freshness of writing that transgresses unabashedly the conventions of academic discourse. It reads like a sophisticated work of hermeneutics, awash with multilingual tags, until one stumbles on comments such as 'The fool!' or 'What a prospect!' Perhaps there are fewer of these in *Narrative Art and Poetry in the Books of Samuel*. But the joy of being an *enfant terrible* will never, I think, entirely leave him. And this, too, is the pleasure of the text.

Francis Landy
University of Alberta
Edmonton, Alberta
Canada

INTRODUCTION

"Curiously enough, literary history has been so preoccupied with the setting of a work of literature that its attempts at an analysis of the works themselves have been slight in comparison with the enormous efforts expended on the study of environment."[1] These lines were written with a view to Western literature, but this fact does not render them less worthy of consideration for Orientalists.

Biblical scholars, too, would do well to heed them. For one or two centuries they have expended such "enormous efforts" in framing theories on the origin of biblical texts and on the history of their transmission that the study of the text itself, which is "only" the final shape of the tradition, but, for all that, the only one given, seems to have suffered somewhat. The diachronic study of texts, carried out under the banner of *Formgeschichte, Ueberlieferungsgeschichte* etc., and the tools[2] that are at its service have been developed to such an extent that the synchronic analysis and description of texts have been neglected, at least in Old Testament studies.

Consequently the interpretation of texts (mostly called exegesis, when religious texts are concerned) is in danger of being subordinated to diachronic study. Although, in my opinion, the interpretation of texts is the normative centre[3] of the various ways of handling texts

[1] R. Wellek and A. Warren, Theory of Literature, 3rd ed. London 1963, p. 139.

[2] A great step forward in the final arrangement of procedures and terminology of diachronic research is Wolfgang Richter's Exegese als Literaturwissenschaft, Entwurf einer alttestamentlichen Literaturtheorie und Methodologie, Göttingen 1971. (The main title is incorrect and a better subtitle would have been: design of a methodology of the diachronic investigation into the OT.)

[3] Around the interpretation I group the various ways of partial and extrinsic approach (questions of a linguistic nature, historical background, theological content, etc.); the text itself stands between its genetic history on one hand and its *Wirkungsgeschichte* on the other hand (cf. Wellek and Warren about perspectivism, at the end of ch. XII).

and deserves independent pursuit, such interpretation is now often considered possible only when subsequent to and based upon the investigation into the origin of the text. Thus the interpretation of a text is commenced only after, and on the grounds of, a complete reconstruction of its origin and process of transmission. From a fundamentally hermeneutic point of view [4] this means that the exegesis rests on a foundation (the genetic history of a text) which will never leave the realm of what is in fact hypothesis. It also means that with quite a few biblical texts exegesis can only be accomplished in an extremely circuitous way.

Is such textual study possible and necessary? Of the possibility we must at once be very sceptical: diachronic research itself maintains that the complete reconstruction of the origin and transmission of many texts is an unattainable ideal.[5] In addition there is the fact that diachronic research has by no means produced a consensus of opinion as to its results, even in outline. Therefore, anyone stating that, for example, the narrative prose of the Old Testament can only be interpreted following genetic explanation is faced with the epistemological consequence that such texts are unknowable.

But is diachronic research necessary to the interpretation of texts? The quotation with which I opened my introduction is found at an important point in Wellek and Warren's theory of literature, the point at which they leave the "extrinsic approach" to texts and turn to the intrinsic study of literature. Before this they had already written, "no causal study can do justice to the analysis, description, and evaluation of a literary work."[6] Not until the interpreter's structural means have been exhausted does the method of genetic explanation seem to me indispensable[7] to an interpretation of texts. However, it is precisely the possibilities and tools of this structural or ergocentric treatment

[4] Hermeneutics h.l. in the sense of theory of exegesis, so the methodology which is the justification and foundation of the craft itself, the act of interpreting. Not hermeneutics as the universal phenomenon which Gadamer has treated in his great work Wahrheit und Methode, Grundzüge einer philosophischen Hermeneutik, Tübingen, 1965 (2nd ed.).

[5] From this it is not to be inferred that this research is useless, undesirable etc.; cf. note 7. Nor is this paragraph meant to be the justification of synchronic or structural research.

[6] op. cit., p. 108.

[7] I do not say: admissible! Diachronic study needs no justification; the origin and tradition of texts are in themselves worthwhile and form an independent object of research.

of texts that in this century have been increasingly applied in the synchronic study of Western literature and that have been neglected by OT scholarship[8] to such an extent that it is time that biblical exegesis availed itself of them. Genetic explanation might turn out to be less immediately necessary than we now imagine, conditioned as we are to asking diachronic questions.

We may also formulate the matter in the following way: a text is a pole in two quite different processes which may be represented thus (A = author, W = work, R = reader, listener)[9]:

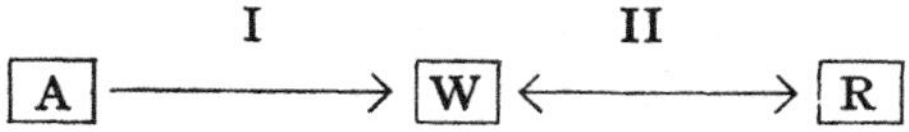

Process I, the creation of a text, may be a complicated and protracted affair, which goes through oral and written stages; often there are no independent data about it or witnesses to it, except for what is to be found in the text itself. This is especially true of many narrative texts from both the Old and the New Testament. The study of process I and any statement about it are thus conceivable and feasible only when process II has been completed. Knowledge of the growth of a text can only be acquired by deduction from the work known, by framing and testing hypotheses, but we acquire the necessary knowledge of a work by first accomplishing II. If our knowledge of a work is poor, for example as a result of a careless or faulty, because biased, reading of a text, our view of I will be faulty in proportion.

Process II, the recreation of a text, which takes place through a successful reading and interpretation, can be independent of the investigation into or knowledge of process I. For the birth of a text resembles that of man: the umbilical cord which connected the text with its time and the man or men who produced it, is severed once its existence has become a fact; the text is going to lead a life of its own,

[8] Cf. the judgement with which L. Alonso-Schökel starts the preface to his *magnum opus* Estudios de Poética Hebrea, Barcelona 1963, p. VII.

[9] Generally speaking I is ontic and II is noetic. But the diagram is a strong simplification; just consider that A can be differentiated in A_1, A_2, A_3 ... A_n (if there was more than one author or if the author himself changed his text more than once in various stages of his authorship) and W in W_1, W_2 ... W_n. Besides, the author is also the first reader of his work, and so II also takes place between A and W.

for whenever a reader grants it an adequate reading it will come alive and become operative and it usually survives its maker. Whereas the creation of a text is finite, finished after hours, years or centuries, its re-creation is infinite. It is a task for each new age, each new generation, each new reader, never to be considered complete.

The examination of texts, so II, can be regarded as and carried out as an end (IIa) or as a means (IIb). It becomes an end when considered a means of getting to know the text itself and of judging it on its merits. On the other hand, it can be regarded as a means to various ends, such as increased knowledge of the period in which a work was written, or greater insight into the author's psyche, his system of metaphysical values or that of his time, etc. The text is then seen as a document and is used in order to reconstruct and to investigate something other than the text. It is used as a transparency through which one looks, for example, at the historical Jesus or at the origin of the text and its development to its final given shape.[10]

Textual research which is a means (IIb) and has knowledge of I as an end is in danger of being distorted and limited in its treatment of the text because of its specific goal and thus is in danger of being aprioristic. My impression is that OT scholarship has made a great deal of study of the growth and transmission of texts on the tacit presupposition that the text is not to be interpreted from itself, because it is stratified or composite, and that to understand it we must first reconstruct its genesis and its process of growth. This is why only research of type IIb is being done. However it is necessary that the validity of such an a priori judgement be tested by granting the texts a painstaking and unbiased examination of type IIa; this is the only equitable treatment one can accord these texts.

Before using the text as a transparency we should recognize its intrinsic values and give it a chance to speak for itself. One form of such research, which judges the text on its own merits, is the analysis

[10] This paragraph holds good for perfect texts such as the ones dealt with in this book. The hermeneutic situation becomes considerably more complicated when a damaged or poorly transmitted text is concerned (which is often the case in classical texts). Then a special form of II should come first: investigation into the text, its material substratum (e.g. clay tablets), and its tradition, which investigation aims at purging, correcting or completing what has come down to us. Not until then can IIa, as best it may, be carried out. For all that, one should – as early as the stage of constituting the object – also take stylistic criteria into account.

of style and structure. Its only concern is with the process work – reader, it is above all descriptive and so it does not aim at a causal interpretation or deduction.

The realization of a text runs a linear course in that it occurs in time. The signs of language succeed each other and each one of them leaves its impression on us; the sum total of those impressions, which make many connections on several levels, is our experience of the work. By describing style and structure we can put this experience into words – our interpretation of the work.[11]

This collection serves a double purpose: to contribute to the interpretation of texts from the Book of Genesis, but, in doing so, to demonstrate especially a method of structural explication which starts from the principle that these texts belong to narrative art and which consistently takes this fact into account.

If to the creators of the prose of the so-called historical books of the Old Testament it was of fundamental importance to express themselves in narrative art and if to the prophets this was also important in poetry (and it *was* of fundamental importance to them), then for the interpretation of the texts it is equally fundamental to understand these texts as literary[12] creations and to recognize their mode of existence as linguistic works of art. This may even be the most fruitful means of gaining direct access to the literary texts of which the bulk of the Old Testament consists.

In the analyses offered here the question of artistic shaping will be as central as it was to the prophets and narrators. This approach, however, is not exclusive, as is the case with much exegesis, the only aim of which is to take the shell off the "theological message", but,

[11] Such a description, when isolated from the question as to the genesis and development of the given text, can lead to various results. If our experience leads to the conclusion that we have found an organic whole which invites us to a positive opinion of its value, we can call the text a literary work of art. If, on the contrary, we hit – in our interpretation – upon the irreconcilability of elements in the work, we may soon feel the need of an examination of type IIb: we can try to account for the discrepancies by explaining them genetically from the complicated process of the genesis of the text (which process must first be reconstructed). Of all methods an independent analysis of style and structure provides us with the motives and justification of diachronic research and indicates the points of application for it.

[12] "Literary" not in the modern (and stale) sense of merely "aesthetic", but in the inclusive sense of the next paragraph.

on the contrary, inclusive: as the fine "form" cannot be detached from a serious "content", so stylistic analysis brings to light not only aesthetic qualities and results, but all substantive aspects of the work as well. In religious texts, for example, the analysis particularly opens the way to theological conclusions. This comprehensiveness[13] is possible owing to the idiosyncratic coherence, the special correlation between the whole and the parts which marks the linguistic work of art as an organism.[14] In it language is not used *up*, with the result that the haphazard words no longer matter, once the information has been conveyed; no, we find *use* of language, so that we begin with, always return to and end with the words.[15] The work – and now I am thinking of the stories about the patriarchs – is not only (and perhaps not even primarily) a denotation of the historically real world (no matter how many listeners may think so) or an unbroken reflection of it, it is a world-in-words. This world exists, and this is fundamental, in the mode of language.[16]

We may say, in other words and anticipating the results of this collection, that the stories from Genesis have the ontological status of the literary work of art.[17] That is why these stories can be readily

[13] M. Weiss speaks, in an original way, of אינטרפריטאציה כוליית, "integral(izing) interpretation", pp. 38ff of his book המקרא כדמותו, שיטת מחקר והסתכלות במקרא על פי עיקרי מדע הספרות החדש Jerusalem, 1963; and of "Total-Interpretation" in SVT 22 (1972).

[14] Cf. the term "sphärische Geschlossenheit des Erzählwerks" used by E. Lämmert, Bauformen des Erzählens, Stuttgart, 1955.

[15] Cf. Martin Heidegger, Holzwege (Frankfurt, 1950), p. 36: "Zwar gebraucht auch der Dichter das Wort, aber nicht so wie die gewöhnlich Redenden und Schreibenden die Worte verbrauchen müssen, sondern so, dass das Wort erst wahrhaft ein Wort wird und bleibt."

[16] It is interesting to see how similar insights are formulated, quite independently of literary scholarship, by an authority on the Old Testament: see the quotation from G. von Rad in note 17 of ch. I (*infra*).
Lämmert, op. cit., p. 26: "Grundsatzlich besitzt die erzählerische Fiktion ebenso eine eigene Zeit-Raum-Konstellation wie sie überhaupt einen Lebenszusammenhang darbietet, der von der realen Wirklichkeit schon durch seine Abrundung kategorial verschieden ist." This is well illustrated by Genesis 11, which creates its own space; see my § 16.

[17] This statement is a) the intuitive judgement with which we start as readers of literary texts and which is only of a tentative validity, b) the result of my interpretative work, which is 360^0 further in the hermeneutic circle which I have come round, and which therefore covers a).
About "ontological status" see Wellek & Warren, Ch. XII.

analyzed as works of fiction, so like the novel or the lyric in European literature; this is valid even for such a work as II Sam. 6-20 + I Kings 1 and 2, which deals with the succession to the throne after David. This last-mentioned text, which everyone concedes is largely "*geschichtsnah*", is an example clearly illustrating that the narrative prose of the Old Testament is characterized by an "intentionality" which differs from that of the works of fiction of Western literature. It has a claim to two other sorts of truth,[18] apart from that of fiction. Thus, no doubt, the listeners/readers were convinced that the people, relationships and events had existed just as they were told. The patriarchs as they appear in Genesis signified to the Israelites their own national history. So the specific "fictionality" of OT prose may not be represented as opposed to what ancient Israel meant by historicity; rather it can be said to include that historicity – another aspect of inclusiveness.[19] The narrators themselves, though, will have had a considerably subtler opinion of the historicity of what they told. The exact shaping power we find in the Chapters I and II renders it highly probable that they were conscious of the fact that by shaping and by creating structures their own contribution was considerable, if not decisive.[20] They felt perfectly justified in re-fashioning the raw "historical" material they had and in putting it into the service of a higher truth, mostly that of their faith. Their creative work arranges

[18] Erich Auerbach, Mimesis, dargestellte Wirklichkeit in der abendländischen Literatur, Bern, 1959 (2nd ed.) says in Ch. I, p. 16 about "die biblischen Geschichten: Die religiöse Absicht bedingt aber einen absoluten Anspruch auf geschichtliche Wahrheit." Also see p. 17.

[19] Quite another problem is of course that by history and historicity we understand something very different from antiquity. To us the historical relevance of Jona, Gen. 4, Ruth, II Sam., Esther etc. varies greatly. But it is interesting that those differences are not displayed by the texts, or hardly so. Cf. Auerbach op. cit., p. 16: "Was er [i.e. the narrator of Gen. 22, but this is true of many OT narratives] hervorbrachte, zielte zunächst nicht auf "Wirklichkeit" – wenn ihm auch diese gelang, so war dies doch nur Mittel, nicht Zweck –, sondern auf Wahrheit."

[20] Tzvetan Todorov, Grammaire du Décaméron, den Haag 1969, p. 12: "Aucune histoire n'est, et ne peut être une invention totalement originale. Tout récit renvoie à un récit précédent: le récit est toujours un écho de récits. L'originalité d'un texte littéraire ne peut pas consister dans l'absence de renvois à d'autres textes antérieurs. Boccace lui-même a indiqué la voie à suivre dans la conclusion du livre: il n'a pas *inventé* ces histoires, dit-il, mais il les a *écrites*. C'est, en effet, dans l'écriture que se crée l'unité; ..."

the historical, the fictional and the religious truths[21] in one perspective.

The first part of this collection contains detailed analyses of two texts which OT scholarship has acknowledged as specimens of the so-called "smallest literary units", i.e., they consist of one scene.

We are about to enter the hermeneutic circle. In fact, it is a spiral which begins in wide curves and – if success befalls our reading – winding about, narrows its circles and takes us to the core. But how to make a start? Not a single method warrants our access to the work in advance; every text requires its own hermeneutics and the annoying thing is that the outlines cannot be drawn until after the event. Yet perhaps one guideline of general validity can be given: go into the text carefully, in an attitude of confidence,[22] thus hoping to find an entrance to the work, those keys to its understanding, which the stylistic means of the text offer to us. On this basis a provisional structure can be designed, which in turn integrates and interprets the stylistic means.

[21] Literary scholarship occasionally has the term "mythical truth" for the third case; for New Testament scholars this is intelligible, cf. Bultmann.

[22] Leo Spitzer, Stilstudien II (München, 1928) p. 17: "Tatsächlich scheint mir Lesen, gründliches Lesen der beste Handwerkskniff, um hinter Geheimnisse der Sprachkunst zu dringen."

Alonso, Estudios p. 56, says: "... el método (...) compromete la personalidad íntegra del investigador."

E. Staiger, die Kunst der Interpretation, Zürich 1955 (2nd ed.), p. 12, says of poems by Mörike: "Ich liebe sie; sie sprechen mich an; und im Vertrauen auf diese Begegnung wage ich es, sie zu interpretieren.

Es ist mir klar, dass ein solches Geständnis im Raum der Wissenschaft Anstoss erregt. Das allersubjektivste Gefühl gilt als Basis der wissenschaftlichen Arbeit! Ich kann und will es nicht leugnen. Ich glaube jedoch, dieses "subjektive" Gefühl vertrage sich mit der Wissenschaft – der Literaturwissenschaft – sehr wohl, ja sie komme nur so zu ihrem Recht."

PART I

STYLISTIC AND STRUCTURAL ANALYSIS OF TWO "SMALL LITERARY UNITS"

CHAPTER I

GENESIS 11.1-9: THE TOWER OF BABEL

§ 1 It is already known to Old Testament scholarship that the narrator of Gen. 11.1-9 did his job within the square meter. He who has something to say and must, speaking in terms of sound and time, do so in 121 words or two minutes, or, in terms of writing and space, within half a page of thirteen lines, is forced to confine himself.[1] To quote Gunkel, the passage mentioned is a clear example of a "sehr kurze Erzählung". Just contrast it to the lovely calm of Gen. 24, in which the narrator inserts an elaborate da capo (in the verses 35-48, which alone are twice the length of the story with which we are now concerned!) by having the servant tell his host what he himself has already presented in verses 1-27, thus developing what Gunkel rightly distinguishes from the short story as "ausgeführtere Erzählung".[2]

What has not yet come to the fore in biblical studies is that the narrator of Gen. 11.1-9 did his job within the square centimeter. Or rather, to put it in non-figurative language: the main stylistic means within this text have been noted, most carefully so in Cassuto's commentary[3] but hardly any one of them has been interpreted – which is what is important.

[1] "Der geringe Umfang, innerhalb dessen der Erzähler sich bewegen muss, hat ihn dazu gezwungen, seine ganze künstlerische Kraft am kleinsten Punkte zu sammeln; so klein auch diese Schöpfungen sind, so *konzentriert* sind sie, und so stark ist ihre Wirkung." H. Gunkel, Genesis, Handkommentar, 3rd (= 5th) ed.; Göttingen, 1910, Einleitung § 3.7, S. XXXIV. Unfortunately these words are preceded by: "Solche Kürze der Sagen ist (...) das Zeichen der *Armut* dieser alten Kunst" (for which he cannot make amends with:) "aber zugleich hat gerade diese Armut ihre besonderen *Vorzüge*." (Italics by Gunkel).

[2] *Ibid.* § 3.7 and § 3.21. The distinction, at first sight only slightly conspicuous, is much more than a merely quantitative one.

[3] U. Cassuto, פרוש על ספר בראשית, חלק ב׳׳: מנח עד אברהם Jerusalem, 1953. p. 159f. (There is a translation: A Commentary on the Book of Genesis. II. From Noach to Abraham. London, 1964.)

In polishing the form the narrator did not scorn scrupulous patient labour; the interpreter – anyone observing the demands of the story as best as he can – must not therefore neglect studying the ingenuity of form. Through such work he will gain an insight into the structure which governs the words, a structure which will be seen as the motor of the narration and the narrator's view. Only in this way can it be made evident to the reader what in the beginning can only be an assumption, that Gen. 11.1-9 is a unity and a literary text, a specimen of narrative art. Perhaps a work of art will give up its secrets only to him who works with the "*Vorgriff der Vollkommenheit*", and to others it will remain a book with seven seals. It is not a foregone conclusion that Gen. 11.1-9 is a linguistic work of art, but if the following analysis is correct, i.e., if our interpretation becomes, step by step, self-evident to the reader, then what happens is that our working hypothesis will prove itself.

§ 2 Babel lies in ruins! The tremendous metropolis has become a desolate ruin and therewith its name has become transparent for Israel, after the event. "Babel" is the product of "*bālal*", so Babel means "muddle". This is the conclusion which the Israelitic observer has left us and for which he has drawn on etymological sources. Thus he muses from what is now a safe distance on how the fortune of the most feared and most powerful city can change, and he does so with a sneering pun, not without malicious pleasure, not without relief.

Was this narrator a Palestine farmer, who sees himself surrounded by too many rather than too few stones; a peasant who on the one hand finds his material ready at hand for his modest building achievements and who on the other hand hopes, when full of years, he will be spared the punishment which an unwished-for invader has in store for him: scattering stones all over his farmland?[4] Or was he one of the semi-nomads, a class which, not excelling in architectonic ambitions, observes in anxiety mingled with wonder how the people in the river area, each a tiny wheel in a gigantic organisation, must slave away to build houses, towers and temples from clay and pitch?

"From whatever consciousness" this story may have been written, so much is certain,[5] that our narrator belonged to a simple small

[4] Cf. II Kings 3.25, Is. 5.2.

[5] Cf., however, note 11 of § 5 which produces as a third possibility: a new-fangled citizen with his ambivalence about the growth of court and machinery in (for example Salomonic, rising) Jerusalem.

community and that either the country village or the clan was his social horizon. This life must have signified great freedom for him when compared with the complicated and in his opinion oppressing hierarchy of "classes", functions and tasks in Mesopotamian society, with the impressive and pretentious administration and organisation of the city-states founded by the Sumerians in the Country between the Rivers.

Although all this has little bearing on the text and although it remains a speculative view of the text, we cannot dismiss it because this sense of freedom can still be perceived in the story of fallen Babel. The narrator seems to be released from a certain pressure, a pressure which his age experienced at the sight of the variety of that social polity, its pretensions, inspiring shudders and aversion, and also possibly its expansionism.

These paragraphs may suffice for Gen. 11.9 with its widely known and transparent folk-etymology. They focused only on the pun itself, but through this pun the narrator exerts criticism, the spear-head of which we do not clearly see until the structure of the whole has been unfolded. The narrator talks not only about the world of the people and the earthly polity, his pun is also essentially connected with his view of the relationship between God and men and his view of history; that is why we shall have to return to this point.

§ 3 A pun is a generally recognized example of a phonological phenomenon which carries meaning and asks for an explanation. It seems to us that the one in v. 9, perhaps the most conspicuous formal fact from the passage, can be used as a gate to the story and primarily to its sound stratum. Let us enter through this gate then: the story of Gen. 11.1-9 occupies a special position in OT narrative art by the density of its stylistically relevant phonological phenomena which are closely connected or coincide with remarkable verbal repetitions. The degree of density is much higher than is usual for narrative prose and is only equalled, and seldom surpassed, in Hebrew lyric poetry.

These stylistic means we must now indicate and exploit, i.e. interpret. If Gen. 11.1-9 is an authentic work of art, we may expect to land *in medias res*, in other words to gain a first important insight into the structure. We start with two well-known points, discussed in the commentaries, and from there move on to what is less self-evident, and obscure.

"Come, let us ... !" (v. 3)
"Come, let us ... !" (v. 4)

Twice the clear *hābā* rings out, followed by an exhortative. Quickly and strikingly the narrator introduces the people from Sinear: look at their energy, their enthusiasm and their ambitious plans! For one moment we might fancy that the narrator approves of these intentions and activities, to which he dedicates the first half (esp. vss. 2-4). But then he surprises us when he dedicates the second half to God's activity, with:

"Come, let us ...!" (v. 7)

What humour to have the tune which people started with "hābā ..-ā" completed by God with the same "hābā ..ā", but also, what a blow, what disillusion for man and his plans ,which are, as it were, ridiculed from within by God's singing *with* the people and working *against* them. In fact, the humour is subtle, corroding irony.[6]

And sure enough, the same kind of irony is betrayed by the story in another repetition.[7] The words indicating most clearly the motive for man's building passion are these: "Let us make a name for ourselves, lest we be scattered abroad ..". Besides the important factor of fear ("lest we be ..") the point at issue is a kind of superhuman fame which they want to attain. People want a name? Well, they can have it, but how different it will be from the name they had dreamt of: "... therefore its name was called Babel, "Muddle"! This unexpected turn is like a judgement, so biting is its sarcasm.

When we consider the position of these two cases of irony within the whole, then the surmise is raised of a sort of parallelism of construction. To test this surmise we consider the principal phonological phenomena first: There are three striking paronomasias: *nilb^{e}nā l^{e}benīm, nisr^{e}fā lisrefā, ḥemār - ḥomer*; there is the alliteration *l^{e}benā* – *l^{e}'āben*; the repetition of *šām* (five times), alliterating with *šem*, and the repetition of *kol hā'āreṣ*.

§ 4 First consider the paronomasia *nilb^{e}nā l^{e}benīm*, a turn which does not occur anywhere else in Tenakh. Is it therefore exceptional? We are urged to wariness by the Akkadian, which very frequently

[6] The irony of Gen. 11 has been emphasized by Benno Jacob in his commentary on Genesis, Berlin, 1934.

[7] Cassuto, op. cit., p. 165 about נעשה לנו שם: בהמשך הסיפור נאמר, מתוך אירוניה מרה, שבאמת זכו לשם (פס׳ ט׳: על כן קרא שמה בבל) אבל רק לשם הניתן להתפרש לגנאי, כרמז לבלבול הלשונות שבתוכם.

exhibits the combination of *libittam labānu* not only in the world-of-its-own of our story, but also in the historical reality of Ancient Mesopotamia, where making bricks was the order of day! But even if the phrase *l*^{e}*bon l*^{e}*benīm* was common in classical Hebrew[8] we cannot dismiss this paronomasia in v. 3. And for this reason, that it is part of a chain of repetitions. The combination of the sounds L, B, N occurs no less than six times in our short passage. This means that the problem shifts to that of defining the purpose of these excessive repetitions. Certainly, in the first place it is emphasized to us how important an activity building is for the men, but the real point of the chain of repetitions cannot become clear until we realize that sound effects often serve the purpose of focusing the attention on the sounds themselves. So with the (root)consonants *l-b-n* in mind we read the story once more. Then we come upon the decisive word from God: *nāb*^{e}*lā*, "let us confuse". We have found a sound-chiasmus[9]:

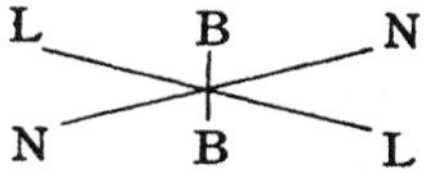

Interpreting this, we see that the reversal of the order of sounds reveals another reversal: God reverses what the men make; the men build, God pulls down; opposed to the men's construction we find, hard and direct, God's destruction. Even without this chiasmus the reversal was in the story, but in this way it becomes pressing, of a particular directness, almost oppressing. Out of inner necessity the narrator not only has this confrontation, this contrast pervade the stratum of sentence content and word meaning, but he even has it crystallize in the sound stratum. And thus the strata become interconnected and organically put into one uniting perspective.

But the necessity of this sound-chiasmus becomes even more ob-

[8] Which its Akkadian sister does not *prove!*

[9] Narrators and poets do not think in linguistic, but in stylistic categories. To the relation of *lbn* – *nbl* one cannot object that *l-b-n* are root consonants and that the *n* of *nbl* is not. The whole theory of the root's consisting of three consonants, for that matter, was not discovered until 1500 or 2000 years later by people who themselves spoke a Semitic language! So the *n* is equally "operative" in *nbl* and *lbn*. That sounds in the reality of the narrator's language are equivalent, even if they fall into linguistically different classes, appears, needless to say, from the folk-etymology *bbl* $< \sqrt{bll}$.

vious when we make another step in the interpretation. The chiasmus connects the two actions so tightly that the one can no longer exist without the other. A causal relation is made, as it were, between the construction and the obstruction: the action of these people with such God-displeasing pretensions asks for counteraction, and necessarily provokes this reaction from God on the basis of this concrete motivation. God's repartee following inseparably on man's word has been expressed with a maximum of economy and impact in the chiasmus.

Unconsciously exegesis had missed a chance by overlooking *nābelā*. Does the reader think such a relation and its interpretation merely subjective and too bold for this moment? That it is correct to apply the words of the root LBN, particularly *nilbenā lebenīm* of v. 3 to NBL of v. 7 is already apparent from the above mentioned parallelism between the verses concerned, "wayyomerū: hābā nilbenā.." // wayyōmer: hābā nābelā...", which parallelism also brought about a reversal or contrast in meaning (by surprise: God's *hābā* was ironic). But the true proof is a structural one and is kept for later use. If we are not mistaken we may expect that this stylistic junction in the story will be essentially tied up with or even be part of the structure. It remains to be seen whether the sound-chiasmus does raise the veil overlaying the composition.

§ 5 With the alliteration of *šem* with *šām* and the five-fold occurrence of the latter, exegesis has again missed a chance by only mentioning these facts. One might start by saying that in order to bring themselves everlasting fame (*šem*) it is necessary for the people to combine efforts in one huge project in one place, *šām*, wherever that may be. But this is too shallow an analysis. Here, too, we must, in order to arrive at an interpretation, first see that the frequent repetition of *šām* aims at drawing our attention to the sounds themselves, and next we must reread the story with this word at the back of our minds. Again we come upon a word that turns out to be the missing link in a chain of sounds, *šāmayim*, 'heavens'.

Our story extends between *kol hā'āreṣ* and *kol hā'āreṣ*. "All the world" assembles and the only result is that they are scattered "all over the world"; precisely what "all the world" seeks to avoid happens, dispersion "all over the world" – another flash of the narrator's dialectic irony. It is one of the pillars of biblical theology that the earth has been given to man and that the heavens are God's private domain, the place of his throne and his hosts. The two planes do not meet; they are essentially different and each other's opposites. Two or three unique exceptions prove this rule,[10] which even extends to the final days. *Be'aḥarīt hayyāmīm*, when all things are made new, there is still the division between a new earth and a new heaven.

The earth has been given and assigned to man by God and man must know his place – here on earth. But that is what the men in Gen. 11 rebel against. The earth is not enough for them, they want more than their plane area. Besides, they are afraid of losing their strength because of the horizontal ("lest we be scattered abroad upon the face of the whole earth"). They decide to bring about a revolutionary break-through, up from the plane to the *šāmayim*. They want to break through the god-given order by means of a tower with its top in the heavens to quiet their fear and make their fame everlasting.

What they want to attain, *šem* = make a name, they make conditional on the *šāmayim*, the abode of God. Implicitly they want, perhaps as yet unconsciously, to make impossible the salvation-history,[11] which according to the biblical message is essentially the thrilling dialogue between God and man. Implicitly they want to penetrate the strictly divine and become divine themselves. What drives them is hubris. We see how, in a nutshell, the narrator conveys in language the idea that hubris has not only a 'positive' component, megalomania, wanting-to-be-like-God, but also a negative one, fear, the fear of being scattered abroad, of having to live without safety and existential security, of being lonely and vulnerable.

That is more or less what the alliteration of *šem* – *šāmayim* communicates in sounds. But there is also *šām*. The word has by no means accomplished its task in referring to a certain region, the land of Sinear. It mainly indicates how important that place is for the people a) to use as a base for their storming of heaven (*šāmayīm*) and b) thus to attain fame (*šem*). There, *šām*, at that one spot, people assemble. They assemble their force to start one big project. Unity is strength,

[10] See p. 53 of Ch. II, about Gen. 28.10-22.

[11] This equally massive and vague concept, to which a meaning is often assigned which is assumed a priori but which is not clear-cut, is here used tentatively, and certainly not as a theological presupposition or a thinking-pattern which might influence the analyses of this book. I will come back to it in my conclusion and try to regauge it on the grounds of chs. I-V. W. Richter, Exegese als Literaturwissenschaft, p. 13 note 16, points out that "*Heilsgeschichte*" has had much influence as an aprioristic thinking-pattern, but that it is now a subject for discussion.

concentration is their slogan; otherwise, they are afraid, their gigantic expansion of power will remain unsuccessful, (and for a moment we realize that urbanization, fusions, automatization, rationalization are not only the slogans of our time). There, on this one spot, all attention is focused and there all human potential is organized. But – and for the fourth time the narrator has God parry with his rapier of irony – from that very spot they will be sent into the desert, precisely from there (*miššām*) abandoned to dispersion and disintegration.[12]

§ 6 We shall touch lightly on the question of the meaning of the tower which the men want to build; opinions differ as to the tower itself and as to the significance of the addition of *wᵉrōšō baššāmayim*. Let us start with the tower. Its bare presence in the story of Genesis is an accurate reminder of the ziqqurat, the building which once dominated the features of the old Sumero-Akkadian town (and which still commands the ruins), just as the narrator is also reliable in conveying the local colour when he mentions tiles and pitch, the building material of the people in Sinear. But our story is first and foremost a Hebrew text, a phonological reality, a linguistic work of art[13]; it is not pri-

[12] Is this story an old document of cultural criticism? Not primarily, I think, but one may see a sharp attack within our narrative, launched by an Israelite of either semi-nomadic or agrarian habit and view of life, and aimed at man as city-builder, at the urbanization which of old characterized Sumerian-Akkadian civilization and which had occurred on a less spectacular scale in Israel since King Salomo. The final verses then offer an alternative: the swarming over all the earth is, it is true, interpreted negatively by the ambitious and yet frightened people, but that is because they refuse to play their part in the covenant history and because they want to withdraw from every perspective in sacred history. However, as soon as one bears in mind the history of salvation and looks at this episode not from a self-centred human point of view but from God's point of view, as the narrator seems to teach us, it is possible to arrive at a positive interpretation of the dispersion, dispersion as fulfilment of the commandment: "be fruitful and multiply and fill the earth". Supporting evidence is that such a genealogy as the one in Gen.10 (in particular vv. 5, 11, 18, 20, 30-32) places a positive value on the dispersion "according to their genealogies, their languages, their lands and their nations". To conclude, one can quite rightly regard the dispersion of Gen. 11 as the necessary background against which the individual Abram, who receives a radical commission from God and thus becomes isolated as well as chosen in Gen. 12, is more clearly spotlighted.
[13] Actually, this is as yet a working hypothesis. We anticipate our results; however small it may be, it fully deserves its claim to the title of literary work of art.

marily an historical document about archaeological realia.[14] We shall try to consider the tower from a literary-stylistic point of view and not to tear it from its context of sounds and meanings, i.e. of linguistic phenomena. Let us spell the word *m-i-g-d-a-l*. For the audience of old it must not have been difficult to remember the etymological "derivation" of this word. For the Israelite it must have been but a short step from *migdal* to *gādol* 'great'; to him *migdal* would have sounded as the word "greatening" would to us. This is only the general linguistic reason; but here the concrete context activates the meaning of *great* in the word *migdal*. For what is the point of this tower? It is *the* material proof that the men want to be great, greater than they are or are asked to be, that they want to make a name for themselves by reaching out for the heavens and thus to be like God. This *migdal*, this "greatening" makes the megalomania of our city-builders concrete and manifest. To support this view there is also the literary-historical and biblical-theological argument that in several biblical texts a tower functions as a symbol of megalomania and godless pretensions.[15]

Then there is the question of "its top in the heavens". Some will contend that this *baššāmayim* needn't mean much more than "in the sky".[16] Indeed, a bold statement, to say that a tower has its top in the sky. Others think that *rōšō baššāmayim* "only" (again that reducing term!) means that its top sticks up high in the sky. There may be some truth in this but this reading minimizes *šāmayim*, for fear of saying scientifically too much. I deliberately choose a maximizing reading, for here the heavens must be retained for the sake of contrast to "the earth, the whole earth", which is definitely relevant in a narrative containing a short but fierce struggle for power between man and God.

[14] Regularly exegetes nowadays change colour when they come across the tower, impressed as they are by the findings and discoveries for over a century of Mesopotamian archaeology. And indeed, it is a temptation to write a large treatise in small type on the Mesopotamian city and its centre of all organization: the temple-tower, or ziqqurat. But a change to the ziqqurat would imply leaving the realm of fiction (the idiosyncratic reality of the work of art) and exchanging it for that of historical reality.

[15] Very clearly in Is. 2.12ff side by side with cedar-trees, mountains and walls. Also in Is. 30.25, Ez. 26.4,9. Elsewhere the *migdal* may of course stand for strength and security in a positive sense.

[16] Neither is it useful to refer to Absalom, who in II Sam. 18.9 – his hair caught in the branches – is hanging "*bēn haššāmayim ubēn hā'āreṣ*", so certainly "in the sky": isn't it delightful to leave the expression in its full sense, "between heaven and earth"? Unforgettable!

And apart from the fact that a narrator, if he should want to make the statement that a tower is high, simply has the word גבה at his command, the word *šāmayim* must sound in its full range as "heavens", because the very function of this word is to reveal the action and intentions of the people as *hubris*. This is not certain yet, but I hope to demonstrate structurally that our story is really one of crime and punishment.[17]

§ 7 It is time we uncovered the objective foundation of all our exegesis by unfolding the double symmetry of the structure which governs the story.

More than once it has been observed that the story falls into two more or less equal halves, the first of which deals with man and the second with Yahweh. It appears to be possible to indicate more precisely and in more detail to what extent we may speak of a qualitative equality. What, as far back as § 3, was a surmise of ours because of the parallelism *hābā ..-ā* || *hābā ..-ā*, now turns out to be correct. A parallel symmetry controls the course of events:

A שפה אחת ודברים אחדים
B הבה + coh. (2 ×)
C נבנה — vv. 1-4 about
D נעשה שם — the men
E פן נפוץ על פני כל הארץ
A′ עם אחד ושפה אחת
B′ הבה + coh.
C′ ויחדלו לבנת — vv. 5-9 about — E′ ויפץ אתם על פני כל האדץ
D′ שמה בבל — Yahweh
E′ הפיצם על פני כל הארץ

[17] A methodological *aperçu* on the choice between minimizing or enriching reading. Von Rad hits the mark in the methodic *Vorerwägungen* of his theology of the OT: "Die historische Forschung sucht ein kritisch gesichertes Minimum; das kerygmatische Bild tendiert nach einem theologischen Maximum" (Theologie des AT, Band I, p. 114, München, 1961). Our stylistic analysis will in the end result in the careful drawing of 'das kerygmatische Bild' of Gen. 11.1-9. That for which von Rad had to plead forcibly, viz. "dem Bild, das Israel selbst von seiner Geschichte gezeichnet hat, auch in wissenschaftlicher Hinsicht eine Eigenständigkeit zuzuerkennen und es als etwas für sich Existentes zu nehmen, das, wie es entworfen ist, als ein zentraler Gegenstand unserer theologischen Beurteilung gelten muss" (p. 113) is something which has been known for much longer by that literary scholarship which believes in and starts from the 'auto-

Note that the objectivity of this parallelism of series of words precedes all interpretation, so much so that any reader, not knowing Hebrew but with a transcription of the story at his disposal, can be shown that the members of the series correspond because of the identity of words and he can inspect their order. The relevance, the essentiality of this symmetry, however, can of course be defended only in the course of interpretation.

At least two means of intrinsic verification are at our service if we are to determine whether this parallel symmetry is significant. Firstly, is the distribution of the members over the halves of the story balanced? It is. Secondly, are the words mentioned in A-E, which make up the parallelism, insignificant or important, are they or are they not related to the main points of the story? A short paraphrase of the members A-E may suffice to prove that the pairs do mark the main points: their natural unity (A) is used by the men to formulate energetically a plan (B) for an impressive building (C). Their object is to make a name for themselves (D) and thus at the same time to take away the fear of dispersion (E). God sees their natural unity (A′) and thwarts the men with an energetically formulated plan of his own (B′) which he carries out at once (E′) so that the building is abandoned (C′). The result is an anti-name (D′) and the very dispersion they feared (E′).

This intrinsic examination of the distribution and representativeness of the members is of a general nature in so far that with all similar symmetries it can, indeed, must, be carried out.[18] We can also carry out an intrinsic examination of the parallel symmetry in Gen. 11.1-9 and authenticate it by considering the absolutely idiosyncratic quality of *this* parallelism. It is definitely there, for except for the neutral identity of the pair A-A′ all other four pairs (B-B′, C-C′, etc.) contain some contrast or reversal. And even more important is the fact that in three of them (B, D, E) we find again the narrator's irony, already noticed by us: in B′ God parrots the enthusiasm of the people; the name they want turns into its poignant opposite, a sneering dig at them; their fear of being scattered abroad turns out to be an example

nomy' of literary texts, of the idiosyncratic structure and organization of the world created by narrators and poets. No wonder that von Rad, one paragraph further down (p. 114f.), points to the fact that the faith of Israel has preferred the vehicle of "die Dichtung" (fiction) to speak of Yahweh and his work in history directly.

[18] E.g. in that of Gen. 28.10-22 (see Ch. II, pp. 71ff.) or Jonah 1 (see R. Pesch, Biblica 47 (1966), Zur konzentrischen Struktur von Jona 1, pp. 577-581).

of self-fulfilling prophecy (E′).[19] In short, it is precisely a number of the piquant sound devices of the narrator's which appear in the majority of the elements in the series; therewith the symmetry has been authenticated.

One thing is curious in this symmetry. A formally parallel symmetry might be expected to be indicative of some similarity of parallelism of content,[20] but in this case the contrast, respectively reversal, of B-E in B′-E′, seems to be sharper, more obtrusive than the similarity, which lies only in repetitions of words and the synchronic progress of the second half (this is confirmed in the structure below, § 8). There is a very curious relation between the similarity of the first and second halves of the story, on one hand, and the reversal of the first half to the second half, thus dissimilarity, on the other hand.

§ 8 The symmetry indicated above contained five pairs, thus there were ten members. However, the greater, the number of pairs in a symmetrical structure becomes, the more difficult it is to break away from the iron grip of such a principle of composition, the easier it is to be convinced of the objectivity of such a pattern and the more readily we can recognize the dominance, the structural significance of such a double, continuous thread.

The second and decisive symmetry in Gen. 11.1-9 consists of even six pairs, plus the turning-point flanked by them. It is a concentric symmetry:

A כל הארץ שפה אחת
B שם
C איש אל רעהו — vv. 1-4 about the men
D הבה נלבנה לבנים
E נבנה לנו
F עיר ומגדל

X וירד יהוה לראת

F′ את העיר ואת המגדל
E′ אשר בנו בני האדם — vv. 5-9 about Yahweh
D′ הבה . . . נבלה
C′ איש שפת רעהו
B′ משם
A′ שפת כל הארץ (בלל)

For notes 19 and 20 see pag. 23

Emil Staiger gives us the following statement: "Jedes echte, lebendige Kunstwerk ist in seinen festen Grenzen unendlich".[21] The special point about Gen. 11 is this: what Staiger calls the fixed boundaries is present and demonstrable here, dead-sharp, exact and complete in itself, with an objectivity preceding all interpretation (and it is neither here nor there that this structure can only be defined through interpretative work).[22]

Again we apply the two intrinsic criteria to check the relevance of the pattern of symmetry. Even more clearly than the ten elements of the parallel symmetry the concentrically arranged twelve elements are evenly distributed over the two halves of the story, on both sides of that intervention without corresponding counterpart (X, "then Jahweh came down") which changes the whole situation in one stroke. And again a short paraphrase of the twelve elements, now and then concisely anticipating the explanation proper in §§ 9ff., can demonstrate that they mark the main points of the story: unity of language (A) and place (B) and intensive communication (C) induce the men to plans and inventions (D), especially to building (E) a city and a tower (F). God's intervention is the turning-point (X). He watches the buildings (F′) people make (E′) and launches a counter-plan (D′) because of which communication becomes impossible (C′) and the unity of place (B′) and of language (A′) is broken.

[19] Only C-C′ has a contrast without literary cachet.

[20] Gen. 28.10-22 is a telling example, see Ch. II.

[21] E. Staiger, die Kunst der Interpretation, Zürich, 1955, 2nd ed., p. 33.

[22] The fact that the objective structure has not been brought to light in the interpretative work of the past 2000 years is epistemologically and hermeneutically most curious, because biblical exegesis has, generally speaking, read the story correctly – we readily admit – namely, as crime and punishment: so a correct interpretation has been possible in this case without the support of the objective symmetry for the readers. This does not deny the importance of the story's structure and the narrator's composing it, but is strongly in favour of it: for centuries the story has hidden the compositional qualities of the skilful narrator, but has, by its dormant structure, had such a firm hold on generations of exegetes, that their interpretation was in essence correct. What happens now, now that the structure has been revealed, is only that the interpretation of the story touches ground and that it can, aided by the structure, also gain in nuance and accuracy in quite a few details.

§ 9 We owe the reader something: the structural proof that it is correct and meaningful to interconnect the words of the root LBN and *hābā .. nābᵉlā* (vs. 7). This proof now lies open to us; the two elements of the sound-chiasmus form a pair in the concentric structure, D-D′. If this chiasmus (together with other phonological phenomena) had not led us to the structure, the structure would have led us to this sound-chiasmus (and other phenomena).[23] – Let us now make the most of the symmetry.
A-A′. First there is, as we have already seen in § 5, the irony which the narrator creates by a pregnant use of the stylistic means of ambiguity: ***kol hā'āreṣ, tout le monde***, and ***kol hā'āreṣ, le monde entier***, are the boundary-posts between which the story takes place. The one is the opposite of the other, because the first ***kol hā'āreṣ*** is a sign of bringing together, unity, concentration of power and the other ***kol hā'āreṣ*** means an end to these illusions: dispersion, multiplicity, the splitting of power. Secondly, the people ("all the world") fail in their task proper, i.e., to spread "all over the world", in the framework of a correct relation to God. And precisely because they are, in their fear of the "all over the world" solely self-centred, that "***ʿal pᵉnē kol hā'āreṣ***" becomes their fate, their punishment in the end.

And this is not all there is. Together, the members A-A′ form an effective chiasmus, when examined in their immediate context:

kol hā'āreṣ	ṣāfā 'eḥat
bālal Yahweh sᵉfat	kol hā'āreṣ

[23] Another remark on the heuristics of stylistic analysis, "the finding of an access to the story". Gen. 11 is a gratifying case in point to illustrate that it is fruitful to make use of those elements that are brought to the fore by the story itself. Precisely those sound phenomena and repetitions that have been pushed into a striking position appear to be the best way to the core of the story (here: the symmetrical structure). Heuristically it is either these or those stylistic details which first raise a surmise of a certain regularity in the composition. But once that regularity has been completely revealed, so that we automatically become observant of the other structurally effective details, it is no longer important whether it was the stylistics mentioned under A-A′ or those mentioned under B-B′ (etc., up to F-F′ and including) that set the spiralling going in the fundamental pattern; and in the exegete's report it is no longer essential to begin at those same stylistics that once put him on the track of the structure.

Very strikingly this chiastic construction throughout the entire story expresses the reversal, the radical intervention; opposite one language comes confusion of language. And again, after unity and communication there is multiplicity and the impossibility of communication and expansion of power. That it is a chiasmus is guaranteed by the structural correspondence of A-A′, although at first this strikes us as strange, for the halves are so far away from each other. Nevertheless the figure of speech of such a widely separated quartet, such a chiasmus 'at a distance' is found more often in the Old Testament.[24]

B-B′. The two little words "there .. from there" when isolated do not render much, but when put in their context have more to offer. For along the cord of the alliteration they also draw the words *šem* (2×) and *šāmayim* within the circle of what is structurally significant – and the interpretation of this we have already given. And when we see the reversals of A, C and D, which take place in A′, C′ and D′, then the structure turns out to be the confirmation and elucidation of what we said in § 5: *šām* stands for the unity of place, which is indispensable to the wished-for expansion of power. Ironically *miššām* is opposed to it, standing for the dispersion which stifles the pursuit of power in its birth.

§ 10 A third pole in the magnetic field: *C-C′ and A-A′*.

The narrator's art of composition lifts the modest idiomatic expression of reciprocity in classical Hebrew ("a man to his mate", meaning "one to another, each other") from the dust of triviality and puts it in a pregnant position, which in turn is the key to a series of stylistic elements, as yet hardly mentioned, of paramount structural significance.

First of all the pair C-C′, when read in its immediate context (especially the negative v. 7b) shows us the same correspondence as A-A′, B-B′ and D-D′. For here, too, the second member C′ is the counterpart of the first one. Again the correspondence contains a reversal: from communication to the impossibility thereof. This reversal is not brought about by the pair C-C′ alone but together with A-A′.

What is the relation, then, between the first and the third pair (between A-A′ and C-C′) and what is the meaning of this relation?

[24] See, e.g., Ex. 6.12 with 30; Ex. 3.21.22 with 11:2,3; I K.1.35 with regard to vv. 13/17/24/30: yimlok 'aḥaray ... yešeb 'al kis'ī with regard to wᵉyešeb 'al kis'ī ... yimlok taḥtay.

In order to find out we look at A and C more closely (C′ and A′ will follow automatically, they are 'only' mirror-images) by doing something which up till now we have almost doggedly refused to do: read from front to back. Verse 1(i.e. member A) describes a prehistoric situation which to the old Israelite must have seemed as unique as it does to us modern readers: the absolute unity of language among mankind. Neither he nor we immediately take in its meaning and its consequences. But that is what C in v. 3 is going to make clear to us. There communication is actually taking place, the unity of language and place (v. 2) renders extensive exchange of ideas and plans possible and is the *conditio sine qua non* for man's expansion of power and act of *hubris*. By means of its members A and C our story puts a heavy, and in classical narrative art particular, if not unique, emphasis on the primacy of language in all communication and creativity, and this primacy is clearly demonstrated with the one "primitive language" mentioned here. In amazement and admiration we can further observe that the narrator materializes his linguistic "philosophy in a nutshell" stylistically, for now it appears that his words on language and communication open a third structural perspective. This continuous thread of composition, the third one, also enables us to explain the stylistics which remained from § 3 (ending). A-A′ and C-C′ are the third pole in the magnetic field of the story, which generates the following lines of force:

a)	אחרים	. . . .	אחת	(v. 1)
b)	לבנים	. . . .	נלבנה	(v. 3)
c)	לשרפה	. . . .	ונשרפה	(v. 3)
d)	לאבן	. . . .	הלבנה	(v. 3)
e)	לחמר	. . . .	והחמר	(v. 3)
f)	אחת	. . . .	אחד	(v. 6)

Wonder precedes science; for a long time we mused in wonder on these pairs, which are framed by two pairs "one .. one", and for a moment there is a yawning chasm of numerology before our feet. But once one spots A-A′ and C-C′, comprehension dawns.

The distribution of pairs over the story, which was a hall–mark of the parallel and concentric symmetries, is not at all appropriate here. The pairs are only to be found in verses which are about people, in short in the first half; even f) above is not an exception, for God does not act yet in v. 6 and in God's words, which are a mere statement (v. 6a), f) is purely the echo of a).

It is in the verses about the human plans that pair must follow pair. Verse 3 especially simply crackles with pairs and not accidentally so. The atmosphere in the human community is electrified by the intensive communication which leads to energetic plans: come on, let us do this! come on, let us do that! Standing in the unity of language (the framework a-f!) people exchange ideas. Like sparks they dart to and fro, "backen wir Backsteine ... brennen wir sie zu Brande! So war ihnen der Backstein statt Bausteins und das Roherdpech war ihnen statt Roterdmörtels." Thus Buber tries to retain the alliterations and repetitions in German (although they are a little cumbersome and ungraceful).

The language is a *Fundgrube* for these people, is for them the source of creative thinking. The stock of words which contains the likenesses of *l^{e}benā – l^e'āben* and of *ḥemār – ḥomer* (certainly our narrator's finest find in the series) implants the idea that burning clay can supply them with the building material they urgently need and that bitumen or pitch can be the indispensable mortar. Balancing the word *l^{e}benā* on their tongues they discover to their amazement: *l^e'āben*! Weighing the word *ḥemār* a light dawns upon them: of course, that is our *ḥomer*. By means of association of sounds they drift from one thing to another. Language creates new realities.

In using the word "one" four times, the narrator has created a square (a + f) which forms the framework for four combinations created by unity of sound and/or unity of word-root. Thus he has completely crystallized his concept of the value and primary importance of language. The primary importance of the unity of language has been made manifest stylistically and structurally.

§ 11 *From A BCDEF to F'E'D'C'B'A'.*

Yahweh finds himself confronted with unexpected concentration of power, with a revolution which threatens to subvert the cosmic order created by him. He intervenes and the concentric structure shows in a way which permits no misunderstanding that God is going to fight this evil by destroying it root and branch.

Root and branch, indeed, God strikes at the roots of the threat. Unity of language, unity of place, the maximum communication which they brought about and the inner urge to actions have led to building a city and a tower (ABCD have led to EF). God "sees" this city and its tower. This means, of course, that he studies, he examines the building, values it at its true worth, in short he sees through the evil and strikes at its root. Responding through his own urge to action he breaks and destroys the communication, the unity of place and the unity of language (F′E′ lead to D′C′B′A′). How much he fears the creativity of language and its possibilities for man is evident in the reason for his intervention. He fears "all other things the men propose to do" and wants to stifle at birth the danger that "nothing will now be too difficult for them". Thus v. 6b is further evidence of the primary importance the story attaches to (the unity of) language.

D-D′. The men against God, God against the men: construction followed by destruction, construction may even be said to have invited destruction (see § 4). The frequent repetition of words with the combination *l, b, n* exerts its influence further in the story. Not only has ***nābᵉlā*** become relevant for its sound but also the name of Babel itself has been included in the chain of alliteration. And there is more to it than this.

E-E′. The effect of the alliterations is that the word ***bānā***, to build, is made even more conspicuous; besides, it is brought to our special notice by its structural position in E-E′ and also by the parallelism of ***hābā*** + exhortative (v. 3) and ***hābā*** + exhortative (v. 4). How important the building is need not be said again, but E′ compels us to formulate our analysis even more precisely. There, for the first and only time in our story the men are 'simply' called men, ***bᵉnē hā'ādām***, but this was immediately preceded by ***bānū***. This alliteration expresses that the men are essentially builders, here, ***that*** work is everything to them. That this relationship between ***ben*** = son and ***bānā*** is not too far-fetched, we learn from Gen. 16.2, where Sarai clearly interweaves the two concepts by sighing, "may I be built" ***and*** "may I have a son" in one deliberately ambiguous word, ***'ibbānē***.

The axis. Finally X" and Yahweh came down" is clearly and tellingly the turning-point in the story and the structure.[25] Suddenly a new protagonist is standing before our eyes, who from now on (vv. 6ff.)

[25] In his "attempt to describe the laws governing chiastic [read: concentric, JF] structures" Lund writes (see note 36) under no. 1: "The centre is always the turning point" and under no. 2: "At the centre there is often a change in the trend of thought, and an antithetic idea is introduced. After this the original trend is resumed and continued until the system is concluded. For want of a better name, we shall designate this feature *the law of the shift at the centre*." (p. 40f).

sovereignly decides what is going to happen. At one blow the situation has changed, at one stroke it is made clear that the earth is not the only thing in existence and is not alone in having inhabitants, but that the heavens and their inhabitants cannot be left out and make themselves felt precisely when men shun them and when they ignore God in in their high-handed proceedings.

Interpretation of the whole

§ 12 Up till now we have only used the symmetries as an incitement to interpret those formal phenomena which they brought to our notice. But a symmetrical structure of the kind that we have come across is, taken as a whole, also a formal phenomenon, if of a higher order and just as up till now we have doggedly refused to stop at merely indicating formal details, so we must now not only indicate the more complex formal phenomenon, but interpret it as an independent entity. And because the symmetrical structure is the most powerful and most fundamental formal aspect of our story we may expect that its interpretation will enable us to push through to the last predominating perspective, to that one decisive concept of the narrator's which inspired and guided him in choosing and handling his tools.

Alas, right from the start a serious obstacle seems to rise before us as we work towards this goal. For in our literary analysis, just as any interpreter, unawares at the least, is likely to seek unity in his object and to read for one perspective, we have explicitly acted on the assumption that our text is an elaborate whole crystallized from a structural core. However, in Gen. 11 there is not simply one structure, but two structural symmetries. Does not one symmetry render the other superfluous? Or, to put it more precisely, are not the parallel and the concentric patterns in conflict?[26]

[26] When answering these questions we must steer clear of two dangers, namely of the desire for abstractions and schemata and for (an equally abstracting) formalism. In the first place we may not confine ourselves simply to the two symmetrical series. Not they, but the whole story is our highest authority and our object proper. After the skeleton has been examined separately for a study of details it must, in the end, be considered in its function within the living body of flesh and blood. The schema of the symmetrical structure must, however important it may be, in the end be returned to its position of service, into the anonymity where it belongs and from which it had been taken away temporarily for the purpose of analysis. Secondly we may not handle the symmetrical series

Let us keep our eyes bent on the vivid reality of the language of this story as our final object and judge the series on their own semantic merits and as indicative of the interpretation of the story-as-a-whole, realizing that basically these series are hidden when we experience the story – an experiencing which is an indispensable condition for a literary analysis.

In connection with the parallel symmetry we have already touched upon a peculiar relation between similarity and dissimilarity which the halves of the story display with regard to each other (§ 7, ending). We must now go into this.

Of a narrator who uses both a parallel symmetry and a concentric one we may, *a priori*, expect that by means of the first symmetry he will want to make visible a form of similarity and by means of the second one, some contrast or reversal, thus dissimilarity. Paradoxically enough, however, nearly all the pairs of the parallel symmetry denote, as we have seen, a contrast, because B′, C′, etc. mean a reversal of B, C, etc. And what about the concentric symmetry? There, fewer pairs mark a contrast, for X, on its own drop out, and E′ and F′ are a not very important repetition of E and F. Yet the reversals which D′C′B′A′ imply with regard to ABCD, and the fact that the two wings run together towards a centre would be expected to make on us a predominant impression of contrast. But this is not the case. Paradoxically enough, I personally experience above all in this concentric arrangement the mirroring-effect (F′-A′ mirrors A-F) and so the similarity of the halves.

That is why we venture to bring the effect of the two symmetries into one formula, which, it is true, is as yet much too abstract and tentative and which, as far as we are concerned, may fall into oblivion later, but which nevertheless slightly indicates how much the two schemata belong together, and shows as well that their relationship is too subtle to be interpreted by the narrow presumption that parallelism stands for equality and concentricity stands for contrast. In terms of the structural form the parallel symmetry indicates the equality in the reversal and the concentric symmetry indicates the

with disregard for all semantics; meanings of words and contents of sentences may not be stripped. We take care that the series are not reduced to a merely abstract and formalistic a-b...n//a′-b′...n′ and a-b...n X n′...b′-a′. If we didn't, we could not but come to the conclusion that series which run parallel (of the type abc/abc) and series which run counter (abc-cba) are conflicting as structurally decisive patterns.

reversal in the equality; in terms of the complex of meanings (the content) the parallel symmetry indicates the reversal in the equality and the concentric symmetry indicates the equality in the reversal.

Is this not too glib an interpretation? Can one expect a work of art to be summed up in such a smooth dialectic? It would indeed be a barren pursuit to use the abstract nouns of equality and reversal from now on as a key to further interpretation, cutting up the text into a card-tray and then classing all the parts and elements under the head "equality" and under the heading "reversal". The sum is more than the parts in this case, just as a mosaic is entirely different from the pile of tesserae of which it consists. Then it is more than clear that the "inequality" of the halves is, if by nothing else, caused by a) the course of events (as in every story) and b) the contrasting of two protagonists, the human race and God. But it is much more fascinating to try to indicate concretely in what the equality of the halves and the reversal-in-the-equality consist.[27]

Quite concretely the two symmetries as such, the key-words of which mark in detail the connection and similarity of the halves of the story, mean this:

– The action of the people is closely reflected in God's reaction. The punishment fits the tresspass; communication and concentration are followed by confusion and dispersion. God's reaction and its effects are minutely attuned to man's action and its causes. To the attack he gives – speaking in modern terms of nuclear strategy – his flexible response, adapted to the extent and place of attack, and thus keeps the conflict limited. (The alternative, wholesale destruction, is not far away. When in Gen. 6 the human race degenerated and was going to be a threat to God, by relationship by marriage with "sons of God" among other factors, he struck back, wiping out every thing – counter-city strategy. Only Noah and his household were allowed to escape the flood. In Gen. 11 God chooses the counterforce strategy, he destroys only the potential and the base of attack of his enemy.) That is the story when read from back to front.

– When read from front to back the symmetrical story is as follows. These actions by men cannot fail to provoke these counteractions by God. Precisely because they will have nothing to do with God, they will have to deal with him. The sin of the people who are self-centred in their communication and concentration of power asks for the

[27] See below § 14.

punishment of confusion and dispersion, dealt out to them by God. This hubris of man calls forth this nemesis of God.

– The polarity of the story, with its poles men-God, action-reaction, hubris-nemesis, articulated so delicately and completely by the doubly-symmetrical structure, is the literary realization of a kind of *talio*.

Before we can work this out we shall first give an explanation of the retaliation.

§ 13 In Israel the *ius talionis* has gone through a development of its own. Formerly clans of nomads and semi-nomads proceeding along the Fertile Crescent were in continual danger of being struck by the effects of the vendetta which caused the feuds to spread unlimitedly like a cancer. And similarly, but much later, this is seen in the world of Arab tribes before Mohammed cast up the first dam with his precept of strict retaliation in case of murder or the infliction of wounds, the qiṣāṣ.[28] The Bible preserves unmistakable reminiscences of the unlimited blood–revenge. What Lamech's song of revenge sang of, "I have slain a man for wounding me, a young man for striking me; for sevenfold vengeance is taken for Cain, but seventy-sevenfold for Lamech",[29] continues to exert its effects long after the nomadic stage had passed. In the time of the Judges, when "everyone did what was right in his sight" (which will certainly have been true of the retaliation and its extent), witness the story of Jud. 19-21[30], and even when the national state has made its appearance, note II Sam. 21 about the Gibeonites and Saul's descendants.[31]

Characteristic of OT law, however, is the "eye for eye, tooth for tooth",[32] which drastically restricts the unlimited blood-revenge, drives back arbitrary violence and means an enormous step forward in the history of law. The first purpose of this regulation, which is also founded on Mesopotamian law,[33] but in Israel remains religiously defined, is to see to it that the punishment of the retaliation will not

[28] Koran, sura II, 178f. (173-175).
[29] Gen. 4.24.
[30] There a whole tribe is in danger of perishing because of the crime of a village against one married couple. Also think of such actions as the ones by Simson in Jud. 15.1-7 (especially v. 7) and 16.23-31 (esp. v. 28).
[31] Also see note 48.
[32] Ex. 21.23-25, Lev. 24.17-21, Num. 35.31-34.
[33] Cf. Ex. 21.23-25 and §§ 196, 197 and 200 of the Codex Hammurabi even with regard to the choice of words.

surpass the crime to be revenged, and it says that it must be equal in severity. Being your own judge remains accepted practice but has been regulated and put under the supervision of community or state.

Put down in language, words, the principle that the punishment should fit the crime might very well lead to symmetry, and now we are getting curious to see whether such symmetry is to be found and, if it is, whether this symmetry is parallel or concentric.

There are, indeed, several texts in the OT which concern some kind of talio and which display a symmetry.[34] Precisely one of the principal talionic texts, Lev. 24.17-21, appears to be concentric, and precisely the characteristic words "eye for eye, tooth for tooth", the key formula by which one remembers the principle, are nicely in the middle:

C He who kills a man shall be put to death. (v. 17)
  D He who kills a beast shall make it good, life for life. (v. 18)
    E When a man causes a disfigurement in his neighbour, as he has done it shall be done to him, (v. 19)
      X fracture for fracture, eye for eye, tooth for tooth; (v. 20a)
    E′ as he has disfigured a man, he shall be disfigured. (v. 20b)
  D′ He who kills a beast shall make it good; (v. 21a)
C′ and he who kills a man shall be put to death. (v. 21b)

This text does not seem to us to be of specifically literary value, but this does not relieve the interpreter of his obligation to interpret this concentric composition,[35] a task which is outside the scope of the present work. For the sake of completeness it must be remarked that concentric composition is by no means restricted to texts about crime and punishment and that it is used both in prose and poetry. A patient search may yield good examples of various applications of concentric composition in the material uncritically collected by Lund and Galbi-

[34] Beside the three texts from Gen. 6, Lev. 24 and 1 Sam. 15 which we shall discuss in our treatise, also see e.g. Ps. 7.17, cf. Lund p. 34 (see note 36 below); Is. 17.12-14, cf. Lund p. 80; possibly the symmetry in Amos 9.1-4 (Lund p. 86f.) and Ps. 58 (Lund p. 95) which deal with God's punishment for wicked people.

[35] It is precisely the interpretation which is quite disregarded or nearly so by the first two authors of the following note.

ati,[36] e.g., the text on the Passover night in Ex. 12.43-49,[37] or Gen. 3.9-20,[38] or Ps. 90.1-2[39]; and Lev. 24 itself, too, because the verses 13-16 (= A) and 16 (= B) with v. 22 (B') and v. 23 (A') form two more rings round the verses quoted above.[40]

But it is time we looked at Gen. 11. For this purpose we select two biblical passages which form symmetries not by means of whole sentences but by means of their words. Both passages are themselves verses, strictly speaking, and thus poetic lines, but they belong to the literary context of a narrative.

When the flood is over and Noah can go and give a new beginning to the history of the earth and its inhabitants, God repeats some decrees which had already been set forth at the creation, adds a pronouncement on the importance of the blood of living beings and

[36] Nils Wilhelm Lund, Chiasmus in the New Testament, a Study in Formgeschichte, Chapel Hill, 1942; this is a book which, in spite of its title, first dedicates about 100 (!) pages to the Old Testament, esp. pp. 51-138.
Enrico Galbiati, la Struttura letteraria dell'Esodo, Contributo allo studio dei criteri stilistici dell'A.T. e della composizione del Pentateuco, Alba, 1956. Cf. the concentric composition of poems which according to P. Lamarche, Zacharie IX-XIV, Structure littéraire et Messianisme, Paris, 1961, governs the book of Deutero-Zechariah; his "Plan de Zacharie 9-14" is to be found on p. 112ff. In the individual poems, too, Lamarche often perceives a concentric structure. So does Benedikt Otzen, Studien über Deuterosacharja, Kopenhagen, 1964 (Acta Theologica Danica vol. VI) regarding 9.1-10.12 (p. 220). – A few examples with a better terminology than Lund's are also to be found in N. Lohfink, Das Hauptgebot, eine Untersuchung literarischer Einleitungsfragen zu Dtn 5-11, Rome ,1963, p. 182, 183, 195.

[37] Galbiati p. 141; structure: ABCD X D'C'B'A'.

[38] Lund p. 59: "the third chapter of Genesis, which describes the meeting between the fallen pair and God and relates the meting out of punishment, contains the chiastic order. The participants are introduced as follows: man (v. 9), woman (v. 12), and the serpent (v. 13). The sentence upon them is pronounced in the reversed order: the serpent (v. 13), the woman (v. 16), and the man (v. 17)."
But this had not even escaped Gunkel's notice (commentary on Genesis, Einleitung 3.8, p. XXXV): "Man beachte, wie z.B. bei der Paradiesesgeschichte die Anordnung dem Inhalt vortrefflich entspricht: im Sündenfall ist die Reihenfolge: Schlange Weib Mann;" at the trial "ist die Reihenfolge die umgekehrte: Mann Weib Schlange; die Strafe trifft zuerst die Hauptschuldigen, daher ist hier wieder die ursprüngliche Reihenfolge eingetreten: Schlange Weib Mann." This to illustrate his thesis: "diese Dispositionen sind nicht mühsam erklügelt, sondern sie sind wie völlig selbstverständlich aus der Natur der Sache geflossen."

[39] Lund p. 125, a symmetrical structure of ten members.

[40] Lund p. 57f.

then says – and the typography helps us in visualizing the symmetry:

שפך ישפך
דם דמו
האדם באדם

Most translations of this verse are not correct.[41] The correct translation is, "whoever sheds the blood of man, *for* that man shall his blood be shed" (Gen. 9.6a) – and from what follows, v. 6b, it at once appears why this punishment is so severe, "for God made man in his own image."[42] The rule of law rests on a religious foundation.

The symmetry of this verse, abc-cba, is striking. It is an excellent choice, to formulate this rule of law in this way, absolutely concentric, for by this compelling form the author achieves several things: a matter of factness, compelling validity, irrevocability. The close correspondence between the two half-verses convinces the reader of the fitness of *this* punishment for *this* crime. Because the verse starts from bloodshed (*šofek*) and returns by the same way to bloodshed (*yiššāfek*), the reader becomes imbued with the immutability of this rule, for you cannot get in a word edge-ways, between such an abc-cba. Whoever begins at bloodshed, will end up by paying with his own blood, "all who take the sword, will perish by the sword". (And what reader will be surprised to hear that this quotation from Matth. 26.52 is also concentric in Greek, ab-ba?)

The second text which we want to put beside Gen. 11 relates a concrete case of execution. The Amalekite king Agag who has been captured in a raid by Saul, but has been spared, is put to the ban by the commandment of the prophet Samuel. Therefore Agag is still killed,[43] and apart from giving the background of the putting to the ban, the message of the capital punishment points unambiguously to

[41] Viz. "by man" which is forcing an open door. The structure itself proves that *hā'ādām* from the first half-verse is the same as the one in the second half-verse. See J. Pedersen, Israel, its life and culture, Kopenhagen, 1926, Vol. I/II p. 397. He is right when pointing out in the note on p. 533f. that b^e means "for", as in Deut. 19.21, II Sam. 3.27 and I K. 16.34. I should like to point to II Sam. 14.7 "*b^enefeš 'āḥīw*", too.

[42] Shedding blood is, moreover, obstructing the commandment which is given in Gen. 9.1 and 9.7.

[43] Lev. 27.28f.: "every devoted thing is most holy to the Lord. No one devoted, who is to be utterly destroyed from among men, shall be ransomed; he shall be put to death."

its religious foundation: "Samuel hewed Agag in pieces before the Lord in Gilgal". We are interested in the motivation,[44] the sentence that Samuel passes in two short and telling lines, I Sam.15. 33a:

כאשר שכלה נשים חרבך
כן תשכל מנשים אמך

The mercilessness of these words is uncommon for the many hard pronouncements in *Tenakh*. Occasionally we do find a person acting so unrelentingly, so uncompromisingly[45] in narrative prose, but then the verse is not so horrible, so hermetic. (Not until centuries later do the scriptural prophets appear, whose oracles of evil were indigestible for their auditors.)

The verse is air-tight. For the time of seven words Agag (and we after him) is uncertain of Samuel's intention, though his words about women made childless and about the sword are sinister enough, but what he could amply suspect (and so could we, indeed!) suddenly becomes crushing certainty, when the eighth word (d') is dropped and the precision-lock abcd//abcd snaps to. This postponement of the decision to the last moment, this sustained suspense is one of the qualities which make this verse so powerful and impressive; another factor is that Samuel, however hard he may be, is not so blunt as to say straightaway, "you will be put to death", but subtly chooses the indirect speech ("... your sword ... your mother") and the listener is free to draw his conclusions.

But make no mistake! This cruelty is not a feature of Samuel's personality, but the necessary and for that time self-evident reflection of Agag's own bringing of death and destruction. That is what the symmetry points out to us, "all who take the sword...". What matters is the precise symmetry of crime and punishment.

[44] When we read I Sam 15 as a whole, then talio and *ḥerem* are one in the execution of Agag. But there is good reason to believe that the story has been subject to adaptation by circles of prophets and precisely where Samuel's commandment to Saul concerning the *ḥerem* is concerned – see C. H. W. Brekelmans, De Ḥerem in het OT, Nijmegen, 1959, pp. 106-114 and the literature mentioned in note 176. This problem does not affect our analysis of the ending (which, moreover, is generally regarded as "authentic"), vss. 32f.

[45] Joab to Abner (II Sam. 3.22-27), Ehud to Eglon (Jud. 3.15-22), Elijah to the prophets of Baal (I K. 18), etc.

On the basis of these two texts from Gen. and I Sam. we can infer that the idea of retaliation can be rendered by putting some form of symmetry into the language, a symmetry which mentions crime and punishment, and that it is immaterial whether the symmetry of word-order is parallel or concentric. Both possibilities are in principle equivalent and in the two texts discussed here they seem to us equally effective. The equivalence, by the way, was to be expected, considering that such symmetries are not the monopoly of talionic texts but function in other contexts as well[46] or, in short, are polyvalent.

§ 14 Both the symmetry of sentences or sentence parts in Lev. 24 and the symmetry of words in Gen. 9.6 and I Sam. 15.33 prove to be ideal ways of expressing the ius talionis; thus the two do not differ materially in regard to the significance of their structures, although symmetry of sentences is of a higher order than that of words.

We are now able to answer the question whether the parallel and the concentric symmetries in Gen. 11 are not in conflict as pillars of structure. The answer must be a definite no! Not only is it impossible to experience and feel them as conflicting, because in terms of our experiencing them, they are not independent entities isolated from the story, not even after analysis has made them explicit; but also in themselves, as independent entities they are not conflicting, but on the the contrary, whether considered separately or together, they work to the realization of one all-regulating core, the *talio*.

Now we are also able to justify the use of the concepts of equality and reversal, which we ourselves have criticized for their abstractness. This abstractness derives its sense and value from the principle of the *talio*. Every inequality and reversal noticed – whether these are stylistic details, such as the ironic reversal of sounds *lbn-nbl* and the ironic "all the world/all over the world", one language/confusion of language, concentration/dispersion, the pursuit of fame/the getting of a

[46] One other fine example of another function of concentric arrangement, Gen. 2.23: זאת ... לזאת indicated and

לקחה ... יקרא

מאיש ... אשה

כי

interpreted by Luis Alonso Schökel, Motivos sapienciales y de alianza en Gn 2-3, Biblica 43 (1962), pp. 295-316. – The polyvalence we have already pointed to in the beginning of this section; also see the notes 36-40.

mock-name, or structurally the reversed sequence in the concentric pattern – is caused by the contrast of crime and punishment, by the tension evoked and checked by the talionic relationship, here especially the tension between the men as offenders and God as punisher, between heaven and earth, between the breach of the judicial sphere aiming at dialogic *shalom* and its restoration.

Every equality noticed, whether such stylistically effective repetitions of words as, for example, the "come, let us ..." plus exhortative spoken by men and God, or structurally the symmetries as such, derives from the punishment's being proportionate to the offence, from the demand made by the law of strict retaliation, that the punishment be determined by the extent and nature of the crime.

Equality and reversal are related and are united by the *talio* which implies them, the *talio* which divides and reigns: two actions of two protagonists are side by side, but they are made interrelated. The *talio* subjects them to itself in this relationship of tension and unites them in one complete and finished event.

If we see in Gen. 11 a story of retaliation,[47] we must, however, make a restriction. Whereas the *talio*, however religiously founded, applies primarily to people in their relation to each other, we have come across a variant here, that the person attacked is God himself and he himself is the one who executes the sentence. Nor is this a case of bloodshed or physical injury. Nevertheless we are justified in calling Gen. 11 a talionic text. The Old Testament has passages which clearly show that

[47] For all we know this has never been a starting-point before, not even for Benno Jacob in his commentary, who, to our surprise, mentions the word *talio*, but only casually and without developing the idea or proposing arguments about it. The word occurs in a passage which sums up the meaning of the story, well formulated, on p. 302.
"Die Erzählung ist also die Verurteilung eines extremen Zentralismus, dessen letzte Konsequenz eine einzige Welt-Stadt mit einem möglichst hohen Wolkenkratzer als Symbol der Konzentration ist, eines Herdensinnes, der sich nur in der Masse und Zusammendrängung geborgen fühlt und das Endziel darin sieht, die ganze Menschheit unter Einen Turm zu bringen, und mit geistreicher Ironie wird nach dem Muster der Talion gerade der Ort des erträumten Zusammenschlusses schon im Namen zum Ausgangspunkt der Zerstreuung über die ganze Erde gestempelt. Die Riesenstadt Babel und die "himmelhohen" Tempeltürme haben der Tora ebensowenig imponiert wie die Pyramiden, die sie nicht einmal der Erwähnung wert hält, obgleich sich ihre Geschichtserzählung zu einem grossen Teil in Ägypten abspielt."

God can apply retaliation, as in Gen. 4 (even in two respects)[48] and in other places.[49, 50]

[48] Both actually and potentially. Actually in v. 10f., *contra* Cain: "the voice of your brother's blood is crying out to me from the ground" etc. Potentially in v. 15 *pro* Cain: "If anyone slays Cain, vengeance shall be taken on him sevenfold." For the principle of seven-for-one also see Ps. 79.12; and in II Sam. 21 where the Gibeonites demand for "the man who planned to destroy us" (v. 5) and who did consume them (v. 2: blood-guilt) "seven of his sons" (v. 6). And just as Agag's execution took place "before the Lord in Gilgal", the Gibeonites are going to hang the seven sons of Saul "before the Lord at Gibeah of Saul". The crime is paid off at the very spot; also see I K. 21.19: "in the place where the dogs licked the blood of Naboth, the dogs will lick your blood too."
Benno Jacob, p. 141 about Gen. 4.11.12: v. 12 is "die moralische Konsequenz" of the evil done, worded in the "ועתה" der Schlussfolgerung. Sie vollzieht sich nach dem Prinzip der Talion durch Wortgleichung אדמה–אדמה. Die adama hatte Kain bebaut, von der adama hatte er ein Opfer gebracht und dann hat er sie vergewaltigt und mit dem Blut des Bruders getränkt, so dass sie zu Gott hinaufschrie, wofür ihr ein Mund zugeschrieben wird (...). Die Rede ist hochpoetisch und von prophetischem Pathos."
[49] E.g. the deuteronomistic version of the episode of Abimelech (Jud. 9.22-24, 56f.). Cf. Friedrich Horst, Recht und Religion im Bereich des AT, Evangelische Theologie 16 (1956) pp. 49-75, who says on p. 61:
"Nun [viz. once things have gone so far that "die Theologie der Priesterschrift die Aussage von der Gottesebenbildlichkeit des Menschen machen konnte"] will Gott selbst für jede widerrechtliche Tötung in der Welt als Bluträcher auftreten; nun soll menschlicher Strafvollzug das äusserst bedrohliche Einschreiten Gottes ersetzen:" – to which Horst quotes Gen. 9.6. And rightly so, for how much God is the demanding party in cases of blood vengeance can be seen esp. in in Gen. 9.5: three times God is subject of *dāraš*, to demand. The phenomenon is, by the way, much older than P's theology with its explicitly formulated Gottesebenbildlichkeit; see such old texts as II Sam. 21 and I Sam. 15.32f. Cf. also Gunkel ad Gen. 4.10: "Nach uralter hebräischer Vorstellung erhebt vergossenes Blut die צעקה (term. techn. der "Klage" des Vergewaltigten um Hilfe), es schreit nach Rache an dem Mörder; wenn Menschen nicht rachen können oder wollen, schreit es zu Jahve, und dann übernimmt Jahve selber die Blutrache vgl. die Geschichte Naboths IReg21; in diesem Glauben zeigt sich schön das tiefe Rechtsgefühl des Hebräers." More generally speaking: more than once God is the "God of vengeance"; Ps. 94, for example, is entirely dedicated to the אל נקמות. In his contribution "Zur Talionsformel", ZAW 52 (1934), pp. 303-305, = Kleine Schriften I, München, 1953, pp. 341-344, Alb. Alt writes:
"... auch bei ihr (*sc.* die biblische Talionsformel) handelt es sich nicht, wie man wohl gemeint hat, um die Befriedigung menschlicher Schadenersatzansprüche im Falle von Tötung und Körperverletzung, sondern um eine streng geforderte, die niemals unterlassen werden darf, wenn durch Tötung oder Körperverletzung eines Menschen die Gottheit geschädigt ist, die ihm Leben und Körper gegeben und darum den ersten Besitzanspruch auf beides hat."
[50] An immaterial difference of emphasis between Gen. 11.1-9 and I Sam. 15.33

§ 15 Not only for the man of letters but also for the theologian is our text a striking passage; a narrative composed so tersely and exactly as Gen. 11.1-9 lends itself admirably to biblical-theological elaboration. Whoever should care to do so, could formulate a biblical theology-in-a-nutshell based on this story and support and illustrate it with much more biblical material. This would be especially true of our story should it have been written as an absolutely independent passage; but even if it is only a link in a chain of narratives,[51] it is true. Because it is in the nature of the text to demand of the interpreter a personal union (it requires him to be a man of letters and a theologian), we make some further, mainly theological, notes in the margin.

If we read the narrative books of the OT as the history of the continually changing relationship between God and man, we may call Gen. 11.1-9 a short and brightly illuminated scene on the stage of that history of the covenant. Precisely the brevity of the moment makes light and shadow more glaring; a narrator who chooses a "sehr kurze Erzählung" is, even more than is usual for OT narrative art, forced to make a selection, to distill his material down to the bare essence and to eliminate everything that might be dispensed with. At the same time he is increasingly in danger of being left with the general, non-concrete matters, and of confinement within the pattern to which he had to sacrifice so much, so that the narrative remains a lifeless outline.

Our narrator has not been bound by the yoke of a schema, as the mere history of the exegesis (to which the symmetries were hidden) shows, but he has brought the doubly symmetrical pattern that he used, under his yoke: the symmetries are subject to and have dissolved in the living organism of the story created by him; this story has a very unique individuality. Although the material has been squeezed into tight shackles, the story does not give a forced or artificial impression.

"In der Beschränkung zeigt sich der Meister". For our narrator

on one hand, and Gen. 9.6, on the other hand, is that the latter text is the rule of law in general and the former texts relate two concrete cases; accordingly in Gen. 9.6 attention is drawn to the criminal = victim of the vengeance only, whereas in the other two passages the attention is more or less equally divided between the revenger and his victim(s).

[51] Namely, in the first place the series of stories that make up the *Urgeschichte* and that continually have main features in common (sin and punishment), which has clearly been pointed out by, for example, Claus Westermann, Forschung am AT, Gesammelte Studien, München, 1964, in ch. I: Arten der Erzählung in der Genesis, pp. 9-91, esp. pp. 47-58 "Erzählungen von Schuld und Strafe in Genesis 1-11".

the constraint of the square centimeter has proved no disadvantage, but an advantage: his story is of a very paradigmatic and didactic nature. Describing an absolutely unique episode, adding local colour and preserving what is concrete, he succeeds in making his general theological vision visible in the particular and in showing the universal in the individual.

Very clearly he indicates how the history of salvation contains a human and a divine component and how the two affect each other. Secret rivalry between the two may suddenly become manifest and the contribution of one to the relationship can evoke a fitting contribution from the other. There is a subtle balance between the two and, when it is disturbed, only one partner is capable of restoring the balance sovereignly and of giving the other a new chance to re-establish it through dialogue. When human *hubris* renders a proper relationship within the covenant impossible, only God with his nemesis can restore the relationship. The reverse is also obvious. Those who play at bowls must look out for rubs, those who want to ride on clouds[52] must reckon with cloud-bursts; God stands no nonsense.

Most clearly, however, the story betrays its paradigmatic nature by moving this episode about the tower, which unmistakably draws material from the history of Mesopotamia, back into time, to a previous place, prehistoric times. For the people we are shown to be so busy here are all mankind-of-that-time: they are *ʿam 'eḥad*, one people. And what is almost a myth of prehistoric times appeals even more strongly to us by the representation that they were *sāfā 'aḥat*, that there was one common primitive language.[53] The story proposes to mention all the ancestors of all mankind by this projection back into prehistory and thus to involve all its readers, *tua res agitur*. This retrospective move has released the universal. The same ascendant movement back into time to ancestors who exemplify all of us, the same inclusive way of thinking which pictures all of us as partners of God, can be found in the story of paradise: Gen. 2 and 3 are not about "a"

[52] Just as Yahweh "rides upon the clouds", רכב בערבות Ps. 68:5 (cf. v. 34 and Deut. 33.26), which has become clear after the discovery of Ugarit and its language, from the title of Baal "*rkb bʿrpt*" in Ugaritic.

[53] After Gen. 10 with its precise differentiation of mankind into tribes and languages, the effect of the mythical "one people, one language" in Gen. 11 is the stronger for it. To the redactor(s) of Genesis, 11.1-9 may have been the explanation for the people's swarming off after Noah, captured in precise and detailed names.

person Adam (and Eve) somewhere in history, but about *hā'ādām wᵉ'ištō*, man and his wife, in prehistoric times.[54]

But he who tells about the towerbuilders, their motives and their fate so paradigmatically, is also didactic. The author teaches his listeners and readers a lesson: these people are bad examples; let them be a warning to you, do not be over-bold if you want to be spared God's punishment, know your place and do not be so self-sufficient and self-centred as to withdraw from communication with God! Of course the auditors are presupposedly fellow-believers; the story is religious and edifying and must have fitted the atmosphere of religious education.

Herewith we have at last pushed through to the deepest intentions of the story and to the author's source of inspiration. Once upon a time the narrator saw through the secret order of this moment in history and now he feels called upon to confide his discovery to his auditors. Now he wants to convey to his audience his key vision of broken and restored balance between man and God, of punishment fitting offence, as forcefully as he can. To that purpose he chooses not the discursive way, the giving of explanations by spreading abstract concepts, but the artistic, fictional, concretizing vehicle loaded with implications: literary shaping, the narrative.

The narrator has recognized the quiet but grim struggle for power in the episode of the tower and thus shapes his story in two halves. The antagonists' interrelationship induces him to repetitions of words which the two parts share. He has discovered a coherence and a balance in the contrast which to him seem to form a variant of the talionic mould. That is why he arranges words and repetitions into a sym-

[54] An excellent analysis of the "dirección cognoscitiva ascendente" of this theological thinking Alonso gives on pp. 309ff of his article Motivos sapienciales y de alianza en Gn 2-3, Biblica 43 (1962). Gen. 11, too, we may say in his words, wants to "explicar una situación actual humana extensa remontándome al único hecho original de donde procede", and here, too, "el pecado trae consecuencias a los sucesores [of the builders of the tower]: (...) un dinamismo descendente" (p. 310). "Supongamos ahora un pensador que extiende el horizonte a toda la humanidad, (...). Si medita sobre esta situación, y quiere encontrar la explicación, lo natural es que aplique el ascenso triangular hasta el origen de toda la humanidad, que por hipótesis es su horizonte. En este proceso mental no proyecta en narración allegórica la experiencia de todos los hombres, sino que asciende verdaderamente hasta el hecho original" (p. 311).
Very clear also are the pp. 67-72 of the monograph by O. H. Steck, Die Paradieserzählung, eine Auslegung von Genesis 2,4b-3,24, Neukirchen, 1970.

metrical pattern over the two halves. He has seen both proportion and reversal in the relation between crime and punishment; and therefore he uses both ambiguity and irony. His vision governs and leads the composition of the story, even to minute details, and shapes it even in the sound stratum. Creating an alliteration by means of some well-chosen consonants, the narrator speaks better and more penetratingly, for more beautifully, than the interpreter ever could, no matter how many or few paragraphs of explication he used.

With great difficulty our analysis has come from the periphery (stylistic details) to the core of the story; once there, we have been able to discover and delineate[55] the periphery, returning to it, just as the narrator, with equal effort, would have worked from the core to design the proper periphery. These are the words which were the results of his work and which, as both starting-point and end, marked for us the circle of the explanation:

ויהי כל הארץ שפה אחת ודברים אחדים
ויהי בנסעם מקדם וימצאו בקעה בארץ שנער וישבו שם
ויאמרו איש אל רעהו
הבה נלבנה לבנים ונשרפה לשרפה
ותהי להם הלבנה לאבן
והחמר היה להם לחמר
ויאמרו
הבה נבנה לנו עיר ומגדל וראשו בשמים
ונעשה לנו שם פן נפוץ על פני כל הארץ
וירד יהוה לראות את העיר ואת המגדל אשר בנו בני האדם
ויאמר יהוה
הן עם אחד ושפה אחת לכלם
וזה החלם לעשות
ועתה לא יבצר מהם כל אשר יזמו לעשות
הבה נרדה ונבלה שם שפתם
אשר לא ישמעו איש שפת רעהו
ויפץ יהוה אתם משם על פני כל הארץ
ויחדלו לבנת העיר
על כן קרא שמה בבל
כי שם בלל יהוה שפת כל הארץ
ומשם הפיצם יהוה על פני כל הארץ

[55] "A fuerza de repetidas lecturas – a veces en la primera –, con reflexiones alternas, se llega a una *intuición* de la razón artística del poema, o del punto más fecundo para analizarlo; a partir de esta intuición se desarrolla después el análisis de los diversos recursos, y se muestra cómo se reducen a aquella razón artística." L. Alonso Schökel in his Estudios ..., p. 65.

§ 16 This theological vision of the history and the nature of the dialogue between God and man required and was realized in a rigorously designed composition. Conversely, the structure of this 'very short narrative' also created the possibility for the narrator to speak meaningfully, indeed paradigmatically, within a small compass.

Because the story is meant to be read as exemplar and is didactic in nature, it cannot be included within our concept of history.[56] The fact that it also cannot be dated with certainty is significant in itself. Dating this story is not essential in order to understand it; the text forbids dating, as it were, out of inner necessity.

Not only does the narrator treat time in an interesting way, by putting the episode of Babel's rise and fall in a primeval time which is, in terms of the history of salvation, the porch to history proper, but it is also interesting to see how he treats space. In this too, he works with precision. Describing the space for his readers with simple means, he manages to express himself plastically, to a high degree. First he makes us witnesses of a somewhat vague ("in the east", yes, but where exactly?) and somewhat aimless movement, the *nāsaʿ* in the narrow sense, which is typical of nomadic mobility. More or less accidentally the people seem to arrive at Sinear. Once they are there, there is a maximum of directedness, of concentration at one point, the city. From there a spatial revolution arises all at once: up, to the heavens, by means of a tower. The horizontal plane is not enough for the men, they want to open up a new dimension. That is their hubris, and it is precisely this vertical action which provokes vertical repression. Like a flash of lightning from a clear sky God hits back into the depth, sharply and unexpectedly. This one flash of vertical action has immense consequences for the horizontal plane, like a stone which hits a smooth water-surface. The people are scattered into all directions; nothing is left to them but the horizontal plane. After the maximum concentration maximum 'decentration' sets in; after the feverish massing of energy the (comparative) calm and purposelessness of the dispersion returns. Therewith the story has been framed and is complete.

[56] After the quotation in note 54 Alonso says: "Si a la narración de un hecho sucedido se le llama historia, entonces nuestro narrador escribe historia, aunque dicha historia, en su método de indagación y en sus procedimientos de exposición, no sea la historia técnica de los siglos XIX y XX." This, too, fits Gen. 11.1-9 nearly as well as it does Gen. 2-3.

It is unusual for narratives from the Bible, indeed, narratives in general, to display such a tight structure as the one discovered in Gen. 11, one which can be made objective (because it *is* objective) in an almost mathematical diagram. We realize this as much as does the reader. Moreover, applying such symmetries might soon degenerate into a boring trick. To put it more precisely: such a symmetric structure is in itself no guarantee of the literary worth of the text, does not prove the text a work of art. But technique and ingenuity of form need not exclude inspiration[57] either. And in any case, inspiration, which asks the artist for materialization, needs a vehicle, a style; it must be "externalized" in form. If the inspiration succeeds in finding a suitable outlet the process author → work is to be described as "revelation is style", and then we have found the counterpart of that adage to which our entire analysis is testimony, "Stil ist Offenbarung",[58] as a description of the process work → reader.

In Gen. 11 the technique has served the narrator, not vice versa. The symmetry here applied individually, read in this way and not otherwise, is, as an indissolubly and naturally integrated part of the whole, an important indication (but not the proof!) of the literary nature of the narrative. That Gen. 11 is a literary work of art has, however, been demonstrated by integral analysis.[59]

[57] Books like those by Lund and Galbiati are not ready for this problem, because they hardly attempt at a serious, elaborate explanation of symmetries. At best, the two give a rather formal paraphrase of the patterns and their parts.

[58] Alonso, Die stilistische Analyse bei den Propheten, Suppl. to VT, VII (1959), pp. 154-164. On p. 163 he says: "Stil ist Offenbarung, wenn wir ihn richtig verstehen".

[59] To point to is to point out: "aufweisen heisst hier beweisen", "la única forma de demostrar es mostrar", Alonso wrote; the German is to be found in Erzählkunst im Buche der Richter, Biblica 42 (1961) pp. 143-172 (see p. 171), the Spanish in the Estudios, p. 65. My argument is the objectified account of my personal dealing with the story,which therefore uses more or less scientific terms, and has more or less been depersonalized for the sake of conveying my experience and was written in the hope that the personal experience and recognition of a text as a work of art will become evident to others.

CHAPTER II

GENESIS 28.10-22: JACOB AT BETHEL

In this second analysis I shall arrange my results in a different way by working linearly, parallel to the reading-process proper: accompanied by the reader I intend to follow the text from front to back, listening to its words and style patiently and closely.

§ 1. When Jacob has filched the blessing for the first born from his father and his brother, he sets out for Haran. In four verses some attention is paid to Esau, then we are given the Bethel episode, Gen. 28.10-22. The passage begins by directing our eyes again to the protagonist, Jacob. It is elucidative to read the simple start, v. 10, in contrast to 28.5.

10 wayyeṣē Ya'qob mibB^{e}'er Sheba' wayyelek Ḥārānā	5 wayyišlaḥ Yiṣḥāq 'et Ya'qob wayyelek Paddenā 'Arām 'el Lābān ben B^{e}tū'el hā'^{a}rammī '^{a}ḥī Ribqā 'em Ya'qob w^{e}'Esāw

We note a great difference, a long sentence with many proper names opposite a short one with two geographical indications; the great difference in context determines the selection of the details. In the preceding part a young man is sent to his uncle by his father; there the family tie is of central importance. Here, in the Bethel pericope, the theme is quite different: the relationship between God and Jacob, promise and vow, as connected with *this* place; any names of relatives would be irrelevant. Factual information will do here, hence a short, simple phrase with geographical data. That Jacob is on the way is now the only thing that matters.

Why two sentences, two names? By mentioning the extreme points of the route the narrator has made a selection from many possibilities. Thus he points out to us the enormous distance Jacob has to cover. Because v. 10 is followed by *wayyifga' bammāqōm*, "he set off" comes to mean "he set out for".[1] Presently we are told of a halt in the journey; "place" cannot refer to Haran, so it must be a place on the way. But if there is a halt, then again the question arises, why two names? Why has the ultimate destination already been mentioned before the Bethel scene? Its effect may be paraphrased as follows: Jacob's journey was long, no doubt hard and full of experiences, but we do not hear anything about this, except for one moment which is so important, apparently, that it must be told. The narrator's choice is significant; because the rest is left in darkness, the more glaring is the light shed upon the Bethel scene. This spotlight technique[2] makes the Bethel episode of a representative nature: only Bethel is essential in this journey. The narrator hastens to speak about it and confines himself to a minimum of information. In six words he dismisses the journey lightly; as early as v. 11 the Bethel scene proper begins.[3]

[1] The meaning of *hlk* in a sentence of the type "A went to X", thus in reporting style and with the destination indicated, is not unequivocal. It may mean "set out" or "be on the way", with the destination as yet unattained (Gen. 22.3, 18.22), but it often implies that the destination has been reached and then the narrative proceeds with what happens in X (Gen. 13,3, 22.19, 24.10, 26.1, 26, 27.5, 28.9, 29.1, 36.6, 37.17).

[2] Such a contrast is by no means uncommon; in many biblical stories it strikes us at once how great distances in space and time are skipped in one leap. In "szenische Darstellung" [which predominates in Genesis] "ist die Sukzession des Erzählens der des Erzählten am meisten angenähert. ... Längere Gesamterstreckung [in our case the whole history of Jacob, see note 3 below] bringt somit notwendig eine durch Aussparungen tief zerklüftete Zeitkontur mit sich. Demgemäss wird hier die Gliederung des Erzählablaufs meist durch abrupten Zeitsprung oder Schauplatzwechsel gekennzeichnet; und der Neueinsatz, wofern er nicht sofort direkte Rede gibt, ist in der Regel durch ausdrückliche Zeit- und Raumangaben fixiert." Of all narrative art it is true "dass die monotone Sukzession der erzählten Zeit beim Erzählen auf verschiedene Weise verzerrt, unterbrochen, umgestellt oder gar aufgehoben wird." So it is extremely fruitful to examine the relation between narrative time and narrated time, "einhelliger als an jedem anderen Erzählphänomen wird gerade an der Doppelheit von erzähltem Vorgang und Erzählvorgang jenes Prinzip der Andeutung und Auswahl positiv greifbar. Deshalb ist ein beobachtender und urteilender Vergleich von *erzählter Zeit* und *Erzählzeit*, wenngleich er nur eines unter vielen Mitteln darstellt, der *zunächst sicherste* Weg, das Verhältnis von erzählter Wirklichkeit und sprachlicher Wiedergabe zu fassen!" These quotations are from western literary scholarship: E. Lämmert, Bauformen des Erzählens, Stuttgart, 1955, pp. 92, 32, 23.

[3] Gen. 28.10 can only be judged on its true value against the background of the whole history of Jacob. This whole is marked, articulated by a great coming

Twelve verses narrate the dream, God's promise and Jacob's reaction; only one of them, v. 11, is reserved as an introduction, after which we are quickly led *in medias res*. Thus the narrator forces himself to be selective in mentioning the data about Jacob's stopping-place. We are told two things: twice we are told that Jacob enters the night, *wayyālen šām* ... *wayyiškab*. Somewhat emphatically the text points out to us that what is going to happen will take place in the night. This motif of the nocturnal theophany achieves its full meaning against the background of the wider context: the two great events in Jacob's life are the nocturnal theophany in Bethel, which marks his exodus and the nocturnal theophany in Pnuel, which marks his return.[4] (We shall come back to this later.) Secondly we are given a peculiar detail: Jacob uses a stone as a head-rest. How much other information the text could have given us, but has omitted! We are told nothing about the nature of the stopping-place, not even its name is made known to us, only that there was a stone by way of a pillow! Whether this seemingly grotesque detail is justified we must wait and see.

But if the narrator is really so selective, could he not have confined himself to such details as, "he struck upon a certain place, where he spent the night; he took a stone and put it under his head"? In other words, what is the reason for "because the sun had set" and the threefold "place"? And thirdly: could he not have said "he came" instead of "he struck upon"? Why *wayyifga'*?

The first point we can only explain by again considering the wider context. Twice in the history of Jacob the sun is mentioned *expressis verbis*, here and in 32.32. On the Jabbok Jacob must fight in the night. The crucial moment for "the man", his adversary, is the "breaking of the day" (mentioned twice) and when Jacob, limping but victorious (judgment and mercy), can pass by as all the others had already done,[5] the sun is beaming at him, of course. For for the first time he has at

and going: away from Canaan, back to Canaan. In both journeys the narrated time is of about the same length while the narrative time varies greatly! It is very appropriate that Jacob should go away at breakneck speed, in one verse, and that the only moment worth relating is the theophany in Bethel, whereas his return involves more activity and requires many more verses in the text. For now Jacob is on the run from his brother, presently he will appear with lagging steps, scared to face Esau, and at first even afraid to face God; see Ch. V, §§ 12-13.

[4] See the repetition of the motif of night in Gen. 32.14, 22, 23.

[5] Five occurrences of *'br* in 32.23,24, followed in the end by Jacob's *'br* in 32.32.

last received the blessing from God too,[6] and from Jacob he has become Israel. So the happenings of nature attend, underline and symbolize what happens between God and man.

When Jacob passes through Bethel, a life of toil and the establishment of a family (judgment and mercy) is in store for him. He will have to fight with God and men; not until Pnuel will the sun definitively rise in his life, but now, at Bethel, the sun sets.[7] That all this is not a fantastic explanation, is proved in Gen. 19. There, too, the sequence of distress-and-deliverance is underlined by night-and-sunrise: in the night Lot is warned, again dawn is the crucial moment (vv. 15ff) and when he safely arrives at Zoar, the sun rises, v. 23.[8]

Secondly we have the point that in one verse the word *māqōm* occurs three times. Is that a double, a weakness of the narrator's or is it a justified stylistic device of narrative skill? The repetition, if useful, makes the word a key-word, which here would have to serve the purpose, precisely by its seeming redundancy, of proposing the question of what place it was and what, if anything, was the matter with it. For *māqōm* to be a key-word, integrated in the whole, it must refer to, anticipate, the main theme of the story. In the verses 16-17 we shall come back to this; not until then can we determine retrospectively the full sense of *māqōm* and everything it implies in v. 11. For the time being we shall note only this: the anonymity of "the place" is in contrast with the precise names in v. 10, and is intensified precisely by this contrast. There is also the fact that the many places on the long stretch from Berseba to Haran make it impossible for us to guess the identity of the place; this, too, underlines the anonymity.

[6] Grammatically Jacob had been neither subject nor object of *brk* before; curiously enough not even in 28.14.

[7] In both cases with a contrary effect: the sun sets, but God appears to him and promises to support him; the sun rises, but Jacob limps.

[8] This appears also in such a theologically central text as Ex. 14, where Israel is definitively delivered from Egypt, "the night ... all night ... all night", and then (v. 24) "in the morning" God discomfited the host of the Egyptians; in Ex. 14.27 the destruction itself: wayyāšob hayyām lifnōt boqer, Israel has been delivered. The same indication of time in Ps. 46.6: ya'zerehā 'elōhīm lifnōt boqer. Cf. also the comparison in Jud. 5.31 we'ōhabāw keṣēt haššemeš bigbūrātō; the metaphor wezārehā... šemeš ṣedāqā in Mal. 3.20. Even more direct is the relation in Jer. 15.9 bā šimšāh be'ōd jōmām.
The comparison in Hos. 6.3a, kešaḥar nākōn mōsā'ō, presupposes a positive meaning of *šḥr*, which in God's reply to this song of penance (vv. 1-3) is resumed in v. 5b umišpāṭō kā'ōr jeṣē; here too the rise of morning-light means salvation, in this case directed against Israel's superficial show of penance.

To conclude, what is the effect of the word *wayyifga'*? Compared with the much more neutral "he came" its meaning, "to strike upon", is more sharply profiled, with a certain degree of casualness or unexpectedness. Whereas the narrator dismissed the journey in six words, he now considers it necessary to devote fifteen words to introducing a place which Jacob "happened to" reach; his listeners surmise, as good as understand, his arrival at that place cannot be entirely fortuitous! The narrator sets the scene for the action – otherwise he would not have mentioned it. What is going to happen in that place? In suspense the listeners wait to see whether they will be able to determine that in the "fortuitousness" there is a hidden necessity which is determined by the story. Their expectations come true, the seemingly fortuitous is integrated into the necessity of God's revelation at Bethel.

A more important datum corroborates this. The concordance tells us that *pg'* occurs only twice in the history of Jacob, as does the sun, namely in the stories about Bethel and Pnuel. In Gen. 28 Jacob "strikes" upon a place which will turn out to be a House of God, a place where angels announce the theophany; in Gen. 32.2 angels strike upon Jacob immediately before the crucial moment when Jacob will have to face God and later Esau at his return.[9] These two encounters with angels,[10] then, take place in the course of the two events which mark the wide movement backwards and forwards in his life. Necessity rather than accident!

§ 2. In v. 12 Jacob's dream is described, no, pictured, in three flashes:
wᵉhinnē sullām muṣṣāb 'arṣā wᵉrōšō maggīaʿ haššāmaymā
wᵉhinnē mal'ᵃkē 'ᵉlōhīm 'ōlīm wᵉyōrᵉdīm bō
wᵉhinnē JHWH niṣṣāb 'ālaw
What is the meaning of this considerable change in narrative style, from narratives to a triple repetition of *hinnē* plus participles? For a better understanding of what happens here we shall first make a brief remark on what is called the narrative situation in literary scholar-

[9] H. Eising, Formgeschichtliche Untersuchung zur Jakobserzählung der Genesis, diss. Emsdetten, 1940, p. 255 note 13: "vgl., dass in V. 15 von Gottes Geleit auf dem Hin- und Rückwege die Rede ist. Dem entspricht es gut, dass auch bei der Wiederkunft ins verheissene Land eine Engelerscheinung berichtet wird (32,2f)."
[10] In a dream he sees an angel once more (but there is no plural), 31.11.

ship.[11] When a narrator begins his story anything may yet happen and his hearer can expect just anything: he knows nothing, the narrator knows everything.[12] After a few words already much less is possible; at the same time a world is beginning to grow before the eyes of the listener/reader.

Our narrator knows already that Jacob is to see a ladder with angels in his dream, but, Jacob, retiring, does not nor do we. In the story the narrator now gives shape to this, Jacob is surprised at what he sees, so that we in turn are also surprised when reading the text. He brings this about not by simply continuing the eight already fading narratives with another five, but by a radical change of perspective. Up till now he had been telling us all kinds of things from the superior point of the omniscient[13] narrator, now he abandons this attitude; he withdraws behind his protagonist and in a subordinate position he records what his, Jacob's, eyes see, hinnē ... w^ehinnē ... w^ehinnē.[14]

This has great consequences for the experiencing of time in the narration. There is no longer a narrator who looks back to a past; there is only the present as Jacob experiences it – there, a ladder! oh, angels! and look, the Lord himself! No more narratives but five participles one after another with the strength of a durative present. This past of what the dreamer saw forces itself so strongly upon the narrator that it becomes present. It sweeps away the distance-in-time which is included in narratives;[15] the narrator unites, as it were, with Jacob and shapes this partnership in three vivid images of evocative power.[16] The particle *hinnē* features in this process, thanks

[11] About "Erzählhaltung" see W. Kayser, das sprachliche Kunstwerk, Bern, 1963 (9th ed.) pp. 204-214.

[12] Only modern novelists sometimes inform us emphatically that they find themselves faced with the fact that their characters want to live lives of their own and are inclined to go into a direction other than that which their author had conceived.

[13] On "erzählerische Allwissenheit" see Kayser, op. cit., p. 206, 211f.

[14] Of course this does not run counter to the fact that behind the scenes the narrator directs the show, shaping it and controlling the narrative situation.

[15] Cf. Kayser p. 207: "... der Erzähler überhaupt und grundsätzlich steht seinem Gegenstand als einem Vergangenem gegenüber," to which must be added that his preterites do not (necessarily) report a "real" past: they have been put down as fictional tenses.

[16] A comparable change of perspective is in Gen. 29.25; on this see Weiss, VT 13 (1963) pp. 460ff (*erlebte Rede* / interior monologue) in his article Einiges über die Bauformen des Erzählens in der Bibel.

to its deictic power; it is partly pre- or paralingual, it goes with a lifted arm, an open mouth.[17]

The present-izing style of 28.12 has its own syntaxis, completely dictates the order of words; here it is necessary for the words to be where they are. There is a subtle but substantial difference in the following three sentences in regard to the syntactic unity:

(1)	wᵉhakkōhen niṣṣāb petaḥ haššaʻar	Jud. 18.17
(2)	hinnē 'ānōkī niṣṣāb ʻal ʻēn hammayyim	Gen. 24.13
(3)	hinnē sullām muṣṣāb 'arṣā	Gen. 28.12

In (1) we find a normal nominal sentence, one syntactic unit and an uninterrupted sentence-melody; such a sentence conveys a situation which is composed of several elements as an integrated whole. In (2) there is a comma after *hinnē*; the nominal sentence retains its structure, the syntactic unity and the sentence melody remain as yet intact, a whole.[18] In (3), however, a barely noticeable halt after the first noun interrupts the sentence-melody, the reins of the syntax have here been loosened under the influence of *hinnē*. The particle is here much more deictic than in (2), where its only function is to attract attention; besides, it clearly carries a note of surprise. There is no longer an integrated whole, but successively various elements are mentioned. Here the sequence is sensorily-psychologically determined, the order of words reflects the order in which Jacob observes things.[19] This

[17] This is not less true because of the fact that in the O.T. *hinnē* + part. is frequently used. We must say it the other way about: with simple means, which everyday speech no doubt provided them with, the narrators have succeeded in developing an adequate stylistic response to the demand to render dreams and the like in language. – Cf. for *hinnē* in the poetry of the prophets L. Alonso Schökel, Biblica 37 (1956) pp. 174-180.

[18] *Hinnē 'ānōkī* is not a syntactic unity, contrary to *hinnenī*; it projects forward, requires continuation. This is not the case with *hinnē sullām*, which may very well be a complete phrase.

[19] There are not many dreams in the Bible, strictly speaking, apart from *ḥāzōn/ḥizzāyōn*. Where they do occur there is always *hinnē*. See Wolfgang Richter, Traum und Traumdeutung im AT, ihre Form und Verwendung, Biblische Zeitschrift NF 7 (1963) pp. 203-220. He uses the term "Traumeröffnungsformel". Most hinnē-phrases are as in our example (2), but are even more concerned with an event; thus Gen. 37.7 *ter*; 41 *passim*; Is. 29.7f. With Gen. 28.12 compare 40.9,16 where an observation rather than an event is presented. Therefore Richter considers Jacob's dream "in der Nähe zu einer Vision". His fourth element of the dream-as-a-genre is lacking: "Eine Deutung fehlt. Nach dem Erwachen (...) erkennt Jakob die Bedeutung des Ortes. Damit hat

reading agrees with the slow pace of the sentence to which we are forced by several aspects of sound.[20] So v. 12a is comprised of the following parts, following the dreamer's gaze: (a) hinnē sullām ... (b) muṣṣāb 'arṣā ... (c) w^{e}rōšō maggī$^{a'}$ haššāmaymā. Here especially it is made clear how the narrator stands back in the shadow of his protagonist and how the past becomes present. In the second and third hinnē lines the syntactic unit is tightened again and the pace is quickened. The greatest surprise is now past.

The extent of fame which is lavished upon this vision is inversely proportional to its length, only three lines. Here, too, the most has been made of the words. We shall look at these lines one by one.

In v. 12a there are two clauses of equal form: subject plus predicate plus adjunct. Their contents are all-encompassing: heaven and earth, which here[21] are diametrically opposed to each other. Touching both of these with its extreme ends the ladder builds a bridge between the realm of God and the world of man, a unique fact, the honour for which has solely fallen to the share of the patriarch.[22]

also der Traum keine Bedeutung für die Zukunft des Träumenden, so dass er zu deuten wäre, sondern für den Ort. (...) Das Ziel dieses Traumes ist Erkenntnis; deshalb bedarf er auch keiner Erfüllung. (...) Das eigene Ziel führt auf eine eigene Gattung des Traumes: den Offenbarungstraum." – p. 210.

[20] The succession of similar consonants at the end and in the beginning of a word (sullāM Muṣṣāb); only slow reading can bring out the separate words. Then there are the heavy dark vowels u-a u-a with again and again a doubled consonant in between; and the syncope in muṣṣāb 'arṣā: xx́ x́x.

[21] Also Is. 1.3. They are complementary as halves of the creation in Gen. 1, and show a sharp antithesis in Eccl. 5.1 and, with another shade of meaning, in Paulus.

[22] Cf. Ch. I, section 5. John 3.13 "No one has ascended into heaven but he who has descended from heaven, the Son of Man." Heaven and earth know no way of communication in the O.T.
The Jacob's ladder against the background of all of Genesis: Gen. 1-11 offers a history of the world (in the form of primeval history) which contrasts sharply with the particular history of Abraham and his descendants in 12-50. Things went wrong for mankind as a whole precisely when, in Genesis, people tried to build a bridge from the earth to the heavens, 11.1-9. The point of man's building-scheme was a "tower with its top in the heavens", and this tower provoked God to intervene quickly and to render such work of humans altogether impossible. Opposed to the various human initiatives of primeval history in general comes, from Gen. 12 onwards, God's initiative, he inaugurates the particular tribal history. The patriarch of Israel beholds how God himself provides a connection: heaven and earth are now really connected, but not from below! For this ladder has been let down from heaven.

Bridges are for crossing. "Messengers of God" keep up busy traffic in both directions, *'ōlīm w^eyōr^edīm*. The contact has been made, and the unofficial opening is followed by the official, the Lord himself follows, v. 13a. The sentences have become shorter and shorter, more and more concentrated: first two subjects, each with a predicate and sentence-element of its own; then one subject, in the plural, with two verbs which almost make a hendiadys, and the trio concludes with Yahweh himself, one subject, one predicate. The gaze which began by covering the distance between earth and heaven and by following the up-and-down movement of the angels can now rest on one point, the figure of God.

Parallel to this concentration the three subjects, too, display an increasing tension and importance:
ladder: grammatically non-qualified; neutral utensil;
messengers of God: grammatically qualified; no more; *'elōhīm* common noun; YHWH: maximally qualified, proper noun.
The appearance of YHWH himself is not unexpected. It has been announced in many ways:
- by the ladder, because its top reaches to heaven,
- by the ladder, because it is *muṣṣāb*; Yhwh is *niṢṢAB*! The repetition of the radix makes the reader connect the two. The presence of this root is the key to the interpretation of these verses, particularly of the function of the ladder: the erection of the ladder is the prefiguration, the preliminary symbol of God's raising himself. Later the text will underline this twice again.
- by the angels, which here (and often elsewhere) are mere representatives, so much so that from this passage we can certainly not build up an angelology.[23] They are the servants, whose presence at once reminds one of their boss – and indeed, there is the master himself!

Consequently, when the ladder and the angels have accomplished their task, they do not occur again, just as Moses' burning bush was also a mere eye-catcher. The attention has been fixed and from the primary sensory perception, seeing, the story now proceeds to the

Von Rad (das A. T. Deutsch, ad loc.) and Speiser (comm. in the Anchor Bible) also make a connection with Gen. 11 via *sullām* which would be steps like those of a ziqqurat. But their derivation from √*sll* seems untenable: how to account for -*ām*?

[23] Von Rad (ibid.) takes the plunge into the darkness and informs us that these angels have no wings.

hearing of God's promise. Not till the end of the vision does the theophany proper start. But – is it not strange that precisely this vision, a mere eye-catcher, is the only part of the story which has been put in a different perspective and is presented as taking place now? Is this justifiable? We shall say more about this presently, with v. 18.[24]

The Lord was "above him". This suffix is the only point in the description of the vision where the particular perspective of the (indirect) interior monologue ("*erlebte Rede*") appears. If the narrator had entirely identified himself with Jacob the text would have said "me" instead of "him". It is true, "der Standpunkt der Perspektive ist gleichsam in die Seele der Gestalt selber verlegt" and every word seems to have been said or thought by the protagonist, but still the narrator has not quite disappeared, for he remains perceptible by his use of the third person. Therewith the "*erlebte Rede*" stands midway between direct and indirect speech.[25]

The *hinnē*-constructions now give way to God's speech. Behind Jacob's back the narrator appears to assume control for a while, with the narrative *wayyōmer*.[26] He starts a new stage of the dream, but then at once calls upon God to speak; by means of the direct speech which is now used, the narrator equates past and present. The remnant of the narrator's point of view, which was still perceptible in the interior monologue, disappears completely in the quotation, the direct transmission of God's promise - achieving maximal objectivity.

§ 3. V. 13b starts a new phase, certainly, but it also continues the

[24] One other problem: what does the suffix of *niṣṣāb 'ālāw* refer to? It is conceivable that God is on the ladder: for its top reaches to heaven, God's realm; the sentence-elements concerning the top and the angels are connected with "ladder" by suffixes, so perhaps this is also true of 13a. On the other hand it is common for God to have descended when he appears to people, and then niṣṣāb 'ālāw is not unusual (also *'md 'l*, e.g. Jud. 3.19, Amos 9.1) when the other person is seated (e.g. Abraham in Gen. 18.1) or lying down as Jacob is; the text does not say, for example, "he called to him from heaven" as in Gen. 22.11,15, but *wayyōmer*, which suggests nearness. What Jacob says in v. 16 presupposes that God had descended. Really cogent arguments in favour of one of the two readings do not exist. I myself prefer to have the suffix refer to Jacob.

[25] I translate and quote Kayser, op. cit., p. 146f.

[26] Such a transition of *hinnē* + part. to the narrative is also to be found in Jud. 7.13. In Kings 3.5ff there are only narratives, which is not accidental, because the surprise does not appear until v. 15.

whole. The connection is visible in a chiasmus,[27] which will be followed by several others:

12c	'ᵉlōhīm	Jhwh	(13a)
13b	Jhwh	'ᵉlōhē ... welōhē	

Explicitly it brings up the relation between the words God and Yhwh and answers a question which we have not yet dealt with but which is most central: why does not Jacob, after the messengers of God, see *'ᵉlōhīm* but Yhwh? Is not Yhwh God then? Yes and no. In the second half of the chiasmus Yhwh himself provides the answer; I am the God of Abraham and Isaac ... but this implies a new question, will this Yhwh, who is the God of the grandfather and the father also be the God of the son? Will it come about at Bethel that the famous triplet is completed, "Yhwh, the God of Abraham, Isaac and Jacob"? In the course of the story Yhwh and Jacob will both show their views on and positions in the mutual relationship.

We need not lose sight of the foreground meaning of v. 13b. Yhwh makes himself known to Jacob and does so in a reassuring way, for the names of Abraham and Isaac create a certain degree of familiarity for Jacob. However, in so far as it is God who speaks, the following sentences have maximum weight and Jacob is inspired with awe. Devoutly he listens while loftily the promise sounds:

13c הארץ אשר אתה שכב עליה לך אתננה ולזרעך
14a והיה זרעך כעפר הארץ
b ופרצת ימה וקדמה וצפנה ונגבה
c ונברכו בך כל משפחת האדמה ובזרעך

And at once we as well as Jacob understand that here history is in the making; in surprise the listener recognizes the formulas of the "blessing

[27] The stylistic means of the chiasmus a) can embody, symbolize an intimate relation between the entities arranged in the chiasmus; we shall see this presently in Gen. 28.24.; b) can symbolize a change or radical reversal in the situation; we have already seen this more than once in Gen. 11, we shall come across it in 28.19, and Alonso, Estudios p. 91, has pointed it out in Is. 1.18:

yihyû ... ya'dîmû	Una construcción sonora quiástica subraya la transfor-
ya'dîmû ... yihyû	mación total que Dios promete obrar.

c) can also be represented as a-b-b-a, so concentrically. In Eccl. 1.6 it symbolizes the incessantly continuing never changing cycle of nature (the monotony is moreover evoked by repetition of words and "leading sounds"): hōlek 'el dārōm / wᵉsōbeb 'el ṣāfōn // sōbeb sōbeb / hōlek hārûᵃḥ.

of Abraham".[28] What Jacob's father had wished him only a short time ago and what he had called the "birkat 'abrāhām" is fulfilled. With his father's words of farewell still in his ears, Jacob now hears land and fertility promised to him by God at Bethel.

The very first word sums up the thema, *hā'āreṣ*. Yet Jacob does not know where he stands, not even after five words. His curiosity has, however, been provoked, an expectation has been raised in him. The order of words has turned v. 13 into a slight anacoluthon. Its brokenness, the interval in the middle, can be made to stand out by increasing the effect in paraphrase:
"as regards the land on which you lie ..." (Jacob kept in suspense), "to you I will give it and to your descendants" (his waiting is rewarded). Thus all at once *hā'āreṣ* – because there is no so-called *nota objecti* it could hardly be predicted[29] – has surprisingly become an object of God's acting: "I will give it to you". Owing to the *casus pendens* the splendour of this present and the royal gesture with which it is given are expressed much better than by a smooth line opening with "I will give ...".[30]

[28] Immediately preceding the Bethel scene Isaac had sent his son away with the wish: (28.3) אל שדי יברך אתך ויפרך וירבך והיית לקהל עמים
(v. 4) ויתן לך את ברכת אברהם לך ולזרעך אתך
לרשתך את ארץ מגריך אשר נתן אלהים לאברהם
What we hear are the two parts of the classical patriarchal promise: land and fertility. What is remarkable is that the one wishes the other such a promise; it does not occur elsewhere. Still more remarkable is that the father points away from himself to the grandfather, for twice the name of Abraham is mentioned, and that he defines the promise of land as *birkat 'abrāhām* – something which is also unique. Before Gen. 28 the name El Shadday and the expression *'ereṣ m^egūrīm* occur in ch. 17 only, so in connection with Abraham. *Q^ehal 'ammīm*, too, refers back, to its parallel *h^amōn gōyīm* in 17.4f.

The blessing to Isaac has been given for Abraham's sake – that is what Gen. 26 keeps hammering at (see my ch. III, § 4), cf. also 25.11. Isaac sticks to this view in 28.3ff.

28.13b shows a striking detail: the apposition *'ābīkā* does not stand with Isaac, as was to be expected, but with Abraham. The double function of this apposition is to bring Abraham to the fore as the most important "father" – which he is, being the one with whom God started this family-history – in accordance with Isaac's pointing away from himself; and thus to raise the surmise with Jacob and with us, to make us consider the possibility that Yhwh, by presenting himself in such a way, will now give the *birkat 'abrāhām* to Jacob too; which is exactly what happens.

[29] The same construction in Gen. 13.15 but there less surprising because of the front position of *'et*. Cf. Ex. 3.5.

[30] Thus something like 'etten l^ekā ul^ezar'^akā 'et hā'āreṣ 'ašer ... etc.

"Your seed will be like the dust of the earth". No doubt the *tertium comparationis* is in the first place the numerousness, by this the comparison has become classical. But the analysis has also to find out whether there are any other aspects of meaning in common.[31] We get on the right track by means of the chiasmus which connects this verse and the preceding one:

hā'āreṣ	zar'ᵃkā
zar'ᵃkā	hā'āreṣ

This chiasmus forces us to ask what relation 13c and 14a bear to each other. The multiplying of Jacob and his descendants is furthered, indeed made possible because God gives land to them. Conversely, the land is given with the intention that Jacob's family prosper and be fruitful. We may attach symbolical value to this chiasmus. Here it is symbolic of the intimate, indissoluble relation between the promises of land and progeny, between Promised Land and fruitfulness. At the same time it elicits and makes explicit another aspect of meaning of the comparison "like the dust of the earth": just as self-evidently as dust belongs to the earth, so Jacob's living in the God given country will mean prosperity.

Again and again we come across the words "you and your seed". Their sequence arranges the entire complex 13c-14c. Again we find a chiasmus, even a double one:

13c	-kā	zar'ᵃkā
14a,b	zar'ᵃkā	'attā (present in pāraṣTA)
14c	-kā	zar'ᵃkā

[31] In Gen. 13.16 only the numerousness of ka'afar hā'āreṣ is of importance: that aspect is what v. 16b emphasizes.

Concerning the comparison note the following: hardly anywhere in the OT is dust, *'āfār*, used as a neutrally geological or physical detail. In the great majority of the more than 100 places – and the same holds good for *'efer* – it occurs as a metaphor, a comparison or part of it, with definitely pejorative meanings such as littleness, worthlessness, humiliation, fear, defeat, misery, mortality, death: one heaps up dust on one's head as a sign of mourning, the miserable man is sitting down in dust, dust is the place man goes to, for man himself is nothing but dust, etc. In not quite ten places only *'āfār* is connected with the concept of numerousness (Gen. 13.16 28.14, Num. 23,10, I Ki. 20,10, Zach. 9.3, Ps. 78.27, Job 27,16, II Chron. 1.9) and of these only four places refer to fruitfulness, the verses in Gen., Num., and II Chron. Negatively speaking the least we can infer from these data is: using *'afar* as a comparison for numerous offspring was not a stale cliché in Gen. 28. Whether it was original cannot be made out for certain, but it might well have been.

The function of this chiasmus, too, is to tightly connect the parts of which it consists. In God's promise Jacob and his progeny come to be on a single level, when viewed in perspective. Indeed, one could almost speak of identity, of Jacob as corporate personality. This is perceptible in the smooth transition from 14a to 14b; the change of subject is hardly noticeable. That "your seed" will be numerous, means that "you shall spread abroad".

In this transition a remarkable sound phenomenon occurs:

k‘PR h'RṢ

PRṢt

A fine melting together of consonants, which we might call a sound-fusion. But it is not merely fine. The task of this concentration of alliterations is what matters. One verse explains the other: "be like dust of the earth" means "spread abroad", certainly, but the Hebrew has carefully chosen a verb which renders this correlation sensorily perceptible, like an echo.[32] To put it even more strongly, *prṣ* is the perfect verbal embodiment of the primary aspect of meaning in *ka‘afar hā'āreṣ*. The levels of sound and meaning have become integrated: they point to each other, they explain each other, pervade each other.

After the concentration of alliterations the narrator proceeds with another figure of speech, the enumeration. Elaborately and evenly the four winds are summed up. "En la enumeración se abarca la totalidad, subrayando la multitud".[33] The completeness of this enumeration rhetorically underlines the theme of "fertility".[34] The uniqueness of

[32] Buber says, on p. 304 of the collection made together with Franz Rosenzweig: die Schrift und ihre Verdeutschung, Berlin, 1936: "So ist uns aufgegangen, dass seine nicht seltenen Alliterationen und Assonanzen nicht durch ästhetische Kategorien allein erfasst werden können: es sind, wenn auch nicht immer, so doch immer wieder Stellen von religiöser Wichtigkeit, an denen sie stehen, und sie dienen dazu, diese Wichtigkeit sinnlich hervortreten zu lassen." But one should bear in mind that this is not specifically biblical; it is a feature of much literature. "In many works of art (...) the sound-stratum attracts attention and thus constitutes an integral part of the aesthetic effect", Wellek & Warren op. cit., p. 158 ("aesthetic" in a sense different from Buber's "ästhetisch").

[33] Alonso, Estudios p. 221.

[34] Ibid.: "las enumeraciones no son escasas en Isaías: en general tienen función oratoria, a veces función descriptiva. En cuanto a la contextura o disposición de los elementos, volvemos a encontrar la articulación binaria como recurso formal ordenador. La serie se reparte en binas."

this passage is easily spotted by comparing it to Gen. 13.14-17 to which it is akin:

		sā nā ʻēnẹkā
28.14 ufāraṣtā		ur^{e}'ē min hammāqōm '^{a}šer 'attā
yāmmā wāqedmā w^{e}ṣāfōnā		šām ṣāfōnā wānegbā wāqedmā
wānegbā		wāyāmmā
	17:	qūm hithallek bā'āreṣ
		l^{e}'orkāh ul^{e}roḥbāh

A first difference is that the promise to Abraham concerns the present. He himself must now take part in its (provisional) realization: hence the imperatives in v. 17, hence the horizontal plane is described for a second time. On the other hand, the promise to Jacob concerns a remote future. More important is that in Gen. 13 the promises of land and offspring are independent, side by side, whereas in Gen. 28 the two themes are indissolubly interwoven. Here the land is only background, substratum for the theme of multiplying; with Abraham it has a much more independent value, and indeed, at that moment is the main concern. The junction of the two elements in the promise to Jacob, however, does not occur until that one clause 28.14b. What at first was mentioned separately in 13c (land) and in 14a (like the dust of the earth), but was already connected in the chiasmus hā'āreṣ – zarʻ^{a}kā – zarʻ^{a}kā – hā'āreṣ is now integrated into one organic whole: ufāraṣtā yāmmā wāqedmā ... etc. Now we remember the sound fusion, recalling that precisely at the point where the two parts of the promise merge, there is also the concentration of alliterations! So there is yet another way in which sound level and 'content' refer to each other.

In 14c a climax is reached. Jacob becomes the ferment of the people on all sides, bringing blessing to them. From the *mišpaḥat Yaʻqob* our gaze is led to *kol mišp^{e}ḥōt hā'^{a}dāmā*; "dass 'alle Geschlechter der Erde' in Jakob Segen finden, geschieht nach der Aussage dieses Textes so, dass Israel sich nach allen Richtungen hin verbreitet (v. 14a) und dadurch (...) als lebensförderndes Ferment unter den Völkern wirkt".[35]

[35] Gerhard Wehmeier, der Segen im AT. Eine semasiologische Untersuchung der Wurzel BRK, Basel 1970, p. 179. He tries to circumscribe the *nifal* (3 × in OT), separating it from the *hitpael* (7 times), as middle voice "(für sich) Segen gewinnen", pp. 177-179.
Another point: why do 12.3 and 28.14 have '^{a}*dāmā*, and not, as the blessing in 18.18, 22.18, 26.4 the word *'ereṣ*? The five passages have in common that by God's election a patriarch is put in the centre and that for his sake the whole

§ 4. Just as the first part of God's promise, the second part consists of four lines:

והנה אנכי עמך	15a
ושמרתיך בכל אשר תלך	b
והשבתיך אל האדמה הזאת	c
כי לא אעזבך עד אשר אם עשיתי את אשר דברתי לך	d

First a remote future, a world-wide perspective, four subjects (I – your seed – you – all families). Now the present and the near future, the privateness of a dialogue. Six times God is subject now, in the first person, six times Jacob is the other figure, as direct or indirect object.

The particle *hinnē* brings about a connection with v. 12f. The vision, narrated with *hinnē*, repeated three times, now ends with and finds its cause in the words "I am with you" – the secret of all the promises which like a pivot stands precisely in the middle. Just as it was important to interpret the brevity of v. 10, so is this also true in v. 15a. Here we have the compact pronouncement, I am with you, which is rendered in Hebrew in two words. There is no need of more, for there are no restrictions set, and syntactic adjuncts are given no chance of curtailing the fullness of the pronouncement. Massively, of jewel-like shortness, this pronouncement by God, which might serve as a title for so many passages in the O.T., expresses the unconditional, absolute support and loyalty which Jacob is to experience from God.[36] The words "I am with you" are made concrete twice. On his way to and fro Jacob can rely on God's help, the *waw* before šemartīkā is explicative. V. 15c can refer to what 13c says: so that this land may be given to Jacob, God will bring him back; the near future serves the remote future.

world is blessed. The universal significance of the particular election is always primary. This significance is not in danger of being curtailed in 18.18 and 22.18, because *'ereṣ* does not occur in a limited sense in the immediate vicinity, and in 26,4 there is no danger because there it forms a contrast to the rather rare plural *kol hā'arāṣōt hā'el* (2 times). But because in the passages of Gen. 12.3 and 28.14 the word *'ereṣ* has already been used in the clearly outlined sense of a certain country, namely the country of Canaan, another word, *'adāmā*, is chosen to denote unambiguously the world-wide range of the blessing. In v. 15c *'adāmā*, too, is eventually restricted again by the demonstrative pronoun.

[36] A. L. Strauss, Bedarkē Hassifrūt, p. 68, is the first to analyze (cf. Weiss, Hammiqrā ... p. 131f) how the brevity, the jewel-likeness of the words *Yhwh rō'ī* and *lō 'eḥsar* in Ps. 23 (we may call it the counterpart of *'ānōkī 'immāk*") expresses the psalmist's unshakable faith in God, which not even the critical moment of v. 4 can change (cf. Strauss p. 20 on a poem by Lea Goldberg).

God's promise in vv. 13-15 presupposes that the land, Canaan, is not Jacob's yet. Therewith these sentences lend connotative meaning to v. 10. Berseba, which Jacob left, is foreign land, and he turns his steps to the land of his origin; for from Haran was his father, from there his mother, too, had been taken. But now there is a rebound and v. 10 lends connotative meaning to vv. 13-15. The land of his origin is not the promised land for Jacob, his stay there will be only temporary and foreign Canaan will fall to him.

V. 15d, the fourth clause, resumes the theme of "I am with you", "I will not leave you". This line is made to serve as a conclusion by the exclamatory-assuring *kī* and the general phrasing of the clause ("do ... speak").

§ 5. God has spoken. The story now moves to Jacob – with a sudden turn which is quite common for the O.T. after a theophany – and remains occupied with his reactions. The second part of the pericope has begun:

וייקץ יעקב משנתו ויאמר 16
אכן יש יהוה במקום הזה
ואנכי לא ידעתי
ויירא ויאמר 17
מה נורא המקום הזה
אין זה כי אם בית אלהים
וזה שער השמים

Waking up from his sleep, Jacob reacts to the sum total of his experiences in amazement. Unsuspecting and with an open mind he comes to the conclusion: so Yhwh is in this place, and I, I did not know it. But no sooner has this penetrated his mind than his amazement gives way to fear (*wayyīrā*) and he carefully phrases what this means as to the nature of his stopping-place. The narrator shows psychological insight; he knows very well, that people, when waking up, come "to (the point)" by degrees. After his first artless amazement, when his own position is not yet at stake, Jacob, starting to take deeper soundings and becoming involved in the situation, is himself compromised: "he was afraid".

Both of Jacob's reactions circle round the motif of "place". The word itself is used twice, when the second half of the story begins. But had not it been used three times already, precisely when the first half began? We clearly see the point of that now. Right from the start the story raised an important motif by hammering the word "*māqōm*" home to us, with a threefold repetition, and it created suspense by raising the question at the same time, "but what place?" Now in vv. 16-17 it refers back to the beginning by means of a double *māqōm* and next answers explicitly with a double name, "House of God, Gate of Heaven".[37]

So the word *māqōm* was not a false alarm but indeed a justified stylistic means. As a key-word it marked a leading motif right in the beginning, at least it was precursory to it. For an important part of the complex 'content' of the pericope is that Jacob's stopping-place is *'admat qodeš*! What seemed to be merely "a place", with no face of its own, turns out to be the gate of heaven![38]

But we do not learn this directly from the narrator. He has chosen direct speech, and thus he changes the narrative perspective again. Again he retires behind the back of his protagonist, as with the vision. There is a reason for this. That Jacob himself gives name to the nature of the place shows that at first he also did not know where he had retired to rest. For him, too, the identity of the place was a question-mark, "and I, I did not know".

The narrator has started off ingeniously. For of course he knew in advance that his story was to end in "Beth El"! He could have begun with a sentence like "Jacob came to a place called Bethel and spent the night there; but he did not know that it was a House of God", but then the beginning would have been insipid, without suspense. Because he does not reveal anything other than an always anonymous '*māqōm*' he represents what Jacob saw and knew, i.c. did not know. To this extent the narrator has succeeded in identifying with Jacob.

Another beginning would have produced another content. In literary use of language the shape is not an interchangeable garment but the necessary form of this content.[39] The content determines the

[37] The same stylistic method (first pass over a quality or identity on purpose, only later fix it) we find in the Jabbok scene: the "man" turns out to be "God". (It is striking that there, too, the identity is revealed by the protagonist himself, not by his narrator). It is also found in Gen. 22.8,14.

[38] The definite article with the first *māqōm* in v. 11 may have had the function of arousing surprise and raising a question; but it is better to read, as does Ehrlich (Randglossen zur Hebräischen Bibel, Leipzig, 1908, vol. I p. 135), "a certain place". So does P. Joüon, Grammaire de l'Hébreu biblique, Rome, 1947, § 137n (3) about this shade of meaning in the article.

[39] So say Buber and Rosenzweig, op. cit. pp. 311, 257; Alonso, SVT 7, p. 163; Weiss, Biblica 1961, p. 257, and Hammiqrā Kidmūtō pp. 35-38; Wellek & Warren p. 28, W. Kayser p. 240; Dámaso Alonso, Poesía Española, ensayo de métodos y límites estilísticos, Madrid, 1957 (3rd ed.) p. 32f.

form, and the other way around, form has substance. This is very clear in this case: the place was anonymous and actually, was not in the least a House of God of its own accord, but could only become one by virtue of an action by God. The place as such was not holy, not awesome (mind you, we are talking about the *māqōm* in Gen. 28!), but it took on that quality by the theophany, as the 'form' conveys. If the narrator had dropped a name in the beginning, things would have been quite different! Now Bethel owes this quality solely to a once and only moment from the history of salvation.

Therefore it is not enough to say that the narrator has avoided an insipid opening by raising a question, an expectation. We should add that this phenomenon of the 'form' (first the anonymous *māqōm* used three times, much further down *māqōm* = Bethel) has been determined by a fundamental theological conception and it embodies this in the language. This conception, as we can read from the 'form', concerns the nature and the origin of this *'admat qodeš*. The form itself is immediate evidence of the surprising action of God, which converts an anonymous place into *Ša'ar Haššāmayim*[40] and thus it is content.

When we turn our attention to Jacob's words again, we observe yet a third moment in his mood; it lies between the other two and in fact constitutes a transition. After the words of amazement "Yhwh is in this place", Jacob expressly says, "I, I did not know" and we observe a note of shame. In these two lines the two main characters of the story have been put on opposite sides. It is worthwhile to search into their relationship here. Artless as he is at that first moment Jacob sharply registers the short-circuit in the situation. While formulating his own part in this he realizes that it was only a negative part. "I could kick myself" – shame and self-reproach steal in upon him and pave the way for fear, *wayyīrā*. In this fear his eye is sharpened for a deeper insight into the situation.

The result of this he also formulates. We shall consider another three details:

a) There is another repetition of words, twice we see *yr'*. Jacob became scared, but this is not simply a subjective matter, for example fear as a result of a bad conscience. Explicitly he himself points out

[40] No doubt Ehrlich is right, though, when he remarks: "die Wiederholung von זה im zweiten Halbvers wäre völlig unerklärlich, wenn Jakob nur auf *eine* Stätte hinwiese (...). Tatsächlich aber wird hier auf zwei verschiedene Stätten hingewiesen, nämlich auf die Stelle auf der Erde, wo die Leiter stand, und dann auf den Punkt am Himmel" (Randglossen, Vol. I p. 136).

that the cause of his fear is outside himself and objective: it is the place which is frightful. After his first spontaneous reaction, formulated on the spur of the moment, Jacob has come to objectify things and this is expressed in strictly factual statements and conclusions.
b) In this way we can also find an explanation for the fact that in the second instance the main characters have disappeared as subjects, and more particularly that Jacob does not mention himself anymore. His thoughts lead him to discern the nature of the place, which is defined by the theophany only, whether he, Jacob, *yd'* or not. The place is a House of God, and he cannot do anything about it. In his continued objectifying Jacob has no use for himself in his conclusions. This is on a level with what the verbal repetition of *māqōm* has already told us earlier: that it is God's action only that converts the anonymous 'place' into Bethel.
c) The use of the phrase *'ēn zę kī 'im* shows that Jacob not only discerns, but almost recognizes with a shock where he is. The scales fall from his eyes: "that I should not have seen it earlier!" The facts allow him but one conclusion, this is no other than a House of God!

V. 18 opens with *wayyaškem Ya'qob babboqer*. This need not conflict with his awakening which takes place earlier in v. 16; nor is it absolutely necessary to suppose that Jacob went to snatch a little sleep after his words in v. 17. That would indeed be evidence of his being unmoved if not apathetic, and that fits neither the image we have of Jacob nor the situation. V. 18a means[41]: "In the morning Jacob got

[41] The verb *škm* has grown away from its etymological root in so far as the aspect of the meaning "shoulder, withers" is not felt anymore; so it has become more abstract – a development which is quite common in language. It is true that in such a case one has to find out from place to place whether the context activates the original meaning again, revives it by means of a connection of sounds, repetition of words etc. or not. (A fine example in Zeph. 3.7,9: there the repetition of *škm* underlines the absolute reversal which God's action brings about, v. 9. *Škm* in v. 9 activates in *hiškīmū*, v. 7, the original "shoulder" as a connotation; the shoulders that first served the evil are now united in the service of the Lord). Usually, however, the concrete aspect of *hiškīm* is dormant, sometimes even totally obsolete: in Hos. 6.4 the dew is *maškīm hōlek*. The primary aspect of meaning has become: "early".

In the stories about the patriarchs the word sometimes assumes a position which it does not have in other places: it immediately follows an appearance by God: Gen. 20.8, 21.14, 28.18 (cf. Ex. 24.4, 34.4; but not in Gen. 19.27, 26.31, 32.1). We find the combination of *wayyaškem babboqer*, and with these words the story starts telling how someone reacts to God's word, or that he is going to perform a command of God. At this turning-point of the action and by the

busy at once," and it is a self-evident continuation of his first reactions, which were verbal.

18 וישכם יעקב בבקר
ויקח את האבן אשר שם מראשתיו וישם אתה מצבה
ויצק שמן על ראשה
19 ויקרא את שם המקום ההוא בית אל
ואולם לוז שם העיר לראשנה

Apart from the anonymous *māqōm* there was one other detail which had attracted our attention in the beginning: the peculiar mention of a stone as Jacob's pillow provoked our curiosity. This thread is now also cast off (for the time being). The stone in v. 11 was justified: it was to be a massebe, a monument, as we now see. To make the connection the narrator takes care to repeat the words wayyiqqaḥ 'et hā'eben ... sām m[e]ra'[a]šōtāw.

But why is it that Jacob set up a massebe, and not, for example, an altar? Let us spell the word *maṣṣebā*; it has a secret to let out. It is from the stem *nṣb* which we have come across twice before in the story, as well as in the beginning. There a ladder was *muṣṣāb* and a little further down Yhwh himself was *niṣṣāb*. This surprising connection makes it clear to us why Jacob needs an erected stone. By setting up a massebe he wants to establish forever that he has seen a ladder with angels *muṣṣāb* and that Yhwh was *niṣṣāb* with him.

Once more, paying attention to a key-word has led us to an important part of the theme. Just as the ladder was a prefiguration of God's appearance, so Jacob now turns an erected stone into a postfiguration of the theophany. The anonymous *māqōm* has changed into Bethel, the simple stone must therefore change into a monument *aere perennius*.

A small thing in v. 11 which we have by-passed now becomes meaningful. Jacob did not take "a stone", but he took [one] "of the

change of subject that goes with it, *hiškīm* clearly acquires the connotation of "react alertly" 20.8 and 28.18, indeed "obey without delay and promptly" in 21.14 and 22.3. For in the two places mentioned last it strikes us that we do not hear about a nightly meeting and that a presupposition to that effect is beside the question; so that the notion of "early" is minimized. Cf. also Erich Auerbach on Gen. 22.3 (Mimesis, dargestellte Wirklichkeit in der abendländischen Literatur, 2nd ed. Bern 1959, p. 12): "Also ist "das Morgens früh" nicht um der Zeitabgrenzung willen gesetzt, sondern um der moralischen Bedeutung willen; es soll das Unverzügliche, Pünktliche und Genaue im Gehorsam des so schwer getroffenen Abraham ausdrücken."

stones of the place". König generally records, "So eilte die Darstellung sehr oft über die Erwähnung des Exemplars zur Nennung der ganzen Kategorie hin".[42] In this concrete text the point is this: by means of the turn *me'abnē*... a maximal indefiniteness is accomplished; the stone has a minimal shape of its own, a minimal "personality", is an anonym. Until it is given a maximal individuality and personality as a milestone in the history of salvation!

The dance of key-words, however, is not over yet. Jacob pours oil on the stone – but not at random; then the text would just have said *'ālẹhā*, as in Gen. 35:14b wayyassek 'ālẹhā nesek wayyiṣoq 'ālẹhā šamen. No, Jacob pours it *'al RŌŠāh*. Is this detail, the mention of *rōš*, useful? In our story there is another *rōš*, in the beginning (for the third time we find a key-word there!), and it is there at a delicate point: where the heaven is touched by the top of the ladder, by its *rōš*. By means of the words *'al rōšāh* in v. 18 the story reminds us of this.[43] By pouring oil "on its top" Jacob commemorates the ladder's reaching to heaven, just as by setting up the massebe he commemorated that this ladder was *muṣṣāb* on earth.

Because the narrator has given the massebe a *rōš*, we have a chance to define the nature of this erected stone. There is more to it than its mere use as a monument. Symbolically the massebe *is* the ladder and that is why the oil must be poured on its top. But in the place where the ladder lasted only the length of a dream, where it was a disappearing prefiguration, there is now the massebe as a postfiguration, eternal and indestructible.

Every massebe is unique in that it has been erected in a special place for a special reason, but at the same time it is only a specimen of the species. But the stone which Jacob has just set up is unique of its kind, because precisely its erectedness, which element has given it the name of massebe, is its most essential part and because precisely this essence is the most adequate embodiment, the perfect symbol of this never to be repeated event, the theophany at Bethel.

"This is a House of God" Jacob realized. Now that the massebe has

[42] E. König, Stilistik, Rhetorik, Poetik in Bezug auf die biblischen Literatur, Leipzig, 1900, p. 201.

[43] The story itself takes care to make us aware of the connection with *r'š*. Key-words are like buoys at sea, they mark the way which the interpreter has to go. The word *r'š* is anchored by the word *mr'šwt*: it occurs in v. 11 and is repeated explicitly in 18, to the point of elaborateness. In other words, it is a thread which we scan until suddenly we feel the knot itself, *r'š*, in our hands.

been set up, the consequences follow: as the place is, so it will be called. Jacob gives it the name of Bethel. It is difficult to find out from case to case where *qārā lᵉ* has been lexicalized and just means, "to give a name to", but in this case it quite agrees with the tension of the pericope and the "archaische Feierlichkeit"[44] of Jacob's actions to preserve the meaning of "to call". It is a solemn, sacral, cultic if you like, proclamation, which Jacob calls out over the place, Beth El, as a fitting continuation and conclusion of the erection and anointment of the massebe.

What was without a name has now been named, but now v. 19b is going to tell us that the place did have a name! Normally we would have heard this as far back as v. 11, in, for example, wayyifga' bᵉmāqōm wᵉšem hammāqōm hahū Lūz, a very frequent turn in the Bible. By postponing[45] mention of the name the narrator completely establishes the relativity of the importance and identity of Luz, indeed he ridicules the place. "Place"? No, he even uses the word "town"! With superior irony this town is presented to us as an anonymous *māqōm*, six times. Canaanite Luz does not stand a chance of existing, not even for a moment! Actually, it is a place without identity, without face, without local colour, a place which has been named Bethel before it has been able to represent itself as an important Canaanite town.

Whence this peculiar exposure of Luz as an actual nonentity? We get on the right track again by a chiasmus, which owes its origin to the less common[46] order of predicate plus subject in the noun clause v. 19b:

šem hammāqōm	Bet 'el
Lūz	šem hā'īr

[44] Von Rad, Theologie des AT, p. 63 (München, 1961, 3rd ed.).

[45] Lämmert, op.cit., p. 32 again: "Die Bauformen des Erzählens erhalten ihre Kontur erst dadurch, dass die monotone Sukzession der erzählten Zeit auf verschiedene Weise verzerrt, (...) umgestellt (...) wird."

[46] The normal order for example we see in Jud. 1.23 "wᵉšem hā'īr lᵉfānīm Lūz". Francis I. Andersen, The Hebrew Verbless Clause in the Pentateuch, New York 1970, on p. 41 points to 54 places with *šem*. "The reverse sequence, that is with šem in S following P occurs only three times in the Pentateuch", among others in Gen. 17.15, where "the inverted sequence secures contrastive focus on the name itself". "Sequence P-S is used also in Gen. 28,19 (= 303; compare Judg. 18.29, contrast Jos. 15.15; Isa. 5.7." See also p. 45.

Here the chiasmus has its maximal symbolical function, as in Is. 1.18. It indicates the complete change that has taken place, the radical reversal from Luz into Bethel.

This radical change, proclaimed by Jacob, originates in the taking place of God's revelation. Before the theophany transformed the *māqōm* into Bethel, it had already accomplished another thing. By the theophany Canaanite Luz has been exposed, leached, purged to the zero-state of "a place". God does not want to appear to Jacob in a Canaanite town, but he wants to appear in a nothing which only his appearing will turn into a something, but then no less than a House of God. Where the history of the covenant between Yhwh and his people begins, all preceding things grow pale. Canaan loses its face, Luz is deprived of its identity papers. The narrator cannot write down this supreme moment in the history of salvation on a pagan clay tablet; only a blank slate is worthy of receiving his account.

Now we have come to a point from where we can look back and find the justification for the fact that it was to the vision that the honour was given of being represented as present. Jacob feels urged to respond, to do something after the revelation. His response, the massebe, is massive – "stone-hard" – so concrete is it; his answer links with the only concretely visible part of the revelation as described in the three *hinnē*-clauses. In no less than three key-words together this link is represented in language. In the narrator's perspective the most concrete part of Jacob's reaction, which does not evaporate and always remains present, urges him to represent the scene to which it is linked, viz. the vision, as present breaking through the past. In the perspective of the narrative and in our perspective: by the overpowering, direct impression which the sight of the vision makes upon him, Jacob is inspired to the thought of and performance of a concrete answer which will always remain present; he succeeds in transforming one of its outstanding moments, the raisedness of the ladder and of God, and to fix it in an erected stone.

A find of genius on Jacob's part; however, only so by the grace of the composition of the narrative. "Die Sachverhalte (...), die Gegenständlichkeit (die natürlich auch Menschen, Gefühle, Vorgänge umfasst) ist nur als Gegenständlichkeit dieser dichterischen Sätze da".[47] He who wants to break through the garment of language to the story, misses the principle behind the formal structure of the Bethel pericope

[47] W. Kayser, op. cit., p. 14. Also see note 49 below.

and will therefore get lost in speculations. Historical research that starts from a literary text is not possible and thus not adequate until it has been determined to what degree the elements signified have been integrated into the structure, how here too "die Sätze der Dichtung sich ihre eigene Gegenständlichkeit schaffen".[47]

A very clear example is our massebe. Religio-phenomenologically and religio-historically it is not possible to say anything meaningful about it until it has been decided and until one is willing to take into account that this massebe here leads its own life, absolutely defined by the story. "Die Sachverhalte haben ein seltsam irreales, auf jeden Fall ein durchaus eigenes Sein, das von dem der Realität grundsätzlich verschieden ist".[48] What is supreme reality to stylistic analysis and exegesis, is to the historian material badly distorted by literature, from which he can draw conclusions only if he is very cautious.[49]

§ 6. We shall now try to localize the principle behind the formal structure of the Bethel scene, its basic stylistic pattern. The stylistic means of keywords has guided us in getting to the essential meaning of the text. Style is not an ornament, for its meaning is found not only at the aesthetical level, not even primarily so. The analysis of all the stylistic aspects automatically brings to light the 'content'. This 'content' is very complex, very composite. But in this compositeness a hierarchy is to be detected, a structure. A basic pattern, a key-thought arranges the levels of the literary work of art, and the interpreter can get to this core by various ways; one way runs via phonological phenomena, another via syntactic elements, etc. By the transparency of a certain detail he intuitively sees the core; from there the entire structure unfolds before his eyes. This happening, this revelation – "Stil ist Offenbarung, wenn wir ihn richtig verstehen"[50] – he can then arrange systematically in a report.

[48] ibid. "Irreal" is not pejorative here!

[49] "Historische und biographische Vorgänge in der Erzählung können mit Hilfe anderer Geschichtsquellen unter Umständen auf ein vollständigeres und sogar relativ objektives Geschichtsbild zurückgeführt werden. Zur historischen Deutung von Dichtungen ist dieser Weg oft beschritten worden (...). Solche Bemühungen zielen jedoch stets mehr auf die Hintergründe eines Werkes als auf das Werk selbst. Grundsätzlich besitzt die erzählerische Fiktion ebenso eine eigene Zeit-Raum-Konstellation wie sie überhaupt einen Lebenszusammenhang darbietet, der von der realen Wirklichkeit schon durch seine Abrundung kategorial verschieden ist." Lämmert, op. cit., p. 26.

[50] Alonso, Suppl. VT vii, 1959, p. 163.

The way from the detail to the core we can now traverse because of the analysis of v. 18. The concentration of key-words makes one expect a priori a centre of meaning for the story in this verse.[51] In the Bethel scene we have noticed close connections between the beginning of the first half and the beginning of the second half. Their "statistical" appearance is as follows, corresponding to their sequence in the text:

verse	1	2	3	4	5	6	7	8	9
11	מקום								
		לקח							
			אבן						
	מקום								
				שים					
					מראשת				
	מקום								
12						מצב			
					ראש		שמים		
								אלהים	
13									יהוה
						נצב			
16									יהוה
	מקום								
17	מקום								
								אלהים	
							שמים		
18		לקח							
			אבן						
				שים	מראשת				
				שים					
						מצבה			
19	מקום				ראש				

[51] "Die biblische Lehre trägt oft ihr Höchstes nicht vor, sondern lässt es sich auftun, – nicht durch Kryptologie und Allegorese, sondern durch diese jedem unbefangen aufmerksamen Hörleser erkennbaren von Stelle zu Stelle geschlagenen Bogen bedeutsamer Wiederholung." Buber, op.cit., p. 32f.
One might replace "biblische Lehre" just as well by any literature. Similarly O. Walzel wrote about repetitions of words in 1923: "Sie binden (...), sie bewirken Zusammenhänge, die ohne sie vielleicht übersehen würden. Sie scheiden sich scharf ab von einer verstandesmässig ausgedrückten, in begriffliche Worte umgesetzten Herstellung solcher Zusammenhänge", Gehalt und Gestalt im Kunstwerk des Dichters, Potsdam, 1923, p. 358.

We can make two more observations, the right interpretation of which will reveal the secret of the narrative form to us: the stream of key-words 1-6 runs parallel in I and II, but that of the numbers 7-9 does not. To start with the latter, we notice that these words occur in concentric sequence, abc-cba. The key-words which finish the beginning of the story, the vision, open the second part. We may not leave it at this formal statement; the three are – of all words! – the words God, *Yhwh*, heaven.

This means that what came last in the dream, the appearance of God himself, and what was of course the most important thing about the dream, is for that reason the first thing Jacob talks about in his reactions, "*Yhwh* is in this place!"

But this series abc-cba is not disconnected from the chain of the first six key-words. Number 1, the word *māqōm* intervenes twice between the names for God, and subsequently sets the entire stream in motion. That means that the occurrence of the revelation, seeing God, is primary for Jacob and this dictates the exact sequence of his reactions. It is nothing particular in itself; but for us the point is that this has been materialized into the far corners of the form, and vice versa: it is only perfectly clear and is only unshakably the essential thing because of this form. The key-words 2-5(6) concern the setting up of the massebe. The formal complex represented in our diagram shows that the vision of the theophany was the force which inspired and made it possible for the stone to be jacked up to a massebe.

We are now justified in arranging the material afresh and to make it dance to the piping of the structure:

māqōm			māqōm
wayyiqqaḥ 'eben	šāmayim	Yhwh	wayyiqqaḥ hā'eben
sām m^{e}ra'^{a}šōtāw	'elōhīm	'elōhīm	sām m^{e}ra'^{a}šōtāw
muṣṣāb	Yhwh	šāmayim	maṣṣebā
rōš			rōš

But this pattern suggests yet that Jacob's actions are a reflection of his experiences; and that is only half true. The other half of the truth is much more essential, that there is also something like progress, development. We can demonstrate this by means of the following well-arranged schema which has also been built up with the parallel series of key-words 1-6, but which shows the development in the story:

I. Staying the night, theophany (vv. 11-13)	II. After the theophany (vv. 16-19)
1. Jacob comes to a *place* stays the night in that *place*	1a. Jacob discerns the *place* as house of God, 1b. he calls the *place* like that: Bethel
2a. He *puts* a *stone* under his head b. He sees a ladder *raised*, then Yhwh himself *raised*.	2. He *sets up* the *stone*: there a monument is *raised*.
3. The *top* of the ladder reaches to *heaven*	3a. "This is the gate of *heaven*." b. He pours oil on the *top* of the stone

Jacob immortalizes the vision in an action, the result of which, the massebe, reflects what he had seen. But what he had done earlier, put down a stone at random, in a place at random, he sets right, he completes under the influence of the vision. It resembles a chemical reaction:

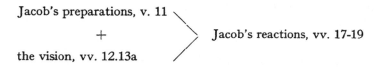

Jacob's preparations, v. 11
+
the vision, vv. 12.13a
→ Jacob's reactions, vv. 17-19

Just as a dull drop of dew is turned into a bright brilliant by the beams of the morning-sun, so, by the theophany, the unimportant trivial action of Jacob is transformed into a historical example in the dialogue of man and his God.

The stylistic core of a text may consist of a verse, a limited number of words. This is true in Isaiah 6, where the vision and hearing the threefold holy effects a chain reaction of triads in the poetry in which the prophet puts down his experience.[52] In the Bethel pericope what we can point to is not so much a centre as a basic pattern underlying the whole. Opposite one half is the other half, a series of words is

[52] Forcefully demonstrated by Alonso, SVT 7 (1959) p. 158, and in the Estudios p. 226.

made a chain of key-words in the second half, by repetition, the parallelism of this repetition structures the halves, there is action and reaction, God appears to a man and man immortalizes this moment. The structure reveals the central thought of the story to us: God starts a dialogue with Jacob and Jacob succeeds in giving the absolutely adequate response to this. It is not only a matter of God, nor only of Jacob. Time and space are structured by the dialogue in which the two find each other.

Their dialogue charges the air, as it were, with an electric tension and transforms the space – from stone to massebe, from "somewhere" on earth to House of God. The whole world has found its centre there; from the country which is to be Jacob's, North and South, East and West will be populated.

Time is structured: the long journey and the dark future after it are in the sign of "I am with you" and thus are transformed into a shielded present and a blessed future of return and prosperity.

The God of Abraham and Isaac will also be the God of Jacob, the *'ōbed '*^{a}*rammī* of the desert will have vine and fig-tree. Taken by surprise Jacob hears the words spoken to him:

החזקתיך מקצות הארץ	ומאציליה קראתיך
ואמר לך עבדי אתה	בחרתיך ולא מאסתיך
אל תירא כי עמך אני	אל תשתע כי אני אלהיך

§ 7. Jacob gives the one adequate response. This is the conclusion we drew from the analysis of part of the story. We have not by-passed the other verses to imply that they belong outside the structure. On the contrary, if the parallelism of the halves is made visible anywhere, then this is certainly so in the verses 20-22 which explicitly link up with v. 15:

20	וידר יעקב נדר לאמר	
	אם יהיה אלהים עמדי	הנה אנכי עמך
	ושמרני בדרך הזה אשר אנכי הלך	ושמרתיך בכל אשר תלך
	ונתן לי לחם לאכל ובגד ללבש	. . . .
21	ושבתי בשלום אל בית אבי	והשבתיך אל האדמה הזאת
	והיה יהוה לי לאלהים	כי לא אעזבך עד אשר אם
22	והאבן הזאת אשר שמתי מצבה יהיה בית אלהים	עשיתי את אשר דברתי לך
	וכל אשר תתן לי עשר אעשרנו לה	

Jacob's vow is an answer to the second half of God's promise, not to the first half of v. 13c-14. But patriarchs never answer promises made to them by God,[53] so that it is not remarkable that Jacob does not go into God's words of vv. 13-14, even less so as they refer to the remote future. What is remarkable is that he does respond at all, and then it is not surprising that he should go into that part of God's promise which refers to the present and the near future. It is a matter of to be or not to be for Jacob, as 20d points out to us.

Before we can start comparing vow and promise, it should be decided where the main clause in the vow starts, in v. 21b or in 22a. We observe the following[54]: the verb in 21b is a so-called "perfectum consecutivum", just as in 20c, d, and 21a, whereas 22a has an imperfect tense; the verb comes first in 20b-21b, whereas 22a opens with the subject; and parallel to this we see that 20b, c, d + 21b are governed by the same subject, so that the inversion of predicate and subject in 22a obviously underlines the change of subject. These three facts render it probable that 21b belongs to the protasis.[55]

If the main clause really started in 21b, the protasis would unmistakably have a note of Jacob calculatingly stating his terms, which is not confirmed anywhere else in the passage. Generally speaking, what tells against such a *hybris* is the biblical-theological argument that man in the O.T. is not in a superior position from which to choose

[53] "Wenn wir bei dieser kritischen Untersuchung auch andere Verheissungen in der Genesis heranziehen, so finden wir dort nie eine Bezugnahme auf den Inhalt der Verheissung ausser in dem einen Fall, wo Abraham die kommende Geburt eines Sohnes nicht meint glauben zu können (17,17). Jede andere Reaktion ist nur äusserlich, indem ähnlich wie hier ein Altarbau (26,25 u.ö.) erfolgt oder eine andere Handlung, die mit dem Inhalt der Verheissung nichts zu tun hat. So gut also unser Gelübde der Situation entspricht, so ist es doch ganz einzigartig." Eising, op. cit., p. 261.

[54] So does Eising, ibid., p. 253f.

[55] To 21b as the main clause one might object that Jacob's vow runs closely parallel to God's promise, so that having the main clause start in 21b seems an arbitrary choice; why not even earlier? And why should Jacob repeat three sentence elements of the promise in his protasis and why should he not include the fourth part? The question remains, however: why is it that the main clause does start in 22a? Chief testimony for the argumentation is, however, the atmosphere, the tone of the passage – and that is in essence theologically defined. Of course it is dangerous to refer to "atmosphere", but the stylistic analysis implies so exact a concentration on all the phenomena of the text that at this stage it is impossible for us to make gross mistakes; literary haziness and stylistic analysis are mutually exclusive.

Yhwh for a God as one of many possibilities, without himself being involved, but he can only either confirm *"Yhwh hū hā'ᵉlōhīm"* or reject it obdurately.[56] Moreover, it would here be in conflict with the tone of the narrative if Jacob in a matter-of-fact and presumptuous manner stipulated what conditions Yhwh would have to fulfil in order to be his God. For some time Jacob has been busy responding to God's appearance and promise in a mood of veneration and gratitude. reacting as befits the occasion; solemnly he has set up a massebe and proclaimed the name of Bethel, and now he is formulating an ending in line with what precedes.

The fundamental question is that concerning the names Yhwh and *'ᵉlōhīm*, and the relationship between Yhwh/God and Jacob. V. 13b implicitly posed the question whether the God of Abraham and Isaac would also be the God of Jacob. For Jacob there was no question that Yhwh is God, certainly not after his vision of God and he acknowledged this God-ness of Yhwh, also implicitly, by saying "Yhwh is in this place" in direct line with "this is the House of God". Once more this acknowledgement is implied in the first words of his vow "If God will be with me ...". For Jacob, however, the point is that Yhwh will really prove himself to be the *Elōhē Ya'qob*, so that he can do something in return.

Just as the words "'ānōkī 'immāk = lō 'e'ezbekkā" framed the promise, so the protasis of Jacob's vow has been framed by "'im yihyẹ 'ᵉlōhīm 'immādī = wᵉhāyā Yhwh lī lelōhịm". Just as v. 15d with its general wordings functioned as an ending, so 21b, too, concludes and summarizes the protasis in general, "If God will be with me (20b) ... when Yhwh has really become my God (by keeping me and bringing me back, etc.)", then I in turn shall be able to see to it that this stone will be a Beth Elohim. The parallelism with v. 15 has

[56] The most important evidence for this argument may well be the formula characteristic of the OT: "I will be your God, and you shall be my people", which occurs again and again in the following: Ex. 6.7, Lev. 26.11f., Deut. 25.12, II Sam. 7.24, Ezech. 11.20, 14.11, 36.28, 37.23, 27, Zach. 8.8 and esp. Jer. 7.23, 11.4, 24.7, 31.1, 33, 32.38. Cf. Hos. 2.25. – "Ein Gott unter den Göttern, für den man sich entscheiden könnte, kommt im AT nicht vor. Aber auch für JHWH entscheidet man sich eigentlich nicht in dem Sinne, dass man ihm vor einem anderen Gott den Vorzug gäbe." There is only "eine reiche Auswahl, sobald der Bund nicht mehr gehalten wird. (...) Von Wählen kan da nur die Rede sein im Sinne einer liturgischen Bestätigung..." K. H. Miskotte, Wenn die Götter schweigen, München 1963, p. 230.

inspired us to this rendering; what God says in 15d means to Jacob: Yhwh will also be *my* God.

There is a ring of zeal and pressure in Jacob's words. It is easy to indicate those points where he rephrases God's promise. For what God calls "this land", neutral and wide words, Jacob's words are, "the house of my father", familiar, intimate, close. In that part of the sentence, v. 21a, Jacob adds: *b^e^šālōm*; the long journey there and back is before his eyes: will he pull through? And there may also be an allusion to the discord with his brother. More than the journey it will worry him to see Esau again. Because the story of Bethel presupposes the presence of the Pnuel scene, as appears at several points later on (we shall come across a verbal connection, in addition to those already mentioned), and because a leading motif in the Pnuel scene is how scared Jacob is of seeing Esau again, and because in Gen. 33, after the reunion, the stem *šlm* is explicitly used once more (v. 18!), it is necessary for *b^e^šālōm* to be read against the background of Jacob's flight from his brother's wrath.[57]

The most striking addition that Jacob makes in his vow is formed by 20d, and here it appears most clearly how Jacob sees his situation and hopes for God's help: even for the bare necessities he is now dependent on God's support, a dependency expressed in the concrete pair bread – clothes. This pair is representative of a totality, as (on a different level, however) "bread and games" was in ancient Rome; we have a merismus here that stands for "all necessities of life, even the barest". The very choice of this pair shows how pressing the situation is for Jacob, a whole clause has been reserved for it.[58]

One more detail deserves our attention. In 20c the word *derek* has been inserted, so for the third time we note a more concrete phrase of Jacob's. He will use it again, when looking back to the Bethel episode, in Gen. 35.3; but for the rest the combination occurs only in one other place in the history of Jacob, again in the story that leads up to Pnuel – and to that another word, *pg'*, had already led us.[59] In the

[57] The emotional tension of this clause is apparent from the effect of emphasis of the numerous alliterations: 2 × šin, 4 × bet, 2 × taw, 2 × lamed, 2 × alef.

[58] Something like this occurs for example in Is. 21.14 (Alonso, Estudios p. 439).

[59] When in Gen. 32.2f for the first time after Gen. 28 it says: "Jacob went on his way", the question implicitly arises: and will God keep, *šmr*, him too, fulfilling his promise in 28.15 (20)? Again he meets, for the first time after Gen. 28, angels (*pg'*) – and the possibility that this meeting is a good omen, as it was

first place the concrete "way" tells us how much Jacob's vow is permeated with the pressing present of the journey; on this situation his eyes are fixed. It also emphasizes the Bethel scene as a milestone in the movement out of the country, after which the movement back to it will be marked in 32.2.

§ 8. Jacob's vow takes up a special position because the words of the protasis have been prompted by God himself in his promise.[60] That is why this structural fact seems to me the strongest among my arguments when I assert that the main clause should not start before v. 22a. But there is another argument, namely that of genre, for the vv. 20-22 are a clear example of the *Gattung neder*.[61] The pattern of this "private Frommigkeitsart" has already been given, "aus der Gesetzmässigkeit der Form lässt sich die Gesetzmässigkeit eines Brauches erschliessen. Danach gelobt eine bestimmte einzelne Person in einer Notlage an einem Kultort, wo es auch eingelöst wird, ein Gelübde."[62] A conditional clause, which begins with *'im*, describes the mercy for which the faithful ask God, and it is followed by a main clause which says what man does in return. In our text it is the founding of a cult at Bethel and the giving of the tithe. Verses 22a and 22b constitute the main clause, and this is marked by the transition to Jacob's role, which transition itself has been indicated especially by inversion.

What exactly does Jacob promise? For the last time we strike upon the stone, and in order to see what, eventually, Jacob does with this very particular massebe, we recall the preceding sentences:

11	wayyiqqaḥ	me'abnē hammāqōm wayyāsem m^{e}ra'^{a}šōtaw
18	wayyiqqaḥ	et hā'eben '^{a}šer sām m^{e}ra'^{a}šōtaw wayyāsem 'ōtah maṣṣebā
22		w^{e}hā'eben hazzōt '^{a}šer samtī maṣṣebā yihyẹ bēt '^{e}lōhīm

Every sentence tells something new, and 22a is the end of this de-

in Bethel, comes true. Jacob leaves Pnuel with God's blessing, a little later Esau embraces him.

[60] Because Richter does not take account of this fundamental fact his interpretation, together with its title, is wildly off the mark:

[61] W. Richter, Das Gelübde als theologische Rahmung der Jakobsüberlieferungen, Biblische Zeitschrift NF 11 (1967) pp. 21-52. It is God's promise which is the frame.

[62] Ibid. p. 31.

velopment. The history of the stone reaches its climax, but it is especially striking that the preceding stages have also been included in 22a. In this one sentence we see the stone grow from *'eben* to massebe, once more, and now also from massebe to temple. The stone will not only function as a monument and a symbol of the ladder and God's appearance, it will be the centre and the seal of this holy ground – without stone there is no House of God. Setting up the stone was the only concretely visible way for Jacob to react. That this concrete element of his response was important, is now confirmed: he knows how to make the most of the stone, and thus, to give it maximum importance, the stone will be a temple.[63]

"Give" is, however, not the right word. We become aware of a subtle difference: the double *sīm* of v. 18 is not repeated in 22a, Jacob does not say "the stone which ..., I shall make it ..." That is to say, we are not explicitly told of an action on his part, but the stone itself is subject of the verb "to be". Together with the proceeding extension in the three sentences quoted, this means that the being-a-temple is an organic continuation, a harmonious and almost self-evident sequel to the promotion from stone to massebe, but now human action is required no longer. Luz has become Bethel, not thanks to Jacob, but to God. The massebe which Jacob had put down as an eternal postfiguration of the theophany has, therefore, acquired such a weighty personality that it is the (obvious) "character" to develop into a temple for God. The natuie of "Bethel", which accrued to the place only on account of the theophany and which Jacob had confirmed by the proclamation of its name, can only be preserved by means of, and remain anchored in, this stone/temple.

The subject in v. 22a is feminine,[64] but the verb is masculine. Why? The narrator has neglected the gender of "stone" because his mind was already so occupied with the final stage, the destination of the stone, that thát (for *bayit* is masculine) determined his choice of the masculine form of the verb. The motif of change and metamorphosis, encountered

[63] Religio-historically the background of this is known: "In *sfire* wurden Vertragsstelen als בתי אלהיא bezeichnet", H. Donner in ZAW 74 (1962), pp. 68ff. And concerning our text Horst Seebass remarks, Der Stammvater Israel, BZAW 98 (1966), p. 13: "Denn dies Wort (viz. house of God) bezeichnet nicht nur Tempel, sondern auch steinerne Stelen. 35 : 14 gehört also untrennbar mit 28 : 22a zusammen."

[64] As the demonstrative in 22a also shows, in this text. And of course "*maṣṣebā*" (the phase mentioned in the attributive clause) is also feminine.

so often in our story already, has left a trace again in a minute detail: Jacob (or, backstage, the narrator; direct speech!) was so obsessed by the thought of a temple for God that this temple, although predicate, simply drives out the influence of the subject on the gender expected in the verb[65]; in his mind the stone has already become a temple before he pronounces the verb.

"House" as an aspect of meaning in *bēt 'ᵉlōhīm* should not be overlooked, the more so as it is activated by its position. For the end of 22a includes the final words of the phrases immediately preceding, just as the whole of 22a combined the verses 11 and 18:

... bēt 'abī	21a
... 'ᵉlōhīm	b
... bēt 'ᵉlōhīm	22a

It is almost like a syllogism: if I come home safe, by which fact Yhwh will have proved himself the God of Jacob too, there will also be a home for God. When the semi-nomad has settled down for good, his God, who went with him and who guided him through the desert, will also have his fixed abode.

In the main clause we had not yet come across a real action by Jacob. Even in the first half of the last sentence he does not speak about himself, but about God: "all that thou givest me ..." Just as in v. 13c, there is a slight anacoluthon here, opening with a *casus pendens* which in the second half turns out to be an object, namely of – at last! – an action by Jacob. In v. 13c God spoke in that way about his giving, now Jacob's reaction is also an anacoluthon ... There the point at issue was the giving of the land, and in 20d Jacob admitted that God is the giver of even his bare necessaries. So "all that thou givest me" is certainly not little, and now Jacob is to pay the tenth of that. As a fraction the number refers to a whole, "all that ...", and so does the act itself: it expresses great gratitude.In other words, the very thing that Jacob undertakes to do, to pay the tithe, is in itself defined and only possible through that which God does and gives. That is why he mentions himself only in the very last place, in the main clause.

[65] P. Joüon, Grammaire ... § 150m, classifies the detail: "Certaines anomalies peuvent s'expliquer par l'influence du prédicat: Gen. 28: 22" and other examples (the section deals with "Accord du verbe"). Here it is made clear that "syntax, ja Grammatik sind nichts als gefrorene Stilistik" (L. Spitzer, Stilstudien II, p. 517, München, 1928). Another example: above p. 67, paragraph 1.

Also significant in this case is a stylistic means which in poetry can be so effective in expressing changes of tone: whereas in the vow God occurs in the third person, even in all the words Jacob had uttered until then, Jacob now, at the very last moment, addresses God in the second person. This transition displays an obvious change of attitude. The thou form establishes a dialogue, the third person may imply distance.[66] After the amazement and fear, after the solemn atmosphere of the setting up and anointment of the massebe and after the name-giving, Jacob frees himself from the formally solemn tone, also discernible in the vow, which now seems too cool and impersonal to him, and he addresses himself straight to God – as a supplicant might who has an urgent prayer to make, or a panegyrist who sings of God's acts of deliverance. Here, in Jacob's case it is gratitude which breaks through and requires the intimacy of the dialogue.[67]

[66] Or something else; Weiss, Hammiqrā ... p. 131: יש שהגוף השלישי, ה״נסתר״, מתפרש כביטוי לוודאות הבטחון שבלב המתפלל, כביטוי למצב שבו אין המתפלל נאבק עוד על קירבתו לאלוהיו, אלא כבר חוסה בצלו. (..) ויש וסיבה דיבור זה בנסתר פירושו שה׳׳ נסתר מן המדבר, שנשתכח ממנו.

[67] There is something like this in Ps. 23; see Strauss op. cit., p. 69 and Weiss, Biblica 1961, p. 277f.

PART II

STYLISTIC AND STRUCTURAL ANALYSIS OF THE CYCLE OF STORIES ABOUT JACOB

INTRODUCTION

We have seen that a structural interpretation of two stories, each comprising one scene, is possible and necessary. This is not so surprising when one considers that these texts had been regarded as literary units for a long time. Now, however, we are forced to wonder whether a stylistic-structural approach is possible at a higher level, that of a much more extended work, a text composed of several scenes. In the second part of this collection we consider, therefore, the cycle of stories in which Jacob is the main subject or object of the action, Gen. 25.19-Gen. 35.

In the short stories of Gen. 11 and 28 we have followed an approach which after detailed study led to the structure. The sound-stratum drew so much attention that even a complete analysis of the stratum of sounds and rhythm might have been profitable. We shrink from this minute method when a text is concerned which is many times longer. This is the case with the Story of Jacob, which consists not of nine or thirteen, but of 298 "verses". For this extended complex of about fifteen scenes we select a broader approach and try to get to the centre of the structure more quickly in order to grasp the whole,* from which we can then discuss only those stylistic details which have an immediate bearing on the structure.

The reading experience which underlies my report in the Chapters III-V followed a different course. The Story of Jacob, too, makes itself especially clear by highlighting stylistic means – especially key-words – which give speed and direction to the circling along the hermeneutic spiral; the *Leitwortstil*, used so skilfully, supports the structure.

* Of course we should be aware that with every new round through the hermeneutic circle this "whole", the structure can be determined with more certainty; thus it changes, unless one is unconsciously swayed by the image of the structure produced by the first reading(s), which image is only an intuitive preconception.

CHAPTER III

GENESIS 25.19-34, 27 AND 28

§ 1 Gen. 25.19-26: *the birth of Jacob and Esau*

The Story of Jacob consists of fifteen scenes, the first of which is Gen. 25.19-26(28). It is true that we call it "the birth of Jacob and Esau", but the story itself uses a different title. It presents our duo from the generation of the father, it uses the name of "begettings by Isaac" and puts this in front as a title.

The rest of v. 19 confirms how we are going to meet Jacob, who is not presented to us, all of a sudden, as an independent adult hero, but as a child, in the framework of the Isaac generation. The Story of Jacob has a narrow but very clear frame, the meaning of which does not become quite clear to us until we arrive at its other half, in Gen. 35.28f, where the birth of Isaac finds its counterpart in Isaac's death at an advanced age.

In the world of the saga[1] there are no isolated individuals, but relatives. In v. 19 we learn that we shall be concerned with the family of Abraham, the exemplarily blessed one on the father's side. Subsequently the record on the mother's side is brought out in v. 20:

[1] Three essential terms on this page are used only with certain reservations: scene, Story of Jacob, saga. The first term must prove itself in the following analyses, the other two will be (re)gauged in my "Conclusion" and are not used as an "Oberbegriff" with which to approach the texts deductively; on the contrary, our method must be inductive, see e.g. Alonso, Erzählkunst .., p. 147 (Biblica 42, 1961). "Saga" is used in the sense which A. Jolles has assigned to it in his Einfache Formen, ch. III (Tübingen, 1930) and which has become common property in OT scholarship. His description is, however, subject to criticism in Germanic scholarship, as W. Richter, Exegese als Literaturwissenschaft, p. 130 note 18, points out, and has been adopted, not without reserve either, by Klaus Koch, Was ist Formgeschichte?, Neukirchen, 1967 (2nd ed.), § 12. Unfortunately it has been adopted without any form of criticism by Claus Westermann, Arten der Erzählung in der Genesis, pp. 36-39 on saga, in his book Forschung am AT, München, 1964.

with rhyme-like precision we are told how the bride Rebekah is the daughter of x "the Aramean" and the sister of y "the Aramean".

As a continuation it is remarkable. For v. 19 says, "these are the *begettings* by Isaac, Abraham's son. Abraham *begot* Isaac." Why is it that the text does not continue with, "and Isaac was forty years when he *begot* Jacob and Esau"? We expect such a sequel more or less, in accordance with the pattern formed for us by v. 19 of this text, which is also the rule in other lists of descendants (*tōledōt*) in Genesis.[2] But the text does not say that; the narrator does not want to dismiss the matter lightly by means of an enumeration, but by means of a separate narrative (vv. 20-26) he wants to show that the coming of Jacob (and Esau) is not a "begetting" (*hōlīd, tōledā,* v. 19), but a "birth" (*yālad,* v. 26). As a deviation of the normal pattern v. 20 means: mind you, with this "generation" something special is the matter. At the end of this scene this will be completely clear to us.

After v. 20 has done its duty – giving factual information on exact personals – the scene can unfold with the required plot as a guide. When reading v. 21 we think for a moment that the story will follow a similar course to that of Gen. 12-24: again a patriarch's wife is barren and again we share the trial of waiting for a son, now for Isaac. But whereas the history of Abraham is tight with the enormous suspense caused by God's reiterated promises of numerous descendants and Abraham's endless waiting until Sarah is old and "worn" (18.12), the Story (not of Isaac but) of Jacob spends as little time, narrative time, as it can on Isaac and his grievous waiting, which, nonetheless, lasted twenty years (vv. 20,26).

For as early as v. 20 we hear Isaac pray humbly to God, before we are informed of Rebekah's barrenness; presently Isaac's prayer has been answered, and in the same verse Rebekah is pregnant! These facts must be quickly given so that in v. 22 the story can proceed to its subject proper, and we are not asked to suffer with Isaac, who really had to go through long years of anxious waiting. We should only realize in passing how the son that was born to Abraham when it

[2] *"Tōledōt"*, which weave a characteristic thread through Genesis, occur thirteen times. Almost everywhere (except for 10.32 and 25.13) they are part of the opening formula "these are the begettings by x" (once, quite extraordinarily, they constitute the ending, in Gen. 2.4a, which belongs to the preceding passage): thus 5.1, 6.9, 10.1, 11.10, 27, 25.12, 19, 36.1, 9, 37.2. Until further notice, viz. our Conclusion, this *tōledōt*-formula also determines the scope of our field of research: 25.19 ↔ 36.1.

had become humanly impossible is also entirely dependent on Yahweh when he in turn wants to be a father.

We may not minimize its importance. The structure of v. 21 is taut and effective. The two halves, each with two sentences, show a clear parallelism. The beginning, (a) "Isaac / prayed / to Yahweh", finds a well-attuned reaction in (c) "by him / was prayed to / Yahweh", and the parallel of (b) and (d) shows how radically Yahweh's answer to a prayer can change a prospectless situation:

(b) "she was barren" turns into

(d) "Rebekah, his wife, conceived".

The Hebrew shows this, even more clearly, in the correspondences of *wy'tr* (qal) – *wy'tr* (*niph*) and the rhyme *'ištō ... 'ištō.* Rebekah shall be a mother, the blessing of her family in 24.60 has not fallen powerless to the ground.

Again the narrator loses no time; "the children struggled together within her", thus months later. At one stroke the real plot of this scene develops, and for eight chapters (to indicate roughly the narrative time) it will hang on us, because for decades (of the narrated time) it scourges and tears a generation, indeed, a family. For Jacob and Esau keep struggling, until their struggle is settled in Gen. 33.

The plot of a story can be developed excellently with the help of a conflict, and in biblical narrative art this conflict is usually present. But what a unique conflict we have here! A conflict of twins which rages even in the womb and so vehemently that their mother is driven to despair. "Behold, how good and pleasant it is when brothers dwell in unity" a psalmist says, but to Jacob and Esau any room is too small when they are together. Their first battlefield is their mother's womb. How cruelly the sweet expectations of children, the greater after twenty years of hope and despair, are dashed for Isaac and Rebekah! As early as the pregnancy their parental happiness is threatened. "What shall I do", Rebekah wonders in despair, in terse and living speech.[3]

In his despair the father had applied to Yahweh (v. 21); in her despair the mother in turn applies to Yahweh, asking for an oracle.[4]

[3] This translation/interpretation I prefer to that of the Revised Standard Version which has, "why do I live?"

[4] *Hālak lidroš 'et Yhwh*: technical term to indicate the consulting of God by means of an oracle; explicitly *drš* (*b*)*dbr Yhwh* in I Kings 22.5 = II Chron. 18.4, II Kings 3.11, 8.8. Also e.g. Is. 8.19, 19.3, I Kings 22.7 (here without *dbr*), 14.5, II Kings 1 (4 × concerning a Baal, cf. I Sam. 28.7).

Now, too, God gives an unambiguous answer, and again the two halves, which are now real verses, contain two sentences. This poetry is short and brisk:

(a) š^{e}nē gōyīm b^{e}biṭnek (b) uš^{e}nē l^{e}'ummīm mimme'áyik yippārédū

(c) l^{e}'om mil'om ye'^{e}maṣ (d) w^{e}rab ya'^{a}bod ṣā'īr.

Most precisely all the four sentences go one step forward in giving information; each one step farther than its predecessor:

—— two children will be born,
—— but they shall be *divided*:
—— they differ in strength,
—— in favour of the *younger*!

The first hemistiche (a and c) explains what is going on and in a sense it is a reassurance to Rebekah, now that God himself speaks. Thus she is the ancestress of two nations! But in both cases there is a barb in the second hemistiche:

(b) ... *yippāredū*: the two cannot live together, they must part, just as *hippāred* was the only solution for the combination Abram – Lot in Gen. 13.[5] The metre shows the importance of this *yippāredū*, for it contrasts most conspicuously with the otherwise quite regular arses in rows of threes; a pattern of 3+3 3+3 it turns into 3+4 3+3. And by the narrowest margin it also turns the nominal clause (b), which is strictly parallel to (a), into a verbal clause.

(d) that one son/tribe will be stronger than the other (c) is not so remarkable, but now (d) brings the sensational tidings that the younger one will prevail. This means that the norm of relationships between brothers is turned topsy-turvy. It is normal for the elder brother to prevail, as the representative of his generation, and that is why the elder son receives a double heritage.[6] On the one side Rebekah can be happy about her progeny's development into nations; on the other side she has reason to face the future full of anxiety, for the reversal in the relationship between elder and younger is bound to carry with it great struggle.

Things happen as God had said they would: v. 24. "*Hinnē*": yes, indeed, they are twins! *Hinnē* makes us share the surprise which the

[5] Gen. 13.9, 11, 14; cf. Gen. 10.5, 32.
[6] Deut. 21.17, cf. II Kings 2.9.

parents experience when their offspring is born – the oracle has really come true. Presently there is a brief description of the two, v. 25f. The beginnings of 25 and 26 constitute a chiasmus, which underlines emphatically who exactly comes first and who comes last:

wayyeṣē	hārīšōn
'aḥ^{a}re ken	yāṣā

(We must bear in mind the choice of words in connection with ch. 27, where the tables will be turned.) V. 25, moreover, first devotes full attention to Esau, before number two is mentioned and described. So we know very well the natural sequence of the brothers.

Peculiar is this description of the two: why does the narrator choose these two qualities for Esau, that he is a) red and b) hairy, and why does he mention only one of Jacob's qualities, viz. the action which accompanied the birth? Reading on, one soon learns the answer to this question. We are being told precisely those outward qualities of Esau's that are essential in the action of scene 2 (Gen. 25.29-34) and scene 3 (Gen. 27). The same is true for the additional remarks on the behaviour of this apparently rough fellow which can be made in v. 27 when he has grown up, Esau is c) a skilful hunter and d) a man of the field. These twin characteristics are also essential in scene 2 and 3.

Striking, though, the difference in description of Esau in v. 25 and of Jacob in v. 26. Of Esau only two qualities are noted, mentioned in an adjunct plus a circumstantial clause which contains nouns only and has a static effect. Jacob, however,[7] is engaged in action at his birth, a revealing action as we shall see. And the quality which here should contrast with Esau's, viz. that Jacob is smooth, is not mentioned. That is significant. His smoothness is in Gen. 27 as essential as Esau's hairiness, and therefore in 27.11 the narrator cannot avoid informing us of this fact any longer; but here, one can safely say, the entirely equivalent counterpart of Esau's hairiness is plainly suppressed by the story. Why? Because at once Jacob himself, as it were, won't acknowledge his lack of hairiness which presently will be the *conditio sine qua non* for acquiring father's blessing. And because here Jacob must solely appear as a man at once engaged in action. For he who knows the sequel knows why *Y'qb* needs must take hold of Esau's heel (*'qb*): even at his birth this chap wants to overtake and outstrip his brother. For Jacob that has been the issue of *wayyitrōṣ^{e}ṣū*: fight for the best

[7] Also in a circumstantial clause, but one with a participle.

starting-position![8] After a months' prenatal race he wants to be the "first" to pass the first important milestone, viz. to come into the world. So he receives his name deservedly, on the ground of these well-timed (though unsuccessful) efforts to be the first-born: Jacob – holder of heels. Of course we must respect the folk-etymological explanation of the proper name in the framework of this story, as it is indeed the only valid one.[9] It is a pity that we do not understand the etymon and the meaning of the name "Esau", anymore than we understand the possible folk etymology in 25.25.

In v. 26, even at his birth, Jacob is in all seriousness busy fulfilling the oracle, and he stubbornly keeps pursuing this object, as far as Gen. 33. "Bent on one purpose" – that appears to be the only possible interpretation of the word *tām* from the further characterization of v. 27, a word which is difficult to define precisely. Among other things *tām* means "sound, unimpaired, of character, incorruptible, sincere", but the moral qualifications at the end of this series are certainly not meant in 25.27. We learn this from the striking parallelism: Esau is a) a skilful hunter and b) a man of the field, and Jacob is a') *tām,* and b') dwelling in tents.

Just as b and b' are in one plane, so a and a' will also be so; then a' will no more aim at passing a moral judgment than a. Whereas the rough man of nature, Esau, does not know how to control himself at crucial moments and forgets his dignity (25.31!), Jacob, the cattle-breeder, calculating and cute as he is, works at one purpose for all he is worth, to become the blessed one who takes the first place. Not for one moment does his attention slacken, until he has found the weak side in the defence of his fellowmen, and one by one they lose: Esau in 25.30f, Isaac and Esau in Gen. 27 and Laban in 30.32-34. This singleness of purpose constitutes Jacob's "integrity", his "being a man of character".[10] Thus it looks as though the only mysterious adjective in the Story of Jacob describes his personality most tersely.

[8] Something that also worries foetuses in Gen. 38.27ff! Who is to be *b^ekor* haunts the family from then on. – There is also Gen. 49, where Jacob consciously shifts '*rab*' and '*ṣā'īr*' though they are his favourite son's children; he does certainly not belie his nature.

[9] The "real" etymology: Jacob is short for *Ya'qob'el,* "God may protect".

[10] Frey interprets tam as "ein Gott hingegebener", although he is a deceiver, for *tām* "bedeutet ja nicht in erster Linie etwas Ethisches. Ein schwerer Charakter voll starker Leidenschaft und erbärmlicher Eigenschaften kann dennoch mit seinem Trachten und Sinnen auf Gott gerichtet sein." H. Frey, das Buch des Kampfes (his commentary on Gen. 25-35), Stuttgart, 1938, *ad loc.*

The unambiguous explanation we gave of 25.26 and of Jacob's entrance, in the preceding two paragraphs, is only to be arrived at from the sequel to the Story of Jacob. Only the further life and actions of Jacob reveal the true significance of his dive for little brother's heel. The forces that dominate Jacob before and during the birth can not be fully understood until afterwards. At this moment, in scene 1, it is by no means simple to get to the bottom of what happens; for the time being v. 26 is equivocal, ambiguous. Like the parents we only presume that the new-born baby wants to suit the action to the word (God's word, v. 23) at once. We do not yet know how cunning and unmitigated Jacob's nature will prove to be, and we think, on the contrary, that his holding his brother exemplifies the devotion and closeness their relationship will have. What softening symbolism there is in such a gesture... That this "holding his heel" should actually be taken unfavourably (suggesting supplanting, deception) cannot be ascertained until much later, in 27.36.[11]

We have come to the end of scene 1. In exactly the same way as does the opening in v. 20a it expresses the father's age:
"Isaac / son of x/y years old" + preposition + infin. constr. + object; in v. 20 at his marriage, in v. 26b when he becomes a father. However, especially revealing in this equality is the variation in the verb in the infinitive. For now we see that the expectations of v. 19 concerning "Isaac's begetting" have been realized in 26b; at last the *"tōlᵉdōt Yiṣḥāq"* can be rounded off.

But even the constructive infinitive in 26b does not tell us that "Isaac has begot", but only that Rebekah has given birth. This repetition of 24a (*lāledet* ... *bᵉledet*) makes it clear to us eventually that this pair of children is not so much begot by Isaac as primarily an affair between Rebekah and Yahweh, an affair of the barren woman who receives children with God's help only. The father has been driven to the edge and, after having performed in 21a one action (which expresses his helplessness!), he does not appear again until v. 26b,

[11] Similarly the whole meaning of "deceive" for the verb *ʿqb* in the Old Testament has probably been derived from and has developed from the folk-etymological interpretation of the name of Israel's patriarch; this narrative may thus have lexically enriched the linguistic history of classical Hebrew. – The cognate form of *ʿqb* in other Semitic languages means "guard, protect", cf. note 9. In the OT *ʿqb* occurs in four places, three of which have a connection with the patriarch's name and know the interpretation of Gen. 25.26: Gen. 27.36, Hos. 12.4, Jer. 9.3 and Job 37.4.

again without action. The rounding-off of this story – truly a story of birth! – with YLD denotes its contents, especially so by the shift from *hōlīd* to *yālad*.

So scene 1 is set in a frame.[12] If we look at this opening passage once more, now from a somewhat greater distance, we observe a tendency to a concentric structure:

A	Isaac was forty years old when he took to wife Rebekah		v. 20
B	Rebekah was barren; prayer for children answered		20/21
C <	his wife Rebekah conceived		21
	the children struggled together within her		22
D	Rebekah asks for	an ORACLE	22
D′	Yahweh grants her		23
C′ <	her days to be delivered were fulfilled		24
	and behold, there were twins in her womb		24
B′	birth and appearance of Jacob and Esau		25, 26a
A′	Isaac was sixty years old when she bore them		26b

This pattern comprises all the moments of the scene, but the concentric structure is not everywhere compelling. It hardly can be, for B′ is not a striking counterpart to B, and the division between B and C and between B′ and C′ is not clear-cut. Nevertheless the structure of this passage betrays what is the heart of the matter in Gen. 25.19-26, that which is the centre of the symmetrical composition, D + D′. The oracle is central, and therefore we should deal with it again. There are structural reasons to believe that it is even more important than we had already thought.

The other members, ABC ... C′B′A′, corroborate once more that we are at the beginning of a story about the new generation and not of a Story of Isaac. They show that it is not Isaac's trial of waiting and the answering of his prayer which constitute the plot, but that the ins and outs of the children's birth are the main point. But the really explosive material, which can lend dramatic force to a story of approximately ten chapters, lies in the kernel which ABC and C′B′A′

[12] Even a double frame, in so far as v. 26b refers to two verses: a) by means of *yld* to v. 19 b) by means of the age-indication to 20a. That an age-indication like the one in 26b closes the circle is to be found elsewhere, too: Gen. 16.16, which concludes the story about Hagar and Ishmael, is pretty much the same as 25.26b; the story of Gen. 17 is framed by an age-indication in 17.1 and v. 24f.

hold in their grip: God's word of v. 23. What food for conflicts is gathered there!

The oracle is also the point that made it worth-while for the narrator to tell the story about the birth. This is not the story of just any twins, but about children whose whole lives are going to pass under a very special sign, whose destiny and mutual relationship were decisively determined and predicted by Providence before their birth. By its centre of power scene 1 also obliges the reader to read all the events of Jacob's life in the light of the oracle, and Gen. 25 does so by raising such questions with us as: could it really happen that "old serves young"? How will it come about? How will the parents behave? These tensions reach far beyond the boundary of the first passage in 25.26, and that means that 25.19-26, well rounded-off though it may be, refers to what follows. It is a fitting opening passage of a much larger whole.

How well scene 1 is integrated into the whole of the history of Jacob needs little argument now. A story about a birth is *eo ipso* only a beginning; the description of v. 25f is attuned to scene 2 and scene 3 and the oracle has the power to extend the conflict of the opening passage to the conflict of all of Gen. 25-35. Need we wonder that this word of God is poetry?

Many things have happened in seven verses, thanks to a rapid pace and concentration on what is essential.

§ 2. Gen. 25.29-34: *Jacob takes the bᵉkōrā from Esau*

The verses 27 and 28 have no action. They are the quiet fading of scene 1, so that at once the relationships in the whole family have been indicated, and a loose transition to the second passage has been made. Fifteen, twenty years of Jacob's and Esau's lives pass, and, v. 27, it dawns upon the parents how greatly the twins differ. Indeed, they themselves react differently. Rebekah's special liking for Jacob and Isaac's preference for Esau (which runs via the stomach and is definitely pre-reflexively rooted ...) reveal something of a gulf between the two married people. Could they grow apart, perhaps, by the coming of these very different children?

We are not told anything else of the long time from birth to adolescence. The narrator skips this narrated time completely, because he only wants to spend narrative time on events that are an essential continuation of the conflict of scene 1. Nothing else is interesting.

Patiently Jacob awaits his opportunity. Suddenly there is an opening, in v. 29ff., and Jacob at once plunges into it, extremely resolute. This is shown by the structure[13] of the second scene:

A Jacob was boiling pottage — v. 29a
 B Esau came in from the field, he was tired — 29b
  C *wayyōmer ʿEsaw*: let me eat some of that red red pottage (...), I am so tired! — 30
   D *wayyōmer Yaʿaqob*: first sell me your *bkrh* — 31
    X *wayyōmer ʿEsaw*: I depart, I die; of what use is a *bkrh* to me? — 32
   D′ *wayyōmer Yaʿaqob*: swear to me first. – So he swore to him and sold his *bkrh* to Jacob. — 33
  C′ Jacob gave Esau bread and pottage of lentils; he ate and he drank — 34aα
 B′ He rose and went his way — 34aβ
A′ Thus Esau despised his birthright (*bkrh*) — 34b

Who is there in X? Esau. He is hemmed in by his brother's cunning design. The centre, X, is the highest point, or rather the lowest point, for it shows (and therefore it is also the turning-point) Esau toppling (over), a prey to his craving for strengthening food, because he is dead tired. He exchanges his own pride and dignity, the ornament of the birthright for ... a mess of pottage. It is a concrete thing, the short-term man thinks, and Jacob, the long-range-planner, has scored his first hit.

The axe ends with the key-word of the scene, *bĕkōrā*, the birthright upon which this event pivots. Jacob desires it, and, speaking as tersely as the desperate Rebekah in 25.23, Esau says most life-like: "Of what use is it to me?" Also his words, "I depart, I die", remind one of his mother's cry of distress. There is a parallel between v. 22 and v. 32, and its function is to underline how Esau is capable of losing sight of proportions – for how ridiculous and childish is Esau's weariness of life compared with his mother's distress!

D and D′ are about Jacob and ... Jacob. That is to say, Jacob turns

[13] This structure comprises no less than the entire action of vv. 29-34, but no more than this either: the aside from the narrator to his listeners, given with an understanding nod, v. 30b, does not belong to the plot/fable and so it falls outside the symmetry. Cf. Gen. 32.33, a similar "etymological verse", and there placed after the plot.

round and round the exhausted Esau, he hems him in. D and D end with "your/my birthright to me/Jacob", for that is our "hero's" object. They begin with pressing imperatives. The rhyme of *mikrā* ... *hiššābeʿā* illustrates how Jacob directs all his persuasive power at Esau. And when he is successful, he wants to secure it: he pins Esau down by asking him to swear. Jacob makes so bold as to invite his brother to take the name of God in vain.[14] Painful, to see how Esau agrees to this request like a shot.

We have seen that D and D′ flank X in order to visualize how Esau is hemmed in. But let us look back for a while to the preceding story, where the struggle rages prenatally and is worded in an oracle. There the hemming in appears to have been visualized too, in the heart, in that oracle, by means of a chiasmus. We see this if we supply the correct identity:

le'om	mil'om ye'emaṣ
(=Israel)	(=Esau/Edom)
(Esau)	(Jacob)
rab	yaʿabod ṣāʿīr

The a-b b-a structure of a chiasmus pictures how Jacob has the first and the final word and how Esau is caught in between.

In C and C′ Esau expresses, again most life-like, his craving for some strengthening food. Or rather he comes, sees and falls; "that red stuff there" fascinates him so much that because of his weariness he loses sight of proportion and of his self-respect. But of course, Esau himself was *'admōnī*, red! Jacob outwits his "red" brother with his own nature. It is no wonder that Esau has received the name of Edom, "Red-man".[15] After the exchange bargain has been confirmed with an oath, Jacob offers him refreshment (v. 34a).

[14] "You shall not take the name of the Lord your God in vain" was certainly known to narrator and listeners as the second commandment; but no doubt the matter was in force before the Decalogue had come out and this commandment had been numbered. – On the swearing Frey remarks, ad loc.: "Es ist schwer zu entscheiden, wer in diesem Augenblick der Verwegenere war: der den Schwur forderte angesichts des Linsengerichtes, oder der ihn leistete um den Linsenbrei."

[15] Now it is also clear to us, why the narrator did not use the name "Edom" in the birth-story. It is more fitting and surprising to drop "Edom" only in connection with *'ādōm 'ādōm*; moreover, 25.25f is in the first place about persons, so that it would be difficult not to put "Esau" but "Edom" side by side of the proper noun "Jacob".

B and B′, *va et vient.* These two members convey movement: enter Esau, exit Esau. The only quality mentioned in 29b is that which is the weak point in Esau's suit of armour: he is dog-tired and loses his discernment.

In v. 29 this scene shows for the first time the qualities mentioned in v. 27 ("man of the field" versus "dwelling in tents") "in operation"; they are part and parcel of the action.

The story is framed with a pair of three words each, which exactly indicate the kernel of the action, for we see the brothers contrasted as antagonists, each with one attribute which belongs to him but which is exchanged:

Jacob + pottage / Esau + *bᵉkōrā*

In the centre they are together for the exchange, on the edges (A + A′) they have been driven wide apart. Are they not wide apart?

A	wayyāzed	Ya'ᵃqob	nāzīd
A′	wayyibez	'Esāw	'et-habbᵉkōrā

We now survey the whole scene. There is not a word too many. At full speed the story makes for its turning-point, nearly as quickly it reaches its end. In the middle the brothers exchange words twice, which is precisely articulated by *wayyōmer* repeated four times. Before we get wind of it, Esau has been floored. The conflict of scene 1 has been continued here, and this first round has been convincingly won by Jacob. Morally speaking there are only losers.

The importance of "coming into the world first" and not after the other (25.25f) is now expressed exactly by the word *bᵉkōrā*, which has been pushed forward as a first class key-word by the members D, X and D′ of the concentric structure. It will remain one in the third story from the Story of Jacob.

§ 3. Gen. 27-28.5: *Jacob takes the fatherly bᵉrākā from Esau*

If we call this story a "scene" we must subdivide it into six "moments". But it sooner reminds us of an act from a play, which consists of six scenes. It has indeed a theatrical preciseness because the moments exclude each other mutually and the transitions come about by the entrance of other characters.

This third passage is about eight times larger than scene 1 and scene 2. The narrative style is broad, balanced and quiet. It needs to be because many and very vehement emotions are released, which must be able to reach their climax and which we must be able to digest: Rebekah and Jacob endure the tension of "will our device be successful?" This tension is greatly increased by Isaac's investigations, made again and again (vv. 20-26), until v. 30 delivers us, Isaac is in gnawing doubt for an equally long time and after that he has to stand the terrible shock of the discovery of the deceit. For Esau the shock is even greater[15]; his intense bitterness finds an outlet in brooding on revenge and that in turn leads to great apprehension on the part of Jacob and Rebekah.

All the members of the family take part in the action but at the same time they must be kept apart in pairs to prevent bloodshed. The action itself is much more complex than in scene 1 and 2, and therefore it is admirable how lucidly this story, too, has been constructued by a narrator who can only work on the principle of a single-strand narrative[16]:

vv. 1-5	A	Isaac + son of the *brkh/bkrh* (= Esau)
6-17	B	Rebekah sends Jacob on the stage
18-29	C	Jacob appears before Isaac, receives blessing
30-40	C′	Esau appears before Isaac, receives anti-blessing
41-45	B′	Rebekah sends Jacob from the stage
46+28.1-5	A′	Isaac + son of the *brkh/bkrh* (= Jacob!)

The conflict of scene 1 and 2 is continued and is here so greatly deepened that the togetherness of the whole family is broken in a tragic way. And all this is because Jacob, now supported by Rebekah, keeps pursuing his own goal. Now he wants to obtain what is the first-born's (*bkr*) right, to be blessed (*brk*), even at the cost of the ties of

[15a] There is a climax in the parallel of v. 33a and 34a:

wayyeḥ^{e}rad ḥ^{a}rādā g^{e}dōlā	ʿad m^{e}'od	33
wayyiṣʿaq ṣ^{e}ʿāqā g^{e}dōlā umārā	ʿad m^{e}'od	34

[16] S. Talmon, Darkē hassippūr bammiqrā (3rd ed., Jerusalem, 1965), p. 24 nearly (see his *kimʿaṭ*) gets the point: שני הזוגות האנטיתטיים הם רבקה–יעקב מכאן ויצחק–עשו משם, לפי סדר ההופעות מתקבל כאן מבנה כמעט סימטרי:

יצחק – עשו		רבקה – יעקב
	יצחק – יעקב	שלב הסיבוך
יצחק – עשו		רבקה – יעקב
	(v. 46) יצחק – רבקה	
	(28.1-7) יצחק – יעקב	שלב ההתרה

The division into scenes is correct in Eising, op. cit., p. 45. (It is true that he adds v. 5 to B, but on p. 65 he corrects himself on this point, though without correcting p. 45).

blood that connect him with Isaac and Esau. Reverence and solidarity, both valuable assets in the world of the saga, he despises, and together with his mother he divides the family quartet into two parties. This discord is also the extreme consequence of the preference which the father and the mother have for, respectively, Esau and Jacob.

The narrative skill in Gen. 27-28.5, in all six moments equally lucid and mature, reaches a stylistic climax in v. 36:

(Esau:) "Is he not rightly named *Ya'qob*?
For he has supplanted me these two times, *ya'qebenī*:
my birthright (*bekōrā*) he took away,
and behold, now he has taken away my blessing (*berākā*)."

This chiasmus (v. 36b) brings the much-desired blessing in line and level with the birthright already acquired. The words *berākā* and *bekōrā* display a maximum alliteration, here they rhyme with the possessive pronoun (*birkātī* – *bekōrātī*) and the chiasmus telescopes the concepts perspectively, as it were. Because it is hermetically rounded off, the cross construction itself visualizes how Jacob's job with Esau is complete and done with. The other aspect that makes v. 36 a climax is Esau's embittered but perfectly correct explanation of his brother's name. The ambiguity around "Ya'qob" when he took hold of his brother's heel at his birth has now disappeared. *Nomen est omen*; here and now is the definite proof that the "taking hold of the heel" is unequivocal and unfavourable, connoting deception. The father has just dropped that word (*mirmā*, v. 35). "Now for the second time" Esau has been supplanted, and exactly when this first occurred, Esau tells us explicitly in "my birthright he had already taken away". So that this story links directly with the scene of the pottage of lentils.

We called v. 36 a climax, not the climax. Even a superficial reading makes that clear, because it is the end of the intrigue instigated by Rebekah and Jacob in this story, their object, the crown of their work: the father's blessing. And again a narrative takes the wings of poetry. That the verses 28 and 29 are the climax is also due to the irrevocability of the blessing. Once it has been given, this word of power becomes effective, it is past retracting – as Isaac himself, shocked and helpless, points out in the end of v. 33.[17] We feel it, too, by the sigh of relief

[17] "In many instances the English 'indeed' is an excellent rendering of the emphasizing *gam*." Hence in Gen. 27.33 "Blessed indeed he shall be". Thus C. J. Labuschagne, The Emphasizing Particle *gam* and its Connotations, Studia Th. Chr. Vriezen (...) dedicata, Wageningen 1966, p. 200.
The irrevocability is pointed out by Wehmeier, op. cit., p. 102f.

which escapes us involuntarily, when we learn immediately after the blessing in v. 30 how Jacob disappears from the stage only just in time (*'ak yāṣō yāṣā*). We cannot bear to think of what would have happened if Esau had returned in time to see his brother, dressed in the skin of kids and in his, Esau's, best garments, leaving his father's tent!

We might think that this story is about Jacob and how he attains his object, the blessing. But that is not correct, as v. 36, discussed above, can tell us. This verse is to be found in moment/scene C' (Esau with Isaac), the definite interpretation of the name of Jacob comes from Esau's mouth, and the gist of the matter has been expressed here. The total of scene C' is a little longer than C (in which the blessing occurs), and how fitting a counterpart C' is appears from the fact that one more blessing – however peculiar that "blessing" may be, v. 39f – is given, viz. to Esau who desperately holds on. This indicates that this story is equally concerned with Esau. And we can add, it is about the whole family. How indispensable Isaac is, needs no argument; even after the blessing he is needed in arranging for a suitable wife for Jacob (27.46, 28.1). But Rebekah? She may claim to be the *auctor intellectualis* of the whole event! She eavesdrops in v. 5[18]; she sets about doing things at once, does not shun responsibility in the least (v. 13 *'ālay qillātᵉkā bᵉnī*) and influences Jacob, who at first mutters objections (v. 11f). She also ensures a "good result" and saves Jacob's life (42f), to that purpose cleverly calling in the help of the father. In short, she manipulates to perfection. Gen. 27 – *cherchez la femme*.

Rebekah and Jacob carry out her plan and win; Isaac and Esau are beaten. But again the winning party is the moral loser. What price is paid here for this guile! The family is torn apart, the latent contrasts come to light completely. It is characteristic that after Rebekah and Jacob's energetic actions nothing is left for Esau to do but to comment. Jacob acts, Esau is left empty-handed. Esau may cry, gnash his teeth, whimper for one more blessing, brood on revenge – the blessing has been given away once and for all. In scene 2 (25.29-34) he had still been the one to whom things happened, now he is no longer even in the picture.

Now his father is the one to whom things happen. What a paradox:

[18] Because she is furtively present, v. 5 belongs to scene A! Linguistically speaking: as a circumstantial clause v. 5a with its participle refers to the preceding part. Besides v. 5b, as the compliance of Isaac's order, belongs to scene A.

Isaac seems to be a subject in ch. 27, for it is he who sends off Esau, it is he who performs the solemn and awe-inspiring ceremonial of the blessing, but how helplessly he is the object of the manipulations. After the event he is left to empty the bitter cup of the discovery of the conspiracy. He has been degraded to a puppet. How could he be? The first verse of Gen. 27 offers the explanation: the old man's blindness is the weak spot which his loving wife and son exploit with great certainty. Nor does the old man see that Rebekah's concern for a cognate bride for her son Jacob, which in itself is undoubtedly sincere, is pure manipulation at this moment (27.46) because it enables her to conceal her real concern, to save her favourite son's naked life, to rescue him from Esau's revenge. Nor has Isaac seen the shadows of Esau's wrath falling over his family. All this reminds one of David, who in I Kings 1 has become too old to notice the fierce intrigues concerning the succession which rage in his own family.

After this, our first round through the story, we shall touch lightly on the message of the symmetrical composition of the story. Its main purpose is to arrange the material (four main characters; a complicated action which occurs partly in the absence of the first-born; vehement emotions) clearly in six scenes of almost equally bright lighting. In the middle the dramatic centre: C + C'; Esau's visit and the anti-blessing he receives are the exact antipole of Jacob's visit which renders him the true blessing. Around it, central between the ascent (A-B-C) and the descent (C'-B'-A') of the story, is the scheming mother who shows her son the way, B and B'. Around that is again the ring formed by A and A', most revealing for the exchange of parts between Jacob and Esau. In both scenes Isaac sends off the "first-born" for the benefit of his life; in the beginning it is the intended ***bārūk*** and natural ***b^ekōr***, thus Esau, but at the end it is Jacob who has usurped Esau's position of ***b^ekōr*** so effectively (as far back as Gen. 25, too!) that he has become the real ***bārūk***. And again he deals Esau a decisive setback, for thanks to a second trick of Rebekah's he sets out in search of a cognate wife on a journey similar to one which had once been undertaken for his father's bride (Gen. 24), and he leaves Esau behind in his undesirable marriage with heathen women.[19] This blow, too, hits Esau hard (28:6-9). He tries to nullify it by marrying a daughter of Ishmael's, but this only demonstrates that he cannot get away from the collateral branch in the family. Esau has been shunted off.

[19] V. 46: b^enōt Ḥet ... mibb^enōt Ḥet ... mibb^enōt hā'āreṣ; this is prepared for by Gen. 26.34f.

How much Jacob has the upper hand and Rebekah has infiltrated herself also appears from the pattern formed by the presence of the parties, which is symmetrical in both lines:

present in scene:	A	B	C +	C′	B′	A′
– parents:	Isaac	Rebekah	Isaac	Isaac	Rebekah	Isaac
– sons:	Esau	Jacob	Jacob	Esau	Jacob	Jacob

What happens in B and B′ must not be known to Isaac and Esau; what takes place in A and A′ is none of, respectively, Jacob's and Esau's business (they only hear of it after the event); and how C and C′ exclude each other is *luce clarius*. Rebekah does not see or meet Esau, and Esau does not see or meet Jacob. In four out of the six scenes one parent is seen in the company of the favourite child. This family knows no harmony anymore.

We go through the story once more, but this time linearly, normally, from beginning to end, and briefly put down the most important points. V. 4/5: "hunt game for me, and prepare for me savoury food, such as I love." Esau can show his strong point, 25.27 turns out to have been preparatory. Vv. 6b,7: In this extensive style Rebekah has ample opportunity to repeat what has happened and what Isaac has said. This is also shown in the repeated words "savoury food, such as I/he love(s)":

v. 4 maṭ'ammīm ka'^{a}šer 'āhabtī
v. 9 maṭ'ammīm ka'^{a}šer 'āheb
v. 14 maṭ'ammīm ka'^{a}šer 'āheb

Here we have a set of three which links readily with 25.27 "kī ṣayid l^{e}fīw". Precisely the predilection which unites father and son is used in the stratagem.

After her résumé in v. 6f. Rebekah speaks to Jacob only about this guile and his part in it. Her argument (vv. 8-13) is framed by the gentle but resolute pressure she exerts on Jacob:

v. 8f w^{e}'attā b^{e}nī š^{e}ma' b^{e}qōlī lek nā ... w^{e}qaḥ lī
13 b^{e}nī 'ak š^{e}ma' b^{e}qōlī w^{e}lek qaḥ lī

(and presently the same in:)

43 w^{e}'attā b^{e}nī š^{e}ma' b^{e}qōlī b^{e}raḥ.

V. 11f: Jacob is a broad-minded man and raises no objections to the proposal to deceive his father. However, there are technical problems, and being discovered would turn the affair into its opposite, no blessing, but a curse. What the birth-story had suppressed is now being told: Jacob is smooth. Rebekah waves all his objections aside and promises to take the blame. V. 16 is a chiastic continuation of 15b.

In 18-26 the meeting takes place which provokes Isaac to a long and painful examination. His eyes function no longer and his ears tell him: Jacob; his groping fingers again tell him: Esau; and in the end the scale is turned when his nose sniffs up the smell of the field: Esau. But before that moment he has had to ask three times, "are you really my son Esau?"[20] V. 23 and v. 27a end with the same *waybārekehū*; that too is striking. His touch speaks for Esau, and now he is about to speak the blessing, *waybārekehū* (ingressive or voluntative), "he was on the point of giving the blessing",[21] but then his voice caught; he was not assured yet. "Come near!" Then Isaac is convinced at once by smell, the smell of the field, and at the same time his kissing lips "taste" shaggy hair; he recognizes Esau's being (25.27 *'īš sādẹ*) as his own being and at last *waybārekehū* – "he blessed him". V. 20, Jacob presents his deceit very piously. He actually takes the name of the Lord in vain, this time he himself, after he had made his brother do so over the pottage of lentils. V. 20 beats all!

V. 30: the words 'ak yāṣō yāṣā Ya'aqob / we'Esāw 'āḥīw bā are most important. They call to mind how Esau "came forth first" and how "afterward his brother came forth". The first round Jacob had lost, but now he has won the second and the third rounds. Now he has been the first to go out, and now his brother Esau comes after him. The tables have been turned and – again! – it has been visualized in a chiasmus. Full of triumphant feelings Jacob thinks he has realized his destiny, prophesied in an oracle.

V. 33f. offer a moving parallel about the shock of the discovery:

33 wayyeḥerad …	ḥarādā gedolā	'ad me'od
34 wayyiṣ'aq	ṣe'āqā gedolā umārā	'ad me'od

In v. 32f there is the discovery by Isaac, in 33 by Esau. Then follows the painful phase of the digestion, which for Isaac begins as early as

[20] V. 18 mī 'attā benī; v. 21 ha'attā zẹ benī 'Esāw 'im lō; v. 24 'attā zẹ benī 'Esāw.
[21] Also e.g., E. A. Speiser, his commentary on Genesis, the Anchor Bible, New York, 1964, ad loc.

v. 33 with the wording of the event, and which for Esau begins in v. 34 and extends to v. 38.

Esau's share in the dialogue is framed by the very sentence that indicates what is the most important thing for him, bārekenī gam 'anī 'ābī (vv. 34b, 38a), "bless me, even me also, my father!" But this demand is enclosed in another ring; in 34a he cries out bitterly before he speaks, and after his entreaty "he lifted up his voice" again "and weeps" (38b). Twice he also asks his father for the impossible, "have you not reserved a blessing for me?" (end of v. 36 and 38a). The structure in scene C′ is as follows:

A He cried out with an exceedingly great and bitter cry	v. 34a
B and said to his father: bless me, even me also, my father?	34b
(Isaac's explanation // Esau's explanation)	35, 36a
C He said: have you not reserved a blessing for me?	36b
blessing summarized by Isaac	37
C′ Esau said to his father: have you but one blessing, my father?	38a
B′ Bless me, even me also, my father!	38a
A′ Esau lifted up his voice and wept	38b
anti-blessing given by Isaac	39

Scene C′ contains, in the form of an explanation both by Isaac and by Esau, the essence of the story. From the mouths of two protagonists themselves we hear already the correct interpretation of the event accurately and concisely related; the two give the interpreter a lead.

Vv. 41-45. That this passage is not the ending of the story is shown by the symmetrical composition alone; v. 46 + 28.1-5 belong to the story as a counterpart to scene A. But not even on the grounds of internal qualities can scene B′ be the ending. As it hardly continues the action and there is no progression, it only shows us people involved in their own considerations, a) Esau considers fratricide, b) Rebekah suggests to Jacob: flee for your life. The question as to the results of all this becomes unbearable after the words at the endings of verses 41 and 45, "I will kill my brother ... why should I be bereft of you both?" and requires an answer. There it is, in scene A′ and thus the considerations in B′ are a preparation for what follows.

V. 45 (end) is a cry of distress from the mother who is terrified of being bereft of her two children. (She fears that Jacob will be murdered by Esau, the latter executed; compare Gen. 4 and II Sam. 14). That is what her own initiative has led to. The course of Jacob's life does leave deep traces. Before this Rebekah had already uttered a cry of distress, also because her children were engaged in combat, as early as her pregnancy (25.22). In opposition to this beginning which was a nadir to Rebekah, a provisional end is set as a pendant, again a nadir to her. The narratives 1, 2 and 3 have now received a frame; the conflict fought even prenatally, continued and intensified postnatally has come to a threatening head: the family cannot stay together any longer. So far have things come, they have reached a life-and-death struggle!

V. 46: the cry of distress of 25.22 is now repeated before Isaac, for the benefit of an endogamous future for her son. Her "bitterness of life" (26.35, the preparation for this moment) has driven her so far that her life has no value for her. She acts quite convincingly before Isaac who is put under the greatest pressure; he gives way easily (28.1); of course (Gen. 24!) he quite agrees with Rebekah on endogamy. Thus she kills two birds with one stone and of necessity (i.e., because Jacob is threatened) she makes a virtue: his flight leads to a marriage that is morally/religiously the only correct one, so that once more Esau is the loser.

Jacob leaves. How will he fare? Will he find a wife, and in what way? Will he ever see his brother again? But how? These questions are raised for us by the story, and they will all be answered. This story "is open to the front"; even by its ending it shows that it is only a part of a much larger whole.

How far Esau is being pushed to one side seems to be reflected by the fact that 28.6-9 hangs by a tack, like a loose end. Vv. 6 and 7 summarize the event with the blessing, the subject of v. 8 is marriage. How stiffly and dependently Esau's mind works. Only now does it sink into him that father Isaac apparently does not approve of a marriage with Canaanite women. He himself, Esau, had never seen any harm in it; his parents' dismay (26.35) had passed unnoticed by the lumpish fellow. These three verses have been written from Esau's point of view and with the repetition of wayyar 'Esāw kī (v. 6) wayyar 'Esāw kī (v. 8) which distinguishes and connects the subjects of blessing and marriage, they convey very well how difficult thinking is for Esau, how he gains perspective by repeating the events in his mind and how he sees in what respects he has been passed over. The result in v. 9, paradoxically enough an action at last, only underlines how far he is lagging behind.

The fact that Esau sees no harm in marrying Hittite women, whereas Jacob (now in a passive part because of the events, as one sent by his parents) and Rebekah think the endogamous marriage an important point, is worth an evaluation. We see that in the domain of morals Esau is rather easy-going – he ignores the usage of semi-nomads – because he has no sense of the special task of his family under the sign of the blessing. He has no sense of history. Isaac, Jacob and Rebekah on the other hand realize that as "blessed people" it is their responsibility to remain pure, apart, *qādōš*, not to become allied to the population of Canaan by marriage. They know that now in particular the nomad usage is valid, because it has been sanctified by God's blessing.

It is time we did justice to the two complementary concepts of BRK and BKR from the chiasmus. We have not discussed the blessing itself yet.

B^{e}kōr. It is useful to have a close look at the titles in the story. How does the narrator present the twins to us? Here is the most important material[22]:

1	Esau is the	b^{e}nō haggādōl	to Isaac
15	Esau is the	b^{e}nāh haggādōl	to Rebekah
	Jacob is the	b^{e}nāh haqqāṭōn	to Rebekah
19	Jacob says	'ānōkī ... b^{e}kōr^{e}kā	to Isaac
32	Esau says	'^{a}nī binkā b^{e}kōr^{e}kā	to Isaac
42	Esau is the	b^{e}nāh haggādōl	to Rebekah
	Jacob is the	b^{e}nāh haqqāṭōn	to Rebekah

That is a remarkable distribution and again we can see a concentric symmetry.[23] Twice in one verse (15 and 42) of the scenes B and B' (where Rebekah manipulates events) "her older son" and "her younger son" are ("brotherly"...) side by side. These are fairly neutral terms, which correspond to the unalterable biological facts. But the word "first-born" is nowhere used descriptively! So it has become a sort of

[22] The rest is of little relevance; for the sake of completeness: Jacob is *b^{e}nī/b^{e}nō* to Isaac in vv. 18,20(bis), 21, 24, 25, 26. 27, and to Rebekah in vv. 6, 8, 13, 17, 43. Esau is *b^{e}nī/b^{e}nō* to Isaac in vv. 1, 5, 31, 37.

[23] Only "his elder son" in the beginning has no counterpart; of course not, for in scene A' Esau has been replaced by usurper Jacob, and he has taken away the *b^{e}kōrā* but not the "elder-sonship". 28.1 abstains from a qualification, when Isaac's (younger) son comes to him as Jacob.

title, or rather a pretension, a claim, for the word is used only in direct speech, by the son who appears before Isaac to receive the blessing, and is used symmetrically, once in scene C, once in scene C′.

What does it mean that the narrator himself expressly refuses to use the word "first-born" as a matter-of-fact description and refrains from having the parents use it? Negatively speaking it means at least that the matter is definite (in Gen. 25) and over. And positively speaking it suggests that nowhere is Esau literally the *b*^{e}*kōr*, only the "elder son", because Jacob is destined to be the first of his generation and accordingly has bought the *b*^{e}*kōrā* in ch. 25. Therefore Rebekah and Jacob do not use the title. (On the other hand it would have been difficult for the narrator to describe Jacob as "*b*^{e}*kōr*".)

So the word *bkr* is not that prominent in this story at all. It is only the claim, the disputed position on the ground of which the struggle rages for the real issue of Gen. 27, the *blessing*.

BRKH. To begin with, the root itself occurs twenty-five times, of which seven times as noun.[24] The blessing itself attracts our attention:

v. 27	ראה ריח בני כריח שדה	אשר ברכו יהוה
28	ויתן לך הא' מטל השמים	ומשמני הארץ ורב דגן ותירש
29	יעבדו עמים	וישתחוו לך לאמים
	הוה גביר לאחיך	וישתחוו לך בני אמך
	ארריך ארור	ומברכיך ברוך

Of these five poetic lines the first one is an introduction, which refers to the moment of the ceremonial, links up with the prose story and thus anchors the blessing proper (lines 2-5) into the surrounding whole. The old man brightens in a short lyrical outpouring: what unites him and Esau (whom he thinks he addresses) as "men of the field" has God's blessing; the smell carries him away and for just one moment he feels how the strength which causes the hunter's heart to palpitate once was his.

Smelling the field Isaac first dwells upon the bounties of nature, which know only one giver: God. His will is the only and determinant power which implants fertility and makes it work in a harmonious ensemble of heaven and earth. The most beautiful poetic lines on this theme are by Hosea[25]:

[24] G. Wehmeier, der Segen im AT. Eine semasiologische Untersuchung der Wurzel brk, Basel, 1970.

[25] Hosea 2.23f. In Martin Buber's translation:
Geschehn wirds an jenem Tag,/ ich willfahre,/ SEIN Erlauten ists,/ ich willfahre

אענה (נאם יהוה) אענה את השמים   והם יענו את הארץ
והארץ תענה את הדגן   ואת התירוש ואת היצהר
והם יענו את יזרעאל

The whole cosmos ("heaven and earth") floods this first-born with its bounties. The heaven gives dew (of vital importance in Palestine!), the earth its exquisite oils, grain and must. At the head the giver (line 2a), linking up with 1b, then follows a long tail of objects (2b,c,d).

The dimension of nature in the Bible is surpassed by the dimension of history. This is equally true in this blessing. Three verses describe how Jacob (supposed to be Esau) will be in the centre of the seething roar of the nations (line 3), will be lord in the midst of all his relatives (4), and how the fate of the others will depend on the question whether they are friends or foes to him (line 5).

The lines 3-5 stand out as an obvious metrical unity.[26] V. 3 displays a perfect "synonymous parallelism"; lines 4 and 5 show a perfect antithetical, perhaps complementary parallelism. Lines 3 and 4 rhyme at the end of the half-verses. Line 5 has a variation with a clear and dark sounding assonance, ... *'ārūr* ... *bārūk*, and creates a powerful ending by using a clenched metre and by putting the light-side in the last half-verse: the root *brk* has, literally, the final word in this *b^{e}rākā*. The last line is also effective, because it consists of two nominal clauses, which appear as matter-of-course statements after the verbs of the preceding lines. The half-verses 3b and 4b begin in exactly the same way (w^{e}yištaḥ^{a}wū l^{e}kā), but the danger of monotony in 3 and 4 (a four-fold "serve") has been prevented, because, all of a sudden, in 4a the reverse side is shown: Jacob is pushed to the front as ruler, but precisely there he is subject, just for once, forcefully fired with the only imperative. All through, without omitting one hemistiche, a chain of suffixes has been strung: ...*-kā* ...*-kā* ...*-kā*, up to seven times; you, you are blessed, Jacob, you will be lord, you will be served.[27]

dem Himmel,/ und der willfährt der Erde,/ und die Erde willfährt/ dem Korn, dem Most, dem Olivensaft,/ und die willfahren Den-Gott-sät.

[26] Without being troubled by the constraint of a system, we might scan as follows: v. 28 3+2 + 2+3
v. 29 2 + 3
3 + 3
2 + 2

[27] We read in Deut. 28.10: "And all the peoples of the earth shall see that you are called by the name of the Lord; and they shall be afraid of you."

Seven times Jacob has been addressed in the poem of v. 29, seven times he has been proclaimed the centre, round which people arrange themselves and are sorted out. Seven is a holy number, a number of plenitude, as our text knows. In Gen. 33.3 Jacob, the man who was described as lord sevenfold, the man "to whom his mother's sons will bow down", will have to bow down himself seven times, as a servant of Esau's! It seems as if eventually the blessing works through the pseudo-Esau to the real Esau and that it shines about him. When we come to Gen. 33 we shall see that this does not only *seem* to be so.

We have now listened to the sounds, the words, the rhythm of the blessing. But what exactly happens in v. 28 and 29? The prose has been left for a while, the words are stiff in their ranks through rhyme, inner rhyme, parallelism and, by the standard of Hebrew, a regular metre; they are *"gebundene Rede"*. Thus they contain great elementary power which will propel Jacob's life and make it exemplary. To bless is to transmit power.

Where does this power come from? The epic diffuseness of the narrative style shows us, by having both Jacob and Esau repeat the sentence in which Isaac expresses his intention:

Isaac: ba'^{a}būr t^{e}bārek-kā nafšī	v. 4
Jacob: ba'^{a}būr t^{e}bār^{a}kannī nafšekā	19
Isaac: l^{e}ma'an t^{e}bārek-kā nafšī	25
Jacob: ba'^{a}būr t^{e}bār^{a}kannī nafšekā	31

This is not simply: "I will bless you, you shall bless me",[28] but expressly the word *nefeš* is used four times: "so that my *nefeš* may bless you", "so that your *nefeš* may bless me". Four times we have that untranslatable word *nefeš*, the whole person with all his resources. With complete sincerity of purpose Isaac transmits all the strength, all the vitality he once possessed, all his destiny, all his blessedness tersely and in powerful language[29] to his son.

Where does Isaac's power come from? On what grounds does he speak such great words with such natural authority? We should realize the pretentiousness of what happens in v. 28 and 29. The world, the universe is pacified and made safe for the son, space and time are conjured and made subservient to Jacob! It is not something that any

[28] Rebekah's paraphrase, however, simply has the word *'^{a}bārek-kā/y^{e}bārek-kā*, v. 10.

[29] Therefore: poetry! prose would not do.

pater familias of a bunch of sheep-nomads brings about! Isaac speaks with absolute authority, with ἐξουσια as the New Testament would say; we would be wildly off the mark if we were to speak of "eastern exaggeration".

Expressing the blessing is a ceremonial, it is a sacral event, "before the Lord" says v. 7.[30] The text itself points out twice that we must start with Yahweh. Yahweh has blessed the field, the smell of which made Isaac forget his gnawing uncertainty and made him free to recite verses (v. 27). He is the one who makes nature fertile for Jacob, and who leads in the blessing proper (v. 28f).[31]

Strictly speaking this blessing is from God.[32] Its fourth line is explicitly in line with the oracle which Rebekah received, and the fifth line is implicitly so; the synonymous "serve and "bow down" of lines 3 and 4 provide a good link with "serve" of 25.23. That Jacob is a chosen one is not a pious wish of Isaac's, but it is a sure and certain hope, which rests on unshakeable foundations.

We may, indeed we must, make use of the material we find in the book of Genesis outside the Story of Jacob. All through Genesis there is a string of words of power, words of blessing, with which Yahweh has chosen the line of Abraham-Isaac-Jacob. Isaac himself is a *bārūk* who knows that he must hand down his destiny to the next generation.[33] The last line of his blessing preserves the oracle, by which Abraham's family is lifted from the nomadic anonymity and placed in the midst of the light of (salvation-)history (Gen. 12.3).[34]

What Isaac is doing here, however, becomes clearer if we see the difference between his blessing and God's blessing to the patriarchs.

[30] Also if it is correct to render this *lifnē* with: "with Yahweh's approval," here and other places, as Speiser argues, pp. 205, 209 (op. cit.). and Wehmeier, op. cit., p. 110 point 3. Thus also Ehrlich, Randglossen ... vol. I, p. 128.

[31] Exemplary cases concerning blessing: Deut. 28 and the history of Balaam, Num. 22-24; concerning curse: the rest of Deut. 28.

[32] Wehmeier, p. 142f.: "Wie die Form h^{a}wē V. 29a wahrscheinlich macht, ist dieser "Segen" in seinen wesentlichen Bestandteilen prekativ zu verstehen: Isaak wirkt den Segen nicht, sondern er erbittet ihn von Gott."

[33] Johs. Pedersen, Israel, its life and culture, Kopenhagen/London, 1926, Vol. I, p. 190: "That the blessing is handed down from father to son is a consequence of its being a power of the soul. It must go with the family, because there is a psychic community in the latter." – On p. 182 he says: "Blessing is the inner strength of the soul and the happiness it creates."

[34] Almost similar to these two is, to conclude, the final line of Num. 24.3-9. There, too, is lyric poetry of the election.

The latter is a promise of land and numerous offspring, the two bounties from which it appears that the patriarchs are blessed. Isaac only speaks about his son's prominent position. His own summary (v. 37) confirms this. The real issue is *gbr* – *'bd*, "rule – serve".

The authority and power with which he speaks he takes from two sources. He is supported by God's blessing and by the oracle. The words of blessing he speaks concern the same thing that the oracle spoke of before the birth. But he also wants to bend the oracle: he intends to bless Esau, he prefers to stick to the "natural right" which says that the one born first is to be the ruler of the generation. And in this way he performs unconsciously the plans of Providence, which wanted to turn the relationship between older-younger upside down. By ignoring God's will he performs it ...!

In v. 39f the desperate Esau does receive a blessing[35] from his father. Blessing indeed. In v. 39 it looks as though he is to enjoy the same abundance of oils and dew as Jacob, but a figure of speech turns this blessing into a curse:

v. 28 May God give you
of the dew of heaven — and *of* the fatness of the earth

v. 39 "of" the fatness of the
earth shall your dwelling be — and "of" the dew of heaven on high

Here the ambiguous meaning of the preposition *min* has been made use of: "part of" (v. 28) becomes "far away from" (v. 39). The chiasmus visualizes that the contrast is maximal. A cruel joke, this verse! The second line (v. 40a) assures Esau, that he will have as hard a life as Ishmael who has also been driven aside, (Gen. 16.12), and makes it painfully clear to him that the matter has to stop at the oracle: serve you shall!

In the third line something remarkable happens. While we move on from patriarch to tribe,[36] in as unremarkable and fluent a transition as

[35] I scan as follows (excluding *hinnē*, just like *rᵉ'ē* in v. 27, via anacrusis): 4+3 2+2 (or 3+3) 3+4.
Westermann, Arten ... p. 77: "auch Esau erhält seinen Segensspruch, aber dieser gibt dem Esau nur einen gebrochenen Segen, der geradezu an den Kain-Fluch erinnert."

[36] At least this is the most plausible explanation. Or v. 40b would refer to Gen. 33, which is not very appropriate.

in 25.23, Isaac wrests from himself a positive note, light at the end of the tunnel: "but once it will come about that you will break his yoke from your neck, when you wander about freely".[37]

28.3f. Burdened by Esau's spite and Rebekah's cunning manipulations the story does not recede quietly, but it develops towards one more blessing. Ch. 28.1-5, just like 27.1-4 well-framed by "call – send" the son, tells us in v. 1 that a) Isaac blessed him and b) charged him. First the charge is mentioned (v. 1b,2), which has a rhyme similar to that in 25.20 (in this case, ... 'ᵃbī 'immekā ... 'ᵃḥī 'immekā) and which, as in 25.20, mentions the home of the patriarchs, Paddan-Aram. *L'histoire se répète,* again an Aramean is going to take a wife from fellow-tribesmen in Haran; the three stories are framed by it. In chiastic sequence the blessing follows – forming an impressive ending. The fulfilment of the charge, Isaac says, will lead to the realization of the blessing which is given you in farewell (vv. 3, 4).[38]

With a new epithet[39] God again is in fiont, and now Isaac wishes Jacob that he, too, may share in God's promises of land and fertility.[40] Isaac emphasizes Abraham, with whom the election has begun, and the "blessing of Abraham" he uses already as a set phrase. V. 4 describes a bow descending from the wished-for *yitten* "that he may give" to the thankful *nātan* "he has given". The land of Canaan is now to be the scene where the blessing to the first-born (27.28f) will be realized, for Canaan is for this family the Promised Land.

[37] To emend *tārīd* is needless. Ps. 55.3 and Jer. 2.31 make it clear that the root RWD means "frei, ungezügelt umherschweifen" as the Hebräisches und Aramäisches Handwörterbuch über das A. T. by W. Gesenius and Fr. Buhl says (this opposed to Koehler, Lexicon in VT libros, Leyden 1953). The fact that *rwd* occurs infrequently in the OT but that it does occur in Hos. 12 (the reflex on Jacob in the literature of the prophets) is an indication, though not evidence, that it also occurs in Genesis.

[38] NB, 28.3 is joined *finally* with v. 2: qūm ... qaḥ ... wᵉ'El Šadday yᵉbārek – take a cognate wife from there, *so that* God *may* give you the blessing of Abraham. Thus also e.g. J. Hoftijzer, die Verheissungen an die drei Erzväter, Leyden 1956, p. 24 note 81, and Wehmeier o.c. p. 142.

[39] El Šadday, of disputed meaning; one of those names which makes one wonder if its etymology had not been forgotten for a long time in the early days of the monarchy.

[40] Here it appears that Isaac cannot give such a blessing and that he has not given one in 27.28f.

§ 4. *Excursus and retrospect*

Excursus on Gen. 26.

Isaac has given Jacob the fatherly blessing and wished him the divine "blessing of Abraham"; he spoke with authority. When we read Gen. 26 now, we understand its place in the Story of Jacob much better.

A. It is true that Gen. 26 is the only chapter in the Bible devoted to the middle generation of the famous set of three, Abraham-Isaac-Jacob, but it shows us Isaac not for his sake, as someone with merits of his own. No, he is expressly described as his father's son, as great Abraham's heir. Whereas in Gen. 27 he appears as the father of this son, as function of the next generation, Gen. 26 describes him as function of the previous generation. Nowhere is he worth a narration for his own sake, and his experiences are not individual but typical. Fighting over wells (vv. 15-22) will certainly occur more often,[41] it may happen to any generation. The other two events are a repetition of what had happened to Abraham: alienship plus *"Gefährdung der Ahnfrau"*[42] (Gen. 26.1-4) and the making of a covenant (vv. 23-33) have parallels in Gen. 20.1-18 (and also Ch. 12.10-20) and 22.22-34.

We will now look at the material in the three parts of Gen. 26:

- Not only does the material of vv. 1-11 have a parallel with Gen. 12 and 20, but Gen. 26 itself points explicitly to the similarity to ch. 12. Immediately v. 1 makes, in so many words, a comparison with famine of Abraham's time (12.10). The prohibition in 26.26 presupposes the journey to Egypt in 12.10b as a precedent.
- God appears to Isaac to support him, "I will be with you". Why? Literally the text says: "because Abraham has obeyed me and kept my charge" (v. 5); and Isaac receives God's blessing for, "I will fulfill the oath which I swore to Abraham your father" (v. 3). Helping Isaac is to God something that necessarily results from his obligations towards Abraham.
- Part b opens with a preparation (v. 15) which just like v. 1 explicitly refers to the days of Abraham, Isaac again digs his father's wells of water, and again the text (v. 18) retraces the track, even three times ("... in the days of Abraham, ... after Abraham's death ... the same names ...").

[41] See, for example, Gen. 21.25f.

[42] An analysis of the three "doublets" is found in Kl. Koch, Was ist Formgeschichte?, Neukirchen, 1967, (2nd ed.), § 10.

- Part c (vv. 23-33) begins with a theophany just as in part a. Again the text says emphatically "I am the God of Abraham your father" (v. 24) and Isaac does not receive the blessing for his sake or on grounds of his own merits, but "for my servant Abraham's sake".
- As a result the king of Gerar wants to share in Isaac's properity by means of a covenant, as eagerly as in Gen. 21, for Isaac's prosperity is guaranteed by that one blessing of Abraham, indivisible and given by God.

B. Using a rather awkward word we could call Gen. 26 "demonstration-material". What is a blessing, how does it work? The answer we find in some exemplary texts, in a sort of covenant-form such as Deut. 28, which has been enclosed in a homiletic framework. But a real report of the working of a blessing, thus in narrative form, we find (apart from Num. 22-24) here in Gen. 26. Being blessed by God means:

- "I am with you" when entering an unknown, perhaps even dangerous territory (vv. 3, 24 and 26!), so that Isaac is under protection;
- Inheriting the land of Canaan (vv. 36, 46).
- Having numerous descendants (vv. 4a, 24b) the fertility and meaning of which will pass into a proverb (v. 4b).
- God's blessing surrounds Isaac as an iron defence, Abimelech cannot hit him with a punishment (v. 10f).
- Mea Shearim: Isaac enjoys a hundred-fold crops by Yahweh's blessing (v. 12) and becomes rich (v. 13) so that he is envied (v. 14).
- In spite of the Philistines' sabotage Isaac finds new wells again and again, and eventually he finds access to "living water" (vv. 19-22), also in the next "land of alienship" (v. 32).
- The climax is found in part c: from the mouths of the Philistines themselves we hear the acknowledgment that nothing can be detracted from the accomplished fact of Isaac's blessedness; their speech (v. 28f) is perfectly framed by "Yahweh is with you ... you are the blessed of Yalweh".
- The blessing is so desirable and so secure a source of prosperity that the lord-servant relationship of Gerar and Isaac becomes reversed: humbly the Philistines come to ask Isaac for a share in his blessing. "Send away in peace" is hypocrisy in their mouths (v. 29); the only one who is free and has power to do so is the patriarch (v. 31).

Now let us read the story of Ch. 27 *after* Ch. 26. Are we surprised that Isaac acts quite naturally with the blessing and that he speaks with authority? He has a life behind him rich with the repeated experience of being rescued by God from difficult situations when he was a stranger (*ger*) among the inhabitants of Canaan or when a shortage of water was threatening, and of being made to appear stronger and richer each time. What Isaac is going to transmit in Gen. 27 is, as it were, a life saturated with blessing. And from 28.3f it appears that he realizes that he is only a link between two generations, the transmitter (no more) of the blessing of Abraham. The self-portrait which the two verses imply agrees with the lines drawn for us in Gen. 26.

And is it any wonder that Esau and Jacob fight so hard for *b*^{e}*kōrā* and *b*^{e}*rākā*? They have heard from their parents how their nomadic life has been made secure and safe. Part of it they have seen with their own eyes!

Thus we understand how the stories about the blessing in Gen. 26 serve as a foil to the next chapter in which the father solemnly transmits the blessing.

Retrospect

So far in our analysis of Gen. 25-28 we have left aside one important question. Who are responsible? The main characters' behaviour asks for a moral judgment, or does it not?

To begin with, as a true artist our narrator does not need to moralize within the story or to add a clumsy ending such as: "the moral of all this is as follows ..." or, "actually, it is my intention to show that ..." As an adult narrator he assumes our adultness, leaving much to our imagination and remaining reticent about making value judgments himself. He presents the events to us in great detail, he tells us what they smell of (of the field, 27.27) and what colour they are (the red man falls for red, 25.30), and there his story ends. We are left to our own discernment by this knotty and subtle narrative style which displays distance and commitment.

Are these stories amoral then, *jenseits von Gut und Böse*? By no means. We are certainly challenged to sharpen and show our moral discernment when we answer such questions as whether Jacob's and Rebekah's actions please God? But we should understand that in biblical (and other) narrative art "the moral" is indissolubly interwoven with the words and actions of the characters, just as our own actions always have moral implications, even if we are innocent of writing moral-theological tracts. The characters, the personalities of the people acting are shown to us "only" by means of what they say and do, but this is no reason the characterizations should be less clear; on the contrary, this is the most effective means available to the artist for he knows that the qualities, the charisma of "his" people leave an unforgettable impression if they have been made concrete. Showing Esau in the act of falling upon the red porridge is terser and more revealing than a discourse of a full page; representing Rebekah as an eavesdropper behind the scenes is more pregnant than dwelling upon her plans and intentions. This style hits the mark immediately and is restrained in its descriptions. Outward appearance and qualities are only mentioned when essential to the action (25.25,27; 27.1.11). Emotions are mainly expressed by the actors' words; they are mentioned explicitly only when they rise to great heat (27.33,34, 41) and when they are essential to the action (25.28 with a view to ch. 27). In view of this restraint we must strain our ears if we are to determine who are responsible.

It seems to be so easy. Is not everything fixed, right from the start, when even before birth the new generation partly fulfils the oracle which describes the fate of the twins powerfully and reverses the usual power relationship between elder and younger? Was not it bound to happen that Jacob took the birthright from his brother and next received the blessing? God himself had prophesied this in an oracle! This is a rare specimen of predestination.

There is a saying that not one sparrow will fall to the ground without God's will – a plastic way of speaking. Things would, however, be very dull if God, as stage-director, let us have a look in his scenario all the time. Fortunately he does not.

The uniqueness of the Story of Jacob is, in any case, that together with the main characters we are allowed to cast a glance at God's scenario. The importance of this for Gen. 25-35 as a whole we shall understand later. How much it dominated 25-27 has already been demonstrated by the structural analysis: God's will is the kernel of the first story, we saw, and the conflict mentioned in it bursts in the second and third stories and supports their structures.

Well, Providence has revealed itself, and everything is settled. The issue is known (who is to become lord of the generation), the result is fixed: not Esau, but Jacob will win. But what can a narrator do with all this? He would not dream of tackling such a life-story, for the suspense – the most important thing that breathes life into a story – has been entirely removed beforehand. The means of surprise has been taken away from him. Once his main characters are in the service of predestination, they are puppets, dummies. They have been deprived of their responsibilities, thus of their dignity and their credibility. Jacob and Rebekah do what they cannot help doing. They perform God's will and so they act in a morally right way – or rather, they do not; as unfree vehicles of predestination their actions are neither right nor wrong for the tension between right and wrong, thus morality itself, has been extinguished, taken away.

How different is our text in reality! The narrator is not a bit embarrassed after scene 1, and the narrative does not give that impression at all. He does not dismiss his subject lightly, as quickly as he can, because it would be foredoomed to dullness; on the contrary, there is enough material to last him to Gen. 33 at the least. An enormous and long bow of tension becomes perceptible, one pole of which is Jacob's life in Canaan (Chs. 25-28) and the other his return and confrontation with his feared brother (Gen. 32f). These poles create suspense over Gen. 29-31, Jacob's twenty-year stay in Haran. The characters, we feel, have n o t been degraded to puppets and are not a bit overshadowed by predestination; they act freely and on their own decision. It is beyond dispute that they have their own responsibility. The fact that God's will is known already does not deprive the people in Gen. 25-27 of their independence and their dignity, it does not relieve them of their responsibility to choose between good and evil all the time, and we in turn can (and so we must) determine if they live God-pleasing lives. Nothing is detracted from this by the fact that narratives two and three are closely connected with the oracle and that Jacob and Rebekah are obviously busy fulfilling the oracle. That the people in the three stories remain independent and morally responsible is, therefore, greatly to the narrator's credit. Presently we shall ask the question as to how it was achieved.

Now, however, we put the main characters on the scales, or rather, we read the scales which the narrative holds before us. Jacob and Rebekah are found to be too light; these two in particular. But so are Isaac and Esau.

The birth story hardly tells us of behaviour which is open to criticism, unless one reckons that of the baby who, holding his brother's heel, seemed to grudge him a start. But here Jacob still deserved the benefit of our doubt.

As early as the transition to scene 2 in 25.28, however, we see the human limitation of the parents. Their predilections offer a point of application to later disaster. In scene 2 we come upon the first obvious value judgment, implied in the final line, "thus Esau despised the *bᵉkōrā*". It is madness to give up your special position which at the same time is a task – the task of representing the family in a new generation – for a momentary whim. And what an absurd equation: a mess of steaming porridge in exchange for the birthright. A despicable, altoghether objectionable exchange and sanctioned in God's name, at that.

This exchange has stamped the other party as the greatest moral loser. Jacob takes advantage of his brother's weak side. As the originator of the painful exchange he is responsible in the first place, as the instigator of a rather indelicate oath he is the first to take God's name in vain.

But must he not work at his destiny? The story clearly puts forward the view that the end does not justify Jacob's means; almost to the contrary, for using an exchange-trick of his own initiative and of his own free will, he makes use of a means which, measured by God's word, appears to be the more repulsive. Jacob may try to shelter behind the oracle, but it unmasks him as a vile deceiver. This judgment on Jacob is not to be found in the text, or hardly so. It is one of those insights which the narrator leaves to our own discernment, relying on a wise reader/listener. – And of course he also enjoys describing a cunning trick, just as we relish it, too.

In the third story the parents are as obviously present as they were absent in the second story. The split which now develops in the family must become manifest to all four members. Let us first follow the father.

We may assume that Rebekah's despair at her seemingly dangerous pregnancy and the explanation given to her by God have not remained unnoticed by Isaac, her husband. This appears in the fact that he does not criticize Esau's questionable choice in marriage (26.34f, 27.46), but at once exerts himself for Jacob's religiously correct marriage (28.1f), and is also seen in that the blessing which can only come from God, viz. the blessing of Abraham, he destines for Jacob. Apparently he has resigned himself to the idea that Jacob has become the first (28.3f).

If this reading is correct, we see Isaac act within the limits for which we were prepared in 25.28. Rather than draw conclusions from an oracle of long ago he sticks to common usage, common law: the elder one, so Esau, he wants to bless; to him, the hunter, he feels essentially akin. To this son only can he transmit the essence of his being, his *nefeš* by means of the blessing; furthermore, Isaac thinks, the line of life of the family is guaranteed best in Esau.

This means, however, that he deals high-handedly with the blessing. He goes against God's plan when he blesses Esau. He does not know that willy-nilly he is accomplishing the course of events desired by God, through the other "Esau".

Morally speaking, Esau himself is not made a target in this story. Even when he has feelings of revenge, for obvious reasons, he displays that much-esteemed quality that Jacob lacks so shockingly, considerateness towards his father (27.41b). But for the rest, both in 27, and in 28.6-9, he is present only as the underdog, the one who has been totally out-maneuvered.

His bitter words take us to his brother, and as a helpless man's comment they are most revealing. Here an explicitly moral judgment is passed by the one who has lost most, a judgment which is as bitter as it is true, "twice he has supplanted me". There is no doubt but that the narrator shares this view. Jacob's guile is especially objectionable with respect to Esau because Esau's nature was usurped in it: the smell of the field, the hairiness, the prepared food are a theft to suggest the hunter to Isaac.

Simply and briefly the narrator has another judgment passed on Jacob's behaviour by the other victim, who is more shocked than harmed: Isaac uses three words (v. 35), "your brother came with guile"; *mirmā* – that word will return like a boomerang in the Story of Jacob![43]

Towards the father Jacob's behaviour is objectionable primarily in his cynical disrespect towards him and in the impudence of his taking advantage of his father's blindness. He is a deceiver by nature – *nomen est omen*, Esau tells us. And he is destined to continue the name of his father, his strength blessed by God, he of all people!

Finally we see scheming behind the scenes the originator of all the misery and the one who is responsible in the first place, Rebekah.[44] She denies her husband and her marriage, she contrives to deprive Esau

[43] See p. 128f. *infra*.

[44] When one emphasizes her part in the combination Rebekah + Jacob too strongly, one arrives at the following: "Von Jakob dagegen wird keine selbständige Handlung ausgesagt. Er soll wohl als kindlich unselbständig und ohne eigene Initiative geschildert werden." (Eising, op. cit., p. 46). This is carrying things too far, it is greatly one-sided.

of his being for her darling's benefit, she urges Jacob to his vile deceit. She is the only one guilty with respect to all the others.

Now we understand why the characters, esp. Jacob and Rebekah, act freely and independently and why they are not puppets of an almighty predestination. Their independence consists in their high-handedness. Their guilt with respect to the other characters also reveals a "vertical" guilt: guilt towards God. Although his word does not fall totally ineffectively to the ground, Rebekah and Jacob want to carry it out in their own way, to suit themselves and they do not shrink from using evil means to that end. They prefer not to wait; once the distress of the pregnancy is over they do not trouble to ask for another oracle or to consider God's will in any other way.

This interpretation is also found in the words of a witness from the seventh century B.C., who expresses his wrath about the corruption among father Jacob's descendants in an oracle that contains key-words from Gen. 25-35.[45] It is Jeremiah who gives his exegesis implicitly, as follows:

3 איש מרעהו השמרו ועל כל אח אל תבטחו
כי כל אח עקוב יעקב וכל רע רכיל יהלך
4 ואיש ברעהו יהתלו ואמת לא ידבר (. . .)
5 שבתך בתוך מרמה במרמה מאנו דעת אותי (נאם יהוה)

Jer. 9.1-8 (in transl. 2-9) is a GV, a word of judgment to the people.[46] The quotations are from the first half, the accusation (*"Scheltwort"*). The last words, which directly precede the announcement of punishment (*"Drohwort"*) beginning in v. 6 are most interesting. In them Jeremiah brings together his bitter reproaches in a powerful conclusion, "they refuse to know me, says the Lord". This quintessence also refers to the patriarch and this interpretation of Jeremiah's we can adopt for Gen. 25-27 without comment.

So Rebekah and Jacob are independent in their sins. But are they free? Plunging into deceit as free people they become slaves to self-deceit. They refuse to be liberated by God's word; in their haste to perform it on their own authority they fall a prey to desire, narrow-mindedness and inconsideration to their fellow-men.

[45] *Hiššāmer*: also in Gen. 31.24, 29; *'āḥ* especially in Gen. 27, but also in Gen. 31.32,37; *"ya'ᵃqob"* adopts Esau's interpretation entirely; *tll* (Hiph): 31.7, *mirmā* in 27.35 and 29.25.

[46] GV: die Gerichtsankündigung gegen das Volk. See, for example, Claus Westermann, Grundformen prophetischer Rede, München, 1964 (2nd ed.).

Thus the first part of the Story of Jacob culminates in delightful paradoxes: the father who goes against the oracle only fulfills it with his own blessing, and Jacob's efforts to become lord ($g^{e}b\bar{i}r$) of his own initiative lead him into slavery, the house of bondage in Haran, Gen. 29-31.

Incorporation of Gen. 28.10-22.

In the horizontal plane, that of human relations, Jacob's life has become stuck, he has made only blunders. Being *persona non grata* in Canaan he is on his way to Haran, lonely, as a refugee; in a yet unknown stopping place he prepares a hard bed for himself. His sun has set.

In that darkness the light of Revelation shines suddenly and surprisingly. The vertical dimension which Rebekah was allowed to glimpse during her pregnancy is now opened up for Jacob himself. Election and blessing prevail over judgment and punishment.

That, too, is a surprise. With regard to Jacob's guilt God does not take a side yet. Once the hour of truth will come, but not until twenty years later will God expose the debit-side of Jacob's actions, Gen. 32f. In Gen. 28.10-22 the judgment on this individual life yields to God's election of Abraham's family.

In the darkness of Bethel, only a short time after Isaac and Jacob have said good-bye, God renews his blessing to this family and therewith carries out Isaac's wish that Jacob may participate in the blessing of Abraham. And by his promise of help in the situation at hand (28.15) the God of Abraham and Isaac shows that he will also be the God of Jacob, quite concretely his protector.

Because of the blessing of Abraham and the promise of help, the Bethel-scene becomes a pillar in the history of Jacob. The event arouses in Jacob, and the narration arouses in us, great and specific expectations as to the future, and by formulating them accurately Jacob's vow underlines these expectations. The rest of his life takes place in the light of the continuing election and under the sign of God's help.

God is completely frank with Jacob in his acts. Jacob, in turn, is a good observer and gives so transparent an interpretation of what happened to him that nothing is lost: his action with the massebe and his words in the vow are, as the perfect reflection of theophany and promise, proof of his frankness with God. Buoyed up he can move on; grateful for the blessing he faces his future.

Although it is hardly desirable to replace a literary text with a paraphrase, it is necessary to replace the analysis of the scene at Bethel, given in the second chapter of this book, by a summary. We have confined ourselves to showing some broad outlines of this story, which mark its place in the whole of Gen. 25-35.

When we reconsider scene 4, this time as a small part in a large whole, we come upon a phenomenon which is hermeneutically fascinating: the idiosyncratic structure of Gen. 28.10-22 makes this scene largely independent and rounded off, so that we were able to devote a detailed study to it. On the other hand the Bethel-scene fits perfectly in the whole of the Story of Jacob. Its composition shows two great movements to and fro on either side of Gen. 29-31, Jacob's stay in Haran, and as a narrative about a stopping-place on the way, "Bethel" is the link between what happens in the family in Canaan (25-28.9) and the period with Laban.

Scene 4 forcefully and renewingly continues the motif of "blessing" of the preceding part and it sets up a clear perspective within which all that is to follow will take place. In fact it is an optical illusion to interpret this so-called "smallest literary unit" entirely within itself. The rest of this study of Gen. 25-35 will discuss links with "Bethel" in many places and will complete the integration of this part into the large whole.

CHAPTER IV

JACOB IN THE SERVICE OF LABAN, GEN. 29-31

§ 5 *Scene 5: arrival at Haran, "Pastorale"* (*Gen.* 29.1-14)

The middle part of Jacob's life is spent at Haran, his family's former home-land. It is a twenty years' period, which in the text takes up six scenes, Gen. 29-31.

The opening passage of this long act, full of complications and conflicts, is about the only scene of Jacob's stay among the people that is harmonious, indeed almost sweet. The act of this scene is not a conflict, but a meeting, and the atmosphere it breathes is especially important.

We can feel the atmosphere if we call to mind Gen. 24. It is one of the most intimate stories of the Bible, and it tells us how God fulfils Abraham's expectation and his faithful servant's devout prayer as soon as Elieser has come to civilization at Haran: at the spring the first girl, hospitable and indefatigably helpful as she is, proves to be the best girl for Abraham's son, allotted by Providence. Rebekah's family, Laban at the head, recognizes God's hand in the meeting and conforms willingly.

Now, in his turn, Abraham's grandson approaches a spring at Haran. The shepherds round it are cognate, and his heart leaps for joy and hope when he hears that they know Laban and that all is well with him, *šālōm lō*. After a long journey he has arrived safe and sound (*šālem*, cf. Gen. 33.18), he feels secure. God has protected him on his way, according to his promise.

He, too, is approached by a girl. Again the first girl is the best girl. Jacob feels that now, too, God's blessing is with him, Providence makes him meet Rachel, his beloved wife-to-be. Then he rolls the stone from the well with gigantic strength and waters her flock, the reverse of Gen. 24, where the girl waters the traveller's animals.[1]

[1] "Gerade bei dieser Handlung zeigt Jakob sich selbst als der Sohn seiner Mutter, die einst den Fremden und seine Kamele getränkt hat." Benno Jacob, Genesis (Berlin, 1934), p. 587.

We have now come to the only element in this story that requires an explanation.[2] All by himself Jacob rolls away a stone which at any other time is removed by at least four men. From where does he get his strength? Is he in love with Rachel at first sight and does he want to make an ineffaceable impression on her? Love calling up gigantic strength – that is a modern, romantic interpretation, cheap enough to leave it to ladies' journals. It is demonstrably incorrect. The text does not say, "when Jacob saw Rachel he went to her and kissed her; he lifted up his voice and wept. Then he rolled ... and watered her flock." In other words, the mere sequence of v. 10b and 11 should make us change our minds.

It does just this and again the "titles" come to lead us in the right direction. The text is as follows:

> When Jacob saw Rachel, bat Laban 'ᵃḥī 'immō
> and the sheep of Laban 'ᵃḥī 'immō
> Jacob went up and rolled the stone from the well,
> and he watered the sheep of Laban 'ᵃḥī 'immō.
> (then follows v. 11)

This "pastorale" at the well is a bit of saga. A wandering sheep-nomad enters the scene, a striking touch of local colour. He recognizes relatives, hears that Laban shares in "šālōm" and then he meets his daughter. The text does not say, "when he saw Rachel, he came nearer, etc.", but explicitly "when he saw Rachel and the sheep of Laban his mother's brother"; and explicitly he gets to work with the sheep first. A real shepherd is Jacob, and he shows the same helpfulness as Rebekah in Gen. 24. And Rachel is presented to us as a shepherdess. Her appearance is not described (for all we know she may have dull eyes ...). What does count is shown by the title, that Rachel is the daughter of and the sheep are the possession of "Laban-his-mother's-brother". In the saga blood-relationship is the cement of society, blood-relationship is what gives Jacob joy, strength and security.[3] Marriage and love are a small, integrated part of this family-world, and are out

[2] We think of the most important criterium that Erich Auerbach uses with respect to Gen. 22, in Mimesis (Bern, 1959, 2nd ed.), Ch. I: *Deutungsbedürftigkeit*; it is obviously true of most other scenes about Jacob.

[3] B. Jacob on 29.10: "Da wallt das verwandschaftliche Gefühl, die Erinnerung an die Heimat und die Mutter daheim im Jakob auf: ..."(p. 587). Eising, p. 164: Jacob's strength and reception are "ausdrücklich aus dem Verwandschafts-verhältnis begründet". Also Gunkel, p. 326.

of order now. Lastly, at a more profound level the explanation for Jacob's strength is, as we saw, Providence. The balance and harmony of this arrival and recognition have been achieved by virtue of the blessing. God is indeed with him, leads him to the circle of relatives and inside it he meets the woman who is to be his bride.

Whenever Jacob acknowledges this and when he feels he is under God's special protection, he makes it clear with stones. When he received the promise of the support of the God of Abraham and the blessing of Abraham, he immortalized that theophany by means of a massebe. Now he feels that his life proceeds along the right track and he rolls the heavy stone away. He has been inspired by the massebe,[4] the water of life can be drunk.

Opposite to the group saying, "we cannot manage, *lō nūkal*", Jacob takes his stand, the man of *yūkal* (Gen. 32.26,29!!). He removes the obstacle, and that seems to be symbolic: presently all other obstacles will have to get out of the way (Jacob is *tām*) and God himself will admit: "you have fought with people and you have been equal to it, *wattūkal*".

The story makes it impossible for the reader and exegete to forget the stone. It is laid before our feet so expressly that we cannot get round it:

– heavy and unmanageable it is lying there in v. 26; the four iteratives of v. 3 have been caused by the very presence of the stone;
– after the first acquaintance of vv. 4-6 the iteratives recur, "collect – roll away – water";
– the surprising fact that Jacob rolls the stone away by himself (v. 10) is the second climax in this scene and, in any case, the only real action.

That it is a climax is underlined by *wayhī ka'ᵃšer* ("and it happened, when ..."), which is also used to indicate *the* turning-point in Gen. 29-31, viz. in 30.25.

The stone makes us aware of a kind of three-stroke story with great regularity:

wᵉgālᵉlū 'et hā'eben meʿal pī habbᵉ'er - v. 3
wᵉgālᵉlū 'et hā'eben meʿal pī habbᵉ'er - v. 8
wayyāgel 'et hā'eben meʿal pī habbᵉ'er - v. 10 climax

[4] Ehrlich, Randglossen ..., I, on 29,2: "Dieser grosse und schwere Stein (...) ist zu dem 28,18.22 genannten Steine in Beziehung zu bringen. Dem zur Masseba errichteten Steine verdankte Jakob die übernatürliche Kraft, mit der er ganz allein den ungeheuer grossen Stein vom Brunnenloch wegwälzen konnte."

Rachel tells her father what has happened to her. That is why tricky Laban knows, even before he has seen Jacob, that a workman is on his way who is worth his weight in gold. At first his thoughts do not tend in that direction; he receives him cordially, thinking of the riches his family had received (Gen. 24) after having welcomed Abraham's messenger. Only at the end of v. 13 does Laban notice that in this way there is nothing to be gained this time. Jacob tells his story – "all these things", a rather vague, flat formula[5] – and Laban will have become aware of the reason why Jacob arrived alone, without the entourage of a prince (Gen. 24!), even without a *mohar*. Laban collapses; as early as v. 14 Laban's first ambivalence appears: "'*ak* ..." is to be translated by "oh well, yet you are my flesh and blood"[6] and it reveals his disappointment: so you do not bring riches, oh well, but I cannot and will not refuse to accommodate you.

We can judge this ambivalence for its true worth retrospectively, from all that is yet to come for Jacob. But Jacob can have no inkling of it yet. To him the beginning is pleasant and full of great expectations; there is no reason to expect difficulties, the sky is still cloudless.[7]

§ 6 *Scene 6: Jacob takes service, le trompeur trompé, Gen. 29.15-30*

The story takes us *in medias res* with the very first sentence, Laban slyly sets a trap, in which he is to hold Jacob, the fox, for twenty years. "Because you are my kinsman, should you therefore serve me for nothing? Tell me, what shall your wages be?"

Wages and *service* – those are the two key-words which dominate the Haran-phase, especially in regard to Laban and his relation with Jacob. The root ʿBD strings nearly all the scenes, the root SKR all of them.

[5] It cannot refer to what is told in vv. 1-11 because Rachel had already transmitted that, v. 12,13a; besides, the formula comprises too much for that, "*all* these things". B. Jacob on v. 14: "Als ihm aber Jakob alle diese Dinge, d.h. die häuslichen Begebenheiten, die ihn hierher getrieben haben, erzählt, sinkt die Freundschaft Labans sofort auf den Nullpunkt." (p. 588)

[6] Ehrlich, Randglossen I p. 141 about Gen. 29.14: "'ak leitet an dieser Stelle ein erzwungenes Zugeständnis ein, das nicht ganz ohne Zweifel gemacht wird." Interesting: the functions of *'ak* in KBL2 are defined as 1. einschränkend, 2. hervorhebend, in KBL3 the other way round.

[7] This interpretation can be based on the text if one recognizes that 29.12 is a parallel to Gen. 24.28f.

Whenever a lord would like to take on a servant (and Laban would like to have Jacob very much) and with mealy mouth invites him to make the first proposal as to the wages (and oh, how winning Laban is!), there exploitation lies in wait. But the encapsulation hidden in Laban's proposal lies deeper. Laban does not want to accept work from Jacob "for nothing", strictly (*ḥinnām*) "by way of favour" (viz. from Jacob to Laban), but "at decent wages". If a stranger receives wages, then you, my dear Jacob, certainly *a fortiori*. But what does this really mean? It means that Laban proclaims the blood-relationship to be irrelevant, that he changes, degrades the uncle-nephew relationship into a lord-servant relationship and makes it poorer. Jacob cannot suspect it at this moment, we must reiterate. We know the sequel and its tricky and bitter "wage-disputes" (Gen. 30.25-34; 31.36-43).

Laban controls the situation. He knows that Jacob has come for negative reasons (on the run from Esau) and for a positive end (marriage) and without *mohar*. When Jacob does make a wage-proposal (v. 18) he is the last to be surprised that Rachel is the object of his desire and that Jacob will stay at Haran for a long time (and thus will not be confronted with Esau). Does he accept Jacob's terms? Yes and no.

Laban now expresses his second ambivalence, which, again, Jacob cannot see through at this moment, but which we can because we know the sequel (the wedding!): v. 19, "Jacob, you will have her". But he does not say, *Rachel* will be the reward for your work" (although he implies it) and by no means, "she will be your reward for the next seven years". Hardly had Jacob mentioned "seven years in your service" (v. 18) when Laban saw his chance in a flash: if I make Jacob marry the first-born, Leah, first (as befits a father-in-law) I can entrap him for another seven years of service! That Jacob after a seven years' loyal service will, during the next seven years, feel bitter at heart about ... all fourteen years is a matter of no concern to the man who has defined himself as an employer (although he tries to pass for benevolent uncle in vv. 15 and 19). Nor does Laban bother about how sad a future he has prepared for Leah who, already scorned for her plainness, is shifted off like a dummy and whose very presence will remind Jacob of his uncle's deceit every day. Laban's self-interest is more important to him. And that is why in v. 19 he cannot be caught in his words. As a matter of fact the text does not put in black and white what he leads Jacob to believe.

Biblical narrative art can minimize narrated time if it is considered irrelevant. An extreme example is given in v. 20, where seven years are skipped. That is, negatively speaking, what happens in this verse: strong selectivity, the stylistic expression of Jacob's resoluteness and ... patience; he is *tām*![8] But, positively speaking, v. 20 is a subtle allusion to the past: the words "[the seven years seemed to him] but a few days" are the very words of the advice given by his mother, 27.44. Indeed, all four words of Rebekah's in 27.44a have reappeared here in Ch. 29, for we find "stay with him" in 29.14b and 19b, "a few days" in 29.20.

Jacob experiences the seven years as running past and thus he acts on Rebekah's advice. After that, Rebekah had said, you must return. The connection between 27.44 and 29.20 tells us that we can expect a) that Jacob will marry Rachel, after the seven years, and b) that he will return to Canaan now that he has completed this term of service.

That things go differently is caused by Laban's deceit and it teaches Jacob a sharp lesson: now it is your turn to be the victim of deceit, cunning heel-catcher! In v. 27 the new deceiver, Laban, does something that Jacob was very good at himself, when he set about his deceit. He makes use of Jacob's weak side, his love of Rachel. There is nothing for him but to do service for another seven years. He has been presented with an accomplished fact.

The story expresses this with subtle humour. The choice of words in the dialogue of v. 26 is a deadly hit:

Jacob to Laban: "why have you deceived me?" (√*rmh*!)

Laban said: "It is not done, in our country, to give the younger before the first-born." (√*bkr*)

"Lātet haṣṣe'īrā lifnē habbekīrā", to put the younger in front – but this is exactly what Jacob had done, that has been his most striking feat so far! As the younger one Jacob had deceived Esau and his father, and thus he had come before the *bekōr*. Now Laban teaches him, do not play such tricks on me, young man!

We realize that Jacob had remained true to himself and his position by preferring Rachel to the elder sister! How much he has tried to reverse the natural order again is also shown in a chiasmus, which connects vv. 16 and 26:

[8] B. Jacob, op. cit., p. 590: "Die sieben Jahre verfliegen Jakob pfeilgeschwind, sie sind jāmīm 'aḥādīm (...). Dem entsprechend lässt sie die Tora auch dem Leser im Fluge vergehen und widmet ihr kaum einen Vers." Eising, p. 171, saw this too.

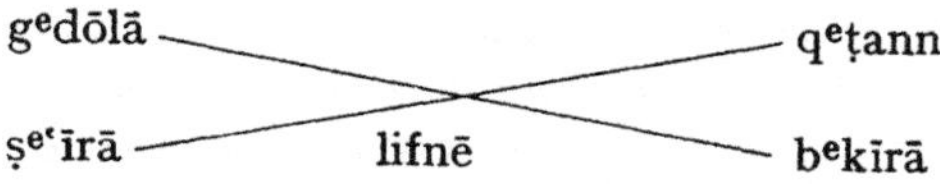

"Such things are not done here", Laban says sharply. This formula always indicates a highly objectionable, action, morally speaking,[9] one contrary to accepted usage. Formally Laban is in his right when he gives Leah in marriage first; morally he is a deceiver. He has followed his nephew's example. In Gen. 27 two brothers were exchanged by means of a trick, before a blind man; in Gen. 29 two sisters are exchanged by a trick in the darkness of night and behind a veil, which eliminate Jacob's ... sight.

Because of this exchange Jacob falls behind by seven years, as is shown by the repetitive connection between the agreement in v. 18 and Jacob's acceptance of the accomplished fact in v. 30:[10]

v. 16 'eʿebodkā šebaʿ šānīm berāḥel
v. 30 wayyaʿabod ʿimmō ʿōd šebaʿ šānīm 'aḥerōt

Jacob, master-deceiver, has found his master. Like a boomerang the word *mirmā* (27.35) comes back to him (29.25 *rimmītānī*) and fells him. Chickens come home to roost.[11]

The narrator has prepared this effect by avoiding the root *bkr* in v. 16. Again[12] he has used the neutral adjectives "big - little" for Leah and Rachel. We are not yet permitted to see the motif of "younger wants to pass over *bkr*". Nor is this allowed in v. 18, where Jacob uses the same word "little"; *he* does not use the word *ṣeʿīrā*, to avoid evoking the assonating *bekīrā*, for *he* wants to ignore normal usage. When, all of a sudden, Laban does not use "little - big" (*qeṭannā - gedōlā*) in his sharp rebuke (v. 26), but when he does use *ṣeʿīrā - bekīrā*, he reveals and parries Jacob's destiny in one blow.

Again a connection has been made from ch. 29 to ch. 25 and ch. 27

[9] The two parallels Gen. 34.7 and II Sam. 13.12 concern a sexual crime, and use the radical words nebālā ʿāsā beYisrā'el (cf. Judg. 19f).

[10] Correct translation of *gam* and *min* in v. 30: "besides, Jacob loved Rachel, and he did not love Leah". The preposition is here used in an excluding sense, which is proved by v. 31 *senū'ā*. Also in *ṣaddīq 'attā mimmennī*, Gen. 38.26, I Sam. 24.18; cf. Gen. 27.1.

[11] This example of Leitwortstil is noted in M. Buber / Fr. Rosenzweig, Die Schrift und ihre Verdeutschung, Berlin, 1936, pp. 224, 251.

[12] To be complete: 29.26 unmasking chiastically with respect to *rab* × *ṣa'īr* (25.23) = *gādōl* × *qāṭōn* (27.15,42) = *gedōlā* × *qeṭannā* (29.16).

and this time it is indissoluble: the core of the first three stories has been resumed. The meaning of this is profound. The *hybris* and high-handedness with which Jacob works at his destiny, to become ruler, have their own faultlessly measured nemesis. The crime receives its own, absolutely fitting punishment. Jacob has been unmasked, he is completely powerless.

Of what is the punishment comprised? What tells us is not one word, which occurs once of five times, not "just" a key-word, but the most frequent key-word, *'bd*, 'work, service, slavery' (in this scene already 7 times; seven!). Qualitatively, too, it is the most important word. It is exactly the counter-weight to the core of "rule" versus "serve" in Gen. 25 and 27 (scene 1: oracle, scene 3: blessing + anti-blessing) and with this *'bd* is the third indissoluble tie between this scene and the previous history. "A threefold cord is not quickly broken."

Jacob, ruler qua destiny, has become a servant, completely entrapped by his uncle. He enters the darkness of the house of bondage,[13] Laban's bēt hā'ᵃbōdā.

Jacob is entrapped very gradually, so much so that only after the wedding with Leah does it appear how much the "service" of the first seven years has already been servitude. Stylistically the imperceptible gradualness with which Jacob has become a wage-earner in chains instead of the "brother" (i.e., relative, v. 15) he was, is visible in the smooth transition of v. 14 into v. 15, which constitutes the transition from scene 5 to scene 6. The "stay with him" (viz. Laban, *wayyešeb 'immō*) of v. 14 and v. 19 passes into a three-fold "serve with him" (v. 25-27-30). And the word that opens this scene 6 is the word that ends it, "serve", v. 15-v. 30. The fox is in the trap with both his hind-legs!

§ 7 *Scene 7: Wives and children, Gen. 29.31-30.24*

Laban has denied the blood-relationship with Jacob by limiting himself to an employer-employee relationship with him; he has denied his fatherhood of Leah by using Leah as an object, so as to bind Jacob for another seven years.

The narrator skips the first seven years in order to make it con-

[13] This is the patriarch; the nation comes into being after it has been brought out of the house of bondage (Egypt) by Yahweh. See p. 188 (ll. 2-3 from bottom), p. 193 (ll. 1-2 from bottom,) and p. 194 (ll. 1-2).

spicuous that they really were "a few days" to Jacob, owing to his sense of purpose. On the next seven years, however, he spends almost thirty verses.

What is shown of this period makes a unique selection. We find ourselves exclusively in the "microcosm" of Jacob's family, whereas the other stories set the scene at Haran, between other shepherds, and describe his relation with Laban. From this outer circle (Gen. 29-31) or "macrocosm" we have now arrived at the intimate inner circle of family life (29.31-30.24). Besides, Jacob is hardly present – in 30.2 he furiously explains why – and he appears only once or twice, in silence, to do his procreative duty (30.4 and 16). About Laban there is not a word.

All the stronger, however, is his influence. He has sown poison in the inner circle by giving Jacob two daughters as wives and by following the natural order, elder before younger. This order, however, is exactly what Jacob rebels against on the ground of his destiny ("big serves little"); he had given priority to the "Jacoba" of the two sisters, Rachel. By means of a trick Laban has imposed "the natural order" on Jacob. Instead of offering harmony the circle of family-life becomes a pit of snakes. Hatred weighs heavy on Leah, envy poisons her's and Rachel's married lives.[14]

Rachel must try to digest what is to her a paradox difficult to accept, to be the beloved wife and ... barren.[15] To Leah is given the priority of fertility by the God of mercy; the "hated" wife becomes at least a mother. And both with the marriage and with the birth of progeny the Jacob-line is broken and Leah, the first-born, precedes. This is so contrary to Jacob's and "Jacoba's" natures that they rebel bitterly; but the only one who suffers is ... the other of the two, for they quarrel in 30.1f. With his words in 30.2 ("Am I in the place of God, who has withheld from you the fruit of the womb?") Jacob acknowledges that God himself has driven him from his high-

[14] The same situation is also in I Sam. 1.5 and Deut. 21.15: parallels from 20th. c. Palestine, Artas, by Hilma Granqvist, Marriage Conditions in a Palestininan Village (2 volumes, Helsingfors 1931/5); Vol. II p. 194: "As a general rule, in relation to the husband one is the favourite, the preferred one (il-maḥḏiyye). the "beloved" (il maḥbūbe) and one is the "not beloved" (muš maḥbūbe), the "hated" (mabġūḍa) one."

[15] She may "uphold the tradition" from Sarah via Rebekah to her, and on to Hannah (I Sam. 1) and Elizabeth (Lk., N.T.)

handed course to his destiny.[16] Herewith a first important indication has been given that this "story" ,too, is well integrated in the whole of the Story of Jacob.

29.31-30.24 gives a curious story. At first sight this seems to be a mechanical enumeration of births, a rather perfunctory excursion. But careful listening shows otherwise.

This story is not a real "scene" and its parts cannot be called scenes either, except 30.14-24. Yet it has a clear construction; there are three passages, devoted to:

A Leah alone, vv. 31-35
B Rachel and Leah, via Bilha and Zilpa, 30.1-13
C "*Dūdā'īm*": Leah and Rachel, 30.14-24.

In each of these passages four children are born. Thus these twelve births are clearly articulated, and the monotony which would only be natural has been largely avoided. What remains of it sinks into insignificance as soon as we have an eye for the uniqueness of this "story".

How extraordinary this series of births is appears when we a) look at the text with regard to its "Personennamen im Rahmen der israelitischen Namengebung" (by way of variation on the title of Noth's famous monograph),[17] b) consider the partly folk-etymological explanations of these names against the background of the many name-givings in Genesis.

In the O.T. stories which are basically etymological aetiologies are rare and if they do occur they are anecdotally short.[18] This is also true of the book of Genesis in which many etymological name-givings occur; neither the "*ätiologische Ortssage*", which was a characterization of e.g. Gen. 32.23ff., nor the "*ätiologische Kultlegende*", as Gen. 28.10ff. was called, occur. These genre-descriptions, popular in the school of A. Alt and M. Noth, have proved to be incorrect; see the accurate

[16] Thus 29.31 and 30.2 are important because they have a direct bearing on Jacob's destiny; they may not be interpreted shallowly, as in: that is the way the narrator says things because the ancient Israelites did believe that fertility and barrenness depend on God. This interpretation of that-is-the-way-things-were-said-at-that-time is taboo because of the significance of the line mentioned in note 15.

[17] M. Noth, Die israelitischen Personennamen im Rahmen der gemeinsemitischen Namengebung, Stuttgart, 1928.

[18] Long, pp. 56-64 of the work mentioned below:

monograph by Burke O. Long.[19] At best a story may contain an etymological aetiology as an illustration or a conclusion, but it is not sustained by it.

In Gen. 29.31-30.24, however, (a text which, by the way, does not contain aetiologies of a cult, settlement or custom) the name-givings are essential. The names with their etymological explanations are the point at issue from paragraph to paragraph: they are the means of revealing the "inner" meaning of the births, that the wives are engaged in keen competition for the favour of Jacob. Each name-giving serves their psychological conduct of war, which is an incessant propaganda-combat.

This seventh story is already exceptional, because eleven names and their interpretations[20] are the main point, like beads on a string. But the uniqueness comes to light even more strongly if we appreciate the interpretations correctly. In ancient Israel a child often received its name from its mother and sometimes from the father. The name could be derived from nature, "Lightning", "Ewe", "Palm" (Barak, Rachel, Tamar). Many more of the names which have been preserved are theophorous. In them the parents confess their faith, thank God or address their wish to him. Thus Elijah, Jonathan and Jojachin, mean respectively, "My God is Yahu", "Yahu has given (us this child)", "may Yahweh strengthen us". The parents show their shared faith, shared thanks etc. But not here! In the first place the father is always absent, which is underlined by the fact that the wives compete for the first place with him by giving birth and sometimes even mention him in their interpretations (29.32b, 34a; 30.20); in the second place every name here serves the happiness and despair of the name-giving mother and is at the same time a malicious shaft to the co-wife. All eleven names are intensely "subjective" cries of pride and expectation. All eleven names are mentioned and interpreted in the framework of the bitter struggle, the poisoining envy between Rachel and Leah. That

[19] The Problem of Etiological Narrative in the Old Testament, Berlin 1968. (=BZAW 108). As does J. Fichtner, Die etymologische Ätiologie in der Namengebung der geschichtlichen Bücher des AT, VT 6 (1956), pp. 372-396, he distinguishes two basic forms (form 1 e.g. in Ex. 2.22, form 2 e.g. in Ex. 15.23), often mixed, which are not constitutive for the whole story. – For criticism of "aetiology" see also W. Richter, Exegese als Literaturwissenschaft, pp. 155 (and note 17), 163; and Cl. Westermann, Arten ... II,3 (= pp. 39-47).

[20] Only Dinah, as a girl apparently less interesting here, is given no interpretation, 30.21 – it would be the same as for Dan, 30,6.

is an extreme variant of the normal name-giving! For that reason especially story seven is unique.

A. *Gen. 29.31-35.* Leah alone. She *is* alone, despised by Jacob, hated by Rachel. Therefore God blesses her. The first name-giving is perhaps the best one, because it contains exactly the three elements that matter all the time: prospectless situation + intervention + prospect. In v. 32 "my affliction" says in one word what v. 30 (Jacob loved Rachel, he did not love Leah) and 31 say: she was hated. V. 32, "truly, God has looked upon ...", links up with the beginning of v. 31 (in Hebrew more than in translation): wayyar Yhwh *kī* ... *kī rā'ā Yhwh*, and she concludes by hoping what a good wife desires, "surely, now my husband will love me!" Thus the name Ruben (literally, "see, a son!" – the proud exclamation of parents) points entirely to Leah's miserable position, by means of the alliteration "*rā'ā* ... *bᵉʿonyī*". It is turned into a name of thanks by a statement which as a hemistiche could be transferred directly to a psalm of lamentation (*kī rā'ā Yhwh bᵉʿonyī*).[21]

"Simeon" approximates "answering" in meaning (viz., of our prayer for a son). Here the meaning is transferred to God's answering of Leah's cry of distress that she is hated – cf. Hagar in Gen. 16.11. And the third name, "Levi", she uses to formulate the prospect of contact with her husband again. Only the fourth name is given the interpretation of a real name of thanks, but the connection with Leah's humiliation remains perceptible when she says "I thank Yahweh."

B. *Gen. 30,1-13.* Leah cannot be ignored any longer. Rachel gets most desperate about the continued absence of any children and utters a cry as weary of life as the former matriarch's, (Rebekah, 25.22) when she went through too much pregnancy. Violently ("*Hābā* ...") she demands children from Jacob, which aggravates his irritation over the disproportion between Leah with children and Rachel without children. He explodes and ... admits, in a way quite different from Isaac's in 25.21, that in Abraham's family births depend on God alone.[16] Then Rachel comes out with an initiative of her own: become a mother via her maid Bilhah, be "built" (*'ibbānẹ*) by receiving *bānīm* via her; with these words she makes the same pun as Sarai in 16.1f.

[21] Also see, for example, Hannah, in I Sam. 1.11.

She, too, explains the name of the son she adopts (v. 6) in terms of herself, "God has judged me" (And has thus put me in the right with respect to my sister, has restored by position, etc.). And in v. 8 we hear of the lamentable competition explicitly when Naphtali is born. *Naftūlē 'ᵉlōhīm*, "twists of God I have twisted (in the fight) with Leah, but I have prevailed".[22] Rachel, in Ch. 29 only passively present as Jacob's favourite wife, now proves to be a real "Jacoba" in her own words, for the proud words "I have prevailed" have a profound meaning in the Story of Jacob, from 32.29. Just as Jacob has fought with people and prevailed, so Rachel has fought with her sister and prevailed. And 32.29 also sheds light on the *naftūlē 'ᵉlōhīm*: by far the best solution is to understand it as an objective "genitive", "wrestlings *for* God I have wrestled with my sister".[23] For this is how things are: the reason why it was so difficult for Rachel to accept her fate of childlessness was that she understood very well that it was God who[24] had closed her womb[25] and opened Leah's womb. After Sarai and

[22] "Naphtali": whatever this name may mean etymologically, the root *ptl* seems to be the only peg for an explanation. *Ptl*: the original meaning is "twist", see the verb in Prov. 8.8, Ps. 18.27, Job 5.13, and the nouns *pātīl* (more than 10×, "twisted" = cord, strand) and *pᵉtaltol* ("twisted" = wrong), Deut. 32,5; the meaning is not exactly "wrestle". But this interpretation is indispensable and there are two strong indications for it: the preposition ("with my sister") and the parallel to Gen. 32.29. Actually, the "genitive" *naftūlē 'ᵉlōhīm* is less of a problem:

[23] Thus also B. Jacob, o.c., p. 596: Kämpfe *um* Gott, *wegen* Elohim. For a subjective genitive I see two possibilities:

a) Mythologically, not applicable here: "wrestlings of God" as a "struggle to which even God has been forced by / which even God must go through with", e.g. Leviathan or Rahab. To such a primeval struggle Rachel would refer using that case.

b) The interpretation of, for example, the Authorized Version: "mighty wrestlings". In my opinion, however, there is much too little evidence in the O.T. to support the theory that "God" (or his proper name) can be used as a superlative in Hebrew. See D. Winton Thomas, Some Unusual Ways of Expressing the Superlative ..., VT 3 (1953), pp. 209-224. On p. 215 he says: "If, when we say that the divine names in Hebrew are used to express the superlative, we mean that they have no religious significance at all and are merely intensifying epithets, I do not find a single example which decisively supports such a view. If, on the other hand, we mean that the divine names have the effect of raising a person or thing to a pre-eminent degree, the person or thing being brought into relationship with God, we may hold that the divine names have in this sense a superlative force." (E.g. Gen. 23.6, I Sam. 14.15)

[24] Psychologically, of course, this does not conflict with 30.1f.

[25] 'ṣr in, among others, Gen. 16.2, 20.18, sgr in I Sam. 5.6.

Rebekah it is now her turn to be tried in this way. Her struggle with Leah is really a struggle for God's favour, and to this extent it can be compared to her husband's struggle. Only, Jacob's struggle *for* God coincides with a struggle *with* God, eventually, on the Jabbok. The interpretation "struggle for God" fits excellently in the framework of the whole of story seven: its text testifies again and again, in six name-givings and in four other places,[26] that God as the true giver of life is the only agent of this story, though a hidden one.

Leah follows Rachel's example and gives Jacob her maid to conceive for her. The explanation "zum Glück" in v. 11[27] is in line with *b^e'ošrī*, "happy am I" in v. 13. In this verse again the explanation of a name is completely applied to the subjective position of the woman-alone, "for the women will call me happy" (cf. Gen. 16.11, 21.6).

After the first series of four children, brought forth by Leah herself, 29.31-35, a second series of four children has been dealt with now, who have come into the world two by two via Rachel's and Leah's body-servants. This second passage is distinguished by an opening of its own with a different main character (30.1), which follows the conclusion of A in 29.35 with two effective words; but 30.1-13 has no conclusion of its own, so C follows smoothly, although it opens with an obviously new moment and a new character. That means that the struggle between the two wives rages on. In 30.14-24 the point is brought to an issue, a most surprising and unique one.

C. *Gen. 30.14-24.* A little chap brings his mother something from the field, "mandrakes"; "*dūdā'īm*" alliterates in a challenging and inviting way with *dōdīm* "caresses". What does v. 14 really mean? The *b^ekīrā* Leah is assisted by Jacob's *b^ekōr*, although the little fellow can have had but little notion of that. Suddenly Leah is in a powerful position, by the possession of the mandrakes she can conquer what seems to have become Rachel's possession exclusively, access to Jacob. Rachel is still the only beloved wife, but she has one weak side, she is still

[26] Not only 30.2 but also and esp. so the structurally important verses of the opening and the conclusion 29.31 (30.17) and 30.22f (what emphasis!).

[27] KBL3 s.v. *b^e* (item 23) and s.v. *gad.* N.B. the Ketib in the MT. On the preposition see B. Hartmann, Zur Kopula im Hebräischen, Oudtestamentische Studiën 14 (Leiden 1965), pp. 115-121, esp. p. 119f: perhaps this *b^e/bi* is a word in itself as a copula, a fossil in ugar./hebr./arab. which is on its retreat. The translation of Gen. 30.11/13 is then: "es ist ein Glücksfall / es bedeutet mein Glück". It hardly differs materially from the explanation of *b^e* as a preposition.

barren. She hopes that she can change this by means of the mandrakes. Thus both wives have a serious "deficiency" – Leah in love and recognition, Rachel in children – which they plan to eliminate for each other by a creative compromise. Yes, "help"; but what sorrow and jealousy are piled up behind the short, very direct dialogue of v. 14b and v. 15! They exchange two things which would seem incompatible, but both have something to do with sexual intercourse with Jacob and conceiving.

V. 16. What a sad, smarting, embarrassing sight, a wife going out to meet her husband with the justification that she may sleep with him on the grounds of a bargain. But what is it that Leah says? Two words give us a start, *sākor sᵉkartīkā*; and the son that is born to her (v. 18) is *sᵉkārī*; therefore she calls him Issachar, < **'īš sākār*.

This birth, this name and these words, "I have hired you", have a profound meaning. They link up with the two key concepts which dominate the outer circle of Jacob's shepherd's life with Laban (29.15.30 at the beginning; presently 30.25-31.43): work (service, servitude), *'ᵃbōdā*, and wages (*sākār*). Servitude and wages are now also in the inner circle, justify the presence of this births-tale and reveal the profundity of it.

Laban had denied the solidarity of the blood-relationship by encapsulating Jacob as a servant, thus degrading and corrupting a human relationship. Now the root *skr* used an emphatic four times reveals that this degradation and corruption have struck from "the outside" to the inside. The family's life is rotten and broken by the dehumanizing atmosphere of SERVICE - WAGES. Things have come so far that the enslaved and oppressed wife must "hire" (skr) her husband to have intercourse, but it does not bring her the loving communication which gives recognition.[28] She must "buy" it from the younger sister, because she, as the only beloved one, is, in spite of her barrenness, the ruler (*gᵉbīrā*[29]). In this family Leah will not get beyond being the *bᵉkīrā*, the one married first or the mother of the first-born. But the first-born (Reuben) helps his mother's position.

The name of Issachar is entirely interpreted by Leah towards herself

[28] Perhaps *yiškab* in v. 15b,16b expresses this. Jacob, it is true, lies/sleeps with her, but does not "know" her; *yāda'* is not used, for Jacob does not want to perform that total, intense knowing with Leah, and in this way he withholds recognition from her.

[29] This word in Gen. 16,4,8f; thirty-five centuries later the *kbīrt il-bēt* with the Palestine Arabs, Granqvist op.cit., II p. 194.

again, which interpretation, by the way, also breathes the atmosphere of "wages-for-work". But the wider context renders the name "Issachar" connotatively much more strikingly relevant. For the name "taints" the father: Jacob himself, we see now, is no longer anything but a "man of wages", i.e. a) someone who must be hired to make his wife a mother, and b) a wage-earner. And he was destined to be *g*e*bīr*, ruler! Owing to the *Leitwortstil* the name "man of *skr*" has a range of action which extends from Laban's kindly proposal (Gen. 29.15), *mskrt*, to Jacob's bitter reproach (Gen. 31.41), *mskrt*. It is by far the most important name in the whole Story of Jacob after that of Jacob himself. Who would have believed that of little son number nine!

Now we see already that this story of births is well integrated in the Haran-episode (Gen. 29-31), owing to a significant key-word. There is an obvious climax in the division into three parts, A (29.31-45), B (30.1-13), C (30.14-24). First there is Leah alone, then Rachel and Leah apart, competing on parallel tracks; but eventually they meet, speak to each other, and decide on an exchange which on Leah's side leads to the revealing "Issachar" and on Rachel's side to the end of barrenness. Joseph's birth, again, makes the next move, Jacob's departure, possible (see the link of vv. 25ff.). The sisters' dialogue reveals that, by means of transformation, Laban's oppression of Jacob brings about, and is reflected in, the oppression of Leah and Rachel. For years Rachel suffered the same sense of inferiority as Sarai in Gen. 16.4 when Hagar had conceived; in 30.23 she, in turn, uses the words of a psalm of lamentation: at last "God has taken away my reproach" (*'āsaf*) and these words are so fundamental to her that she preserves "*'āsaf*" in the alliterating word "*yōsef*", which in v. 24b retains its original meaning. "Vv. 23,24: die Deutungen sind das Begriffspaar W e g t u n - H i n z u f ü g e n",[30] by this perfect combination and also because there are two interpretations of the name of one child, the text underlines the special significance of Joseph's birth; he is not just number twelve, but he is Rachel's first child, and no sooner has he been born than Jacob wants to go.

The creativity of the sisters' contact appears from v. 17 where again it is said: by God's answering, just as in 29.31, Leah's womb became fertile once more. And, of course, it appears from v. 22 especially, where at last the words of 29.31 and 30.17 are also true of Rachel.

[30] B. Jacob, op. cit., p. 600.

To her, too, God hearkens, her womb, too, he opens.[31] God's answering, the message that he alone is responsible for the births in Jacob's family, frame the story strikingly.[32] Moreover, 30.20 rounds the scene off by running strictly parallel to 29.34:

29.34	'attā	happa'am yillāwę̄ 'īšī 'elay	kī yāladtī lō šelōšā bānīm
30.20		happa'am yizbelenī 'īšī	kī yāladtī lō šiššā bānīm

It also shows parallelism of meaning (Leah recognized by Jacob) and again the name (this time of Zebulon) applies exactly to Leah's position.

This tripartite story is also well integrated into the whole of the Story of Jacob. We see this when we answer the question why Rachel bears children now. "God remembers her", the text says, v. 22. The question shifts to: why does God open Rachel's womb now? We have not heard of the *dūdā'īm* again, so they are insignificant and cannot even be defined as the instrument which God uses to grant Rachel fertility.[33] God reacts mercifully to Rachel's actions and because of their profound meaning he is now willing to recognize her.

What, then, happens exactly in 30.14-18? We shall first recapitulate the positions briefly. Leah has a claim to precedence, to being *gebīrā* side by side with *gebīr* Jacob, in three ways: she is the *bekīrā*, she is the first to be married and she is the first to be a mother (even fourfold). Yet she is no match for Rachel. Rachel will be the truly beloved one, qua origin she is "Jacoba" and Jacob recognizes only her. Leah attracts so much hatred from Jacob and envy from Rachel because, as an instrument of the manipulating Laban, she stands in the way of the Jacob principle and is a daily reminder of Laban's deceit. If Jacob and Rachel oppress Leah, it means psychologically that, actually,

[31] B. Jacob on the births in 30.14ff: "Vielmehr werden sie auf die Gottheit zurückgeführt, die noch nachdrücklicher als bei den vorangegangenen zum Subjekt gemacht wird." P. 597.

[32] Just to picture it:

29.31 wayyar Jhwh	wayyiftaḥ 'et raḥmāh
30.22 wayyišma' 'elōhīm	wayyiftaḥ 'et raḥmāh
30.17 wayyišma' 'elōhīm 'el Le'ā	

and 29.32b,33a.

[33] "Die Sache ist sogar umgekehrt: [not: the *dūdā'īm* make fertile, but] Lea bekommt dafür Kinder, dass sie die dudaim fortgegeben hat, und Rachel wird noch lange nicht fruchtbar." B. Jacob, op.cit., p. 597.

they want to oppress Laban and to eliminate him as a major factor in their destiny.

By that one precious treasure, Jacob's love, Rachel gains precedence, has become *haṣṣeʿīrā lifnē habbekīrā* (29.26). In 30.15 she proves to be the one who is privileged (Leah herself admits as much) because she "has" Jacob. The profound sense of her proposal in v. 15 is that now she is prepared, though temporarily, to give up the position of being first to Leah, "then he may lie with you tonight". For the fourth time in the Story of Jacob an exchange takes place, and while exchange number 3 (Jacob gets Leah instead of Rachel) is the response to exchange number 2 (Isaac blesses Jacob instead of Esau), this exchange corresponds with the first one (25.29-34):

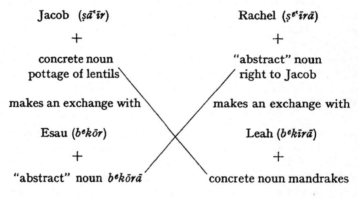

Jacob (*ṣāʿīr*)	Rachel (*ṣeʿīrā*)
+	+
concrete noun pottage of lentils	"abstract" noun right to Jacob
makes an exchange with	makes an exchange with
Esau (*bekōr*)	Leah (*bekīrā*)
+	+
"abstract" noun *bekōrā*	concrete noun mandrakes

In both texts the younger person is the demanding figure, which takes the initiative, wants to get something from the *bkr(h)* and therefore proposes an exchange. But whereas Esau is no match for Jacob and whereas he is put off with an easily forgotten pottage of lentils, Leah receives an equivalent asset for the *dūdāʾīm*: *dōdīm* which lead to pregnancy three times. For once the position of the first is returned to her, Rachel does not block the way any longer; the result is *habbekīrā lifnē haṣṣeʿīrā.*

The meaning of the entire story 29.31-30.24 is, we see now, that the real issue of the sisters' fret and fray is the same as that of the brothers Esau and Jacob's struggle: who will take the lead, who will be the first and who will be he who must serve?

Rachel gives up the only thing that shows her precedence, the access to Jacob, and after that God shows mercy. Now we understand that it is *because* of this he shows mercy. Post hoc propter hoc. As soon as the younger one gives up the high-handedness of Jacob's policy and is prepared to bend, God grants her children. Her barrenness was at the same time a symbol, envy and oppression towards Leah having condemned Rachel to sterility. To conclude, it is elucidative to represent the structure so far visually as follows:

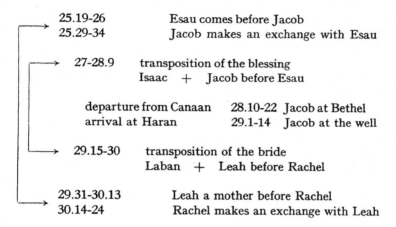

25.19-26	Esau comes before Jacob		
25.29-34	Jacob makes an exchange with Esau		
27-28.9	transposition of the blessing Isaac + Jacob before Esau		
departure from Canaan		28.10-22	Jacob at Bethel
arrival at Haran		29.1-14	Jacob at the well
29.15-30	transposition of the bride Laban + Leah before Rachel		
29.31-30.13	Leah a mother before Rachel		
30.14-24	Rachel makes an exchange with Leah		

§ 8 Scene 8: *Jacob is going to breed his own stock*, Gen. 30.25-43.

At once Jacob goes and hands in his resignation and tells of his intention to go back to Canaan. The beginning of 30.25 indicates that[34] and shows that Jacob has been waiting for one thing, a son by his beloved wife. This links this story directly with the preceding one.

Gen. 30.25-43 is easy to divide into two complementary halves, which at the same time combine fluently with each other[35]:

A) vv. 25-36 Jacob together with Laban: words
B) vv. 37-43 Jacob alone: actions

This tells us little about the contents, but so much is certain, that in B Jacob sets about doing what he had agreed on with Laban in A –

[34] Especially by means of *wayhī ka'ašer*, the same underlining as 29.10 (see p. 125), which indicates an important new initiative.
[35] Fluently; which is proved by the fact that A and B can just as well be divided in a slightly different way. V. 37a and 36b belong together so closely, as do 36b and 36a, that another good division would be: 25-34 / 35-43.

acquiring property of his own, for the first time after fourteen years of faithful service. From the inner circle, the struggle for love, we have returned to the outer circle, the struggle for life.

A. *Gen. 30.25-36.* Jacob is forewarned, he has found his equal in deceit. We see two men opposite each other who are well matched, each intent on "roping in" the adversary. The result is a conversation which is a masterpiece of suspicious wriggle in negotiations, full of ambivalence and false bottoms.

Because Laban soon succeeds in reducing Jacob to negotiations on a new labour contract and because we have gone through a similar arrangement before, in Gen. 29, it is a good thing to have 29.15ff. side by side with this text all the time.

V. 26. Jacob wants to have the free disposal of the wages for which he has worked for fourteen years. Most emphatically, by repeating ʿbd three times, he characterizes this time as *service* to Laban. At once we recognize a key-word vital to most of the preceding stories. He speaks with great emphasis, twice using an imperative plus cohortative:

v. 25 šallᵉḥenī... wᵉʾelᵉkā
v. 25 tᵉnā... wᵉʾelᵉkā

V. 27f. These two honest and straight sentences are followed at once by the first evasion. Laban does not answer Jacob's question as to his departure, but, stalling for time as Jacob threatens to press the button, he says self-righteously, "oh, that I may have found mercy (*ḥen*) in your eyes! By divination I have learned: Yahweh has blessed me (*brk*) because of you! Then he said: name your wages (*skr*) and I will give it."

Most revealing words. From the enemy's mouth we now hear that God's blessing has accompanied Jacob all the time. God has kept his promise made at Bethel, Jacob creates prosperity wherever he appears, just like the servant Joseph in Gen. 39.2f, 5, 23. The *bᵉrākā* shines about him. And who has benefited by it so far? Laban ...

Small wonder that Laban wants to keep this workman. He does his utmost to this end and asks for *ḥen*, "mercy", benevolence. A nice contrast to 29.15 where Laban charmingly refused the "free" (*ḥinnām*) services of Jacob so that he need not ask for "mercy" (*ḥen*).

In the beginning of v. 28 the text places *wayyōmer* between Laban's words, which seems rather annoying. But this "he said" is significant.

It retards the pace of the confrontation with the following effect: after the pious recognition of Yhwh's blessing Laban's mind works feverishly, thinking, how can I keep Jacob as a servant? I know what, I shall ask him to make a wage-proposal himself! We'll see, I shall certainly find an opening, just like 14/7 years ago. And with "then he said" we find a striking parallel to ch. 29:

30.28 noqbā s^{e}kār^{e}kā ʿālay w^e'ettenā
29.15 haggīdā lī ma maskurtekā

L'histoire se répète, Laban trusts to his inventiveness for tricking Jacob later on. But there is a note of embarrassment in his invitation, and this is the point where the situation begins to turn against Laban. It is not the first time that Jacob has heard this ingratiating talk, he is fore-warned and he gives Laban no chance to spring any unpleasant surprises in the form of a gift. Therefore Jacob takes care to put the acquisition of wages into his own hands as much as he can. V. 31 tells of his bitter experiences with presents-from-Laban. V. 32: he makes the proposal by which, as we know, he is going to play a trick upon Laban. *L'histoire ne se répète jamais.*

First (v. 29f) he underlines his faithful labour for Laban and, like his uncle, he points to the workings of the blessing. Using the word *prṣ* (to increase, here concerning Laban's flock which has increased under the blessed hands of Jacob the shepherd) he alludes to God's promise at Bethel (28.14). But the most important word here is *brk,* from Jacob's own mouth. "Yahweh has blessed you wherever I turned" and with that he makes a logical, thus seemingly innocent transition to his wish (v. 30b) to start a business of his own. At the same time he admits – but only we can hear it – that he expects to flourish under oppression.

Laban walks into the trap. Jacob's proposal is very modest, and he seems to assume a secondary position for himself at the beginning of a handicap-race. As Jacob prepares to make a fresh start, all those animals that are not "normally" coloured, viz. the dark[36] sheep and the speckled and spotted goats, are taken from the flock and stay with Laban. Jacob will only feed "normal" animals, i.e. white sheep and uniformly

[36] Fortunately it is not essential to the story whether the right shade is black or dark-brown. R. Gradwohl, die Farben im AT, BZAW 83 (Berlin, 1963), p. 50f., however, speaks in favour of "braunschwarz" – *ḥūm* derived from $\sqrt{}$*ḥmm*.

dark goats and the "abnormally" coloured animals born in these flocks, will be *his* wages; they will be few indeed.

V. 33a: Jacob speaks in solemn juridical terms in order to record this: "my *ṣᵉdāqā* (truth, honesty) will answer for me", my sincere intentions will appear abundantly clear in that I may be judged as a thief (33b) if white sheep and dark goats are found in my flock later.

V. 34: Laban, always on guard, safety-first his motto, is not deceived. Speaking in monosyllables, he is the big man, never committing himself, as for example, in *'ak* in 29.14, *ṭōb* in 29.19 and now *lū*[37] in 30.34. "Oh well, let it be as you have said", but again this is not a clear, unambiguous agreement, in black and white, to the arrangement! You never can tell, Laban thought; just in case Jacob will be blessed by God with many "abnormally" coloured births among the cattle, I want to have room to shift things a little: "no, Jacob, we had arranged that you should have the *'ᵃquddīm*"; "but, Jacob, had we not arranged that you should have the *nᵉquddīm*" etc.

That was hard bargaining for wages! Twice we find "you know how I have served you" (vv. 26,28), and three times *sākār*. Even after these exact negotiations the employer manages to conclude with a hole (v. 34) in the juridical net of the labour-contract; an escape-clause has been provided.

Jacob is likely to have felt this; he has learnt his lesson. But it is all the same to him, for he trusts in the blessing with which he will be able to ward off all Laban's tricks.

B. *Gen. 30.37-43*, Jacob at work.

The features of what now occurs are clear. The shepherd Jacob, having been tricked, manages to increase his property enormously (*mᵉ'od mᵉ'od*, v. 43) at Laban's expense by an ingenious breeding method. Because of the blessing Laban's property had "increased abundantly" (*prṣ*, v. 30), and now this happens to Jacob to an even greater extent (*prṣ*, v. 43).

But what, exactly, do v. 39 and esp. v. 40 say? This difficult text must "mature" before we can explain the whole by means of the parts in a well-founded literary way.

[37] B. Jacob, at his best, as it is, talking of the false bottoms in the wage-dispute speaks strongly in favour of the view that Laban appears unwilling to commit himself when using the word *lū*, pp. 601-605. He translates: "... ja, ja, wenn es doch nach deinem Wort ginge."

Excursus: philological elaboration of the text

We can solve the cruces of v. 40 almost entirely and in any case render them harmless, if we proceed carefully and accurately, step by step from the certain to the uncertain. It is useful to copy out the text into a numbered working translation:

39a the flock bred near the rods
b and the flock brought forth striped[38], speckled and spotted young,
40a Again and again Jacob made the *kᵉsābīm prd,*
b and he gave/set the *pᵉnē haṣṣōn* to/toward the striped and all the dark among Laban's flock;
c he put apart flocks for himself only,
d he did not put them with Laban's flock.
41 Whenever the stronger of the flock were breeding Jacob laid the rods in the runnels before the eyes of the flock, that they might breed near the rods;
42a but when the flock was feeble, he did not lay them there.
b thus the feeble were Laban's
c and the strong were Jacob's.

The following data are beyond all doubt:

- *ṣōn* (passim) and *sę̄* (v. 32) refer to the flock in general, so to sheep and/or goats. Neither the *nomen collectivum* nor the *nomen unitatis* make a distinction.
- opposed to goats are *kᵉsābīm*, "sheep", which is perfectly clear as early as v. 32 and v. 33. The translation (in KBL2) "young ram" is incorrect; the word is not so specific, as is apparent in many places in the O.T. (Deut. 14.4, Num. 18.17; the long series of places in Leviticus, 1.10, 3.7, 4.35, 7.23, 17.3, 22.19,27; also the fem. *kisbā* Lev. 5.6).
  Conclusion: in v. 40a we should read "sheep".

The following is certain, too, if we look at this text closely:

- the actions in 40c and d anticipate the eventual meeting of Jacob and Laban and the determination of Jacob's wages. Jacob, it was arranged, was to have the "abnormal" animals; that is what 40c refers to. Laban will have the "normally" coloured animals, which is what 40d refers to. These two sentences display a *parallelismus membrorum*, c being the precise complement of d. In other words, 40c says, positively, exactly what 40d says negatively.
- 41 and 42 constitute a perfect block, well rounded off. 42a is the negative complement of 41, now briefly formulated. Especially tight, however, is the construction of the four sentences, forming the chiasmus "strong × feeble – feeble × strong".
- 41 and 42 do not give a new breeding-method, which is different from the stock-breeding in 37-39. What they do say is that Jacob applies the breeding-method of vv. 37-39 selectively. Like every stock-breeder he aims at improving the breed, but he applies this improvement in such a way that it is successful only with the animals assigned to him, so that Laban the deceiver is himself deceived with feeble animals.

[38] The root *'qd* means "bind, fetter"; hence KBL2 "with twisted tails". But this context excludes anything but a special colour. Therefore, I, with Ges.-Buhl, prefer: "striped" (meaning, provided with "bands").

– the narrator is not an expert in stock-breeding, obliged to use scientifically correct definitions. In this story it is not difficult to point to such inaccuracies, subtle shifts of terms as in the following:

1. In v. 32 it seems at first as if *kol sę nāqōd wᵉṭālū* (every speckled and spotted head) refers to goats, but it is meant inclusively for all "abnormally" coloured flock, as appears from what follows. Jacob corrects himself after the *waw explicativum*, and also makes a sudden mental leap, as follows: "remove every speckled and spotted head, I mean every dark head among the sheep and the speckled and spotted ones among the goats. [If, later on, any such "abnormal" animals should be brought forth] then those will be my wages."

2. In v. 35 the narrator has no need of a painfully exact symmetry between "he-goats" and "she-goats"; after *'qd* and *ṭlw'* we have not *'qd wṭlw'* again but *nqd* and *ṭlw'*.

3. *'āqod* in 40b is short for *'qd*, *nqd* and *ṭlw'*.

4. An especially subtle shift is the following: in 40b "Laban's flock" comprises "all the flock with which Jacob has been sent out into the steppe and which belongs to Laban. (This equates with 36b "the rest of Laban's flock"). But in 40d "Laban's flock" means exclusively and strictly speaking "the normally coloured animals which (after subtraction of Jacob's wages) will remain Laban's."

However, this list of inaccuracies, is in my opinion, not an obstacle to the patient and kindly disposed reader. The variation is easy to account for: otherwise the narrator would have had to repeat a great many adjectives, which would have produced a tiring and deadly monotony.

Now we approach the three problems: the transition from 39 to 40, plus 40a and 40b. In 37 and 38 we see Jacob busily engaged in a rather hard job. What is he doing? What does he expect from peeling branches? How will he ever come by the wages agreed upon? Such questions are raised within us. In suspense we wait, all through vv. 37 and 38, for an unpredictable outcome. Then, in 39b, the great surprise follows. 39b is the only verse in this story that exactly describes the results Jacob hopes for. It is the climax to which the preceding five sentences have led. After it, v. 41f., the narrator can afford to tell us that this method is only applied with a certain kind of animals, a refinement which can wait. The crown of the work, v. 39b, is stylistically well-marked, because this is the only place in which the set of three adjectives *'ᵃquddīm – nᵉquddīm – ṭᵉlū'īm* appears.

The first problem is that this set of three only describes goats, whereas in the preceding passage the collective noun "flock" was used; so perhaps sheep are included. Or are they not? Should we, from sheer fright, understand the four occurrences of ṣōn in 38f. exclusively as "goats"?

Certainly not. It would be a forced reading and is unnecessary. Such a rigid consistency is not in the narrator's line, as we have just seen from the terminological shifts. There are no signs that "flock" in v. 38 and 39 should suddenly be used in the narrow sense of "goats". It is quite natural to assume that the peeling and putting down of branches is meant for all the animals. 39b only mentions adjectives which, properly speaking, go only with goats, for the sake of euphony and this is appropriate to this crown of the work. The effect would have been completely lost if the narrator had added the monosyllable *ḥūm* to the series; as an apostrophizing singular it does not fit in with the rhyming and abundantly assonant plurals. (For another explanation, a strictly literary one, see below p. 127.)

In 40a the narrator corrects himself, more or less as in 32. It was not his intention to exclude the sheep in 39b, but the adjectives might give rise to misunderstanding. Therefore the story proceeds with "sheep" in 40a, as an addition. Now there are only concluding sentences to be spoken in broad, somewhat vague words.

The verb *hifrīd* in 40a is also unclear in its meaning, *crux* number two, and is usually translated by "Jacob put the sheep apart", or, even less accurately, "... the rams apart". But *prd* always means: "to quit company, to part" of parts from a whole. A fine example: the brothers in Gen. 25.23 (*prd* in the *niphal*). It does not mean the separating (oneself) from a certain unity which was and remains a whole. Accordingly, the *hiphil* always means "to make ... part, to divide, to sort out"; it is unwarranted to use, as Ges.-Buhl and KBL2 do, another sense for Gen. 30.40 only (evidence of the hiph.: Deut. 32.8, II Kings 2.11, Ruth 1.17, Prov. 16.28, 17.9, 18.18).

Therefore the correct translation of 40a is: "the sheep, too, Jacob always sorted out [in this way, in normally and abnormally coloured specimens]". The inversion of object and predicate emphasizes the specifying change of object in respect to v. 39.

Problem number three is the only real crux. What do the multivocal words "give" and "face" mean in v. 40b? In any case, v. 40b does not mean: "he turned the faces of the flock to the striped and all the dark among Laban's flock" (as for example the Bible de Jérusalem still reads). In the first place this interpretation (which has the breeding animals affect their unborn young by what they see, according to the old wives' tale "pregnant woman who sees a hare is going to have a baby with a hare-lip") is not at all viable for shepherds standing in the midst of restless rutting flocks, as Ehrlich (Randglossen I ad loc.) and Eerdmans have already seen.[39] An even greater difficulty is that 40b, in itself, would describe a second, a different breeding method, of which we do hear no more (41f. is about breeding-as-in-vv. 37-39). There is no room for it in this story. The two sentences after 40b are devoted to summarizing results (40c, d), as is the preceding sentence (40a).

Two interpretations remain. The one by Ehrlich is as follows: "und fügte die besten Schafe in den Herden Labens zu den gestreiften und ganz schwarzen Stücken hinzu (...). Wie Jakob das anstellt, dass nur die besten Schafe gestreift oder ganz schwarz geboren wurden, erklärt der Verfasser V. 41 und 42 ausführlich." This translation is certainly worth considering, but there is a serious stylistic objection to the sentence quoted last from Ehrlich. In his view 40b anticipates 41f. But this anticipatory sentence would, then, be premature and isolated, and would thus reveal, only partially and obscurely, the great battle against Laban of 41f. It is a most improbable interpretation as well, because the

[39] Ehrlich, op. cit., p. 151f. On p. 152: *p^e^nē haṣṣōn* = der Ausbund, d.i. die allerbesten, der Schafe.
D. Eerdmans, Alttestamentliche Studien, I. Die Komposition der Genesis (Giessen, 1908), p. 54.

surrounding sentences 40a and c+d are leading towards a conclusion, so that 40b would be an obstacle between them.

The remaining view is preferable, although it is not really certain and for lack of complete information its exact value is not ascertainable. This view can be found in B. Jacob,[40] among others, and in Buber's translation (whose translation of 40a, by the way, is traditional, thus faulty): "er gab zum Vortrab der Tierherde das Gestreifte und alles Braune unter Labans Tieren." This sentence, wayyitten pᵉnē haṣṣōn 'el 'āqod wᵉkol ḥūm bᵉṣōn lābān, presupposes that a) Jacob has already *'āqod*-goats at his disposal, which fits in with v. 39, and b) that he also has the disposal of *ḥūm*-sheep, which is confirmed by our interpretation that 40a has been added to 39b in order to remove misunderstandings. But as this sentence starts from the presupposition that the results desired have been achieved already, the sentence itself is likely to be as much comprising, summarizing as 40c and d (though in a different direction). Therefore I read 39 and 40 as follows, modifying Buber somewhat and explicating the train of thought of the text between brackets:

"... then the flock brought forth striped, speckled and spotted young ones [which Jacob could put apart for himself, separating them from the "normal" goats]. In the same way Jacob separated the sheep [into normal ones for Laban and black/brown ones for himself]. [Now that goats and sheep have been discussed separately, they will be discussed explicitly side by side for the last time, as in vv. 32-35:] He gave the best position among the flock to the striped [goats obtained in this way] and everything black/brown [of the sheep] among Laban's flock. In this way he put [40c and d explain 40b!] flocks apart for himself, which he did not put with Laban's flock."

The only thing for which there is no evidence is the translation of *pānīm*, though there are places in the O.T., where it means "front, position in (the) front"; and how we must picture 40b to ourselves, concretely, remains obscure.

A philological preliminary? Yet an occasional glance at the style and the composition was indispensable! "In Gen. 30:34ff ist eine Fülle von Ausdrücken, die auch zur Quellenscheidung Anlass geben könnten. Sollten diese aber bei der schwerfälligen Schilderung nicht eher stilistischen Erscheinungen sein?" This question of Eising's (p. 202) I answer with a whole-hearted yes on the ground of this excursus, but especially because of the analysis given below.

In story 6 (Gen. 29.15-30) we came across the first wage-dispute. Laban and Jacob spoke six times in all,[41] and Laban took advantage of Jacob.

In this story we find the second wage-dispute. Again the "dialogue", in so far as suspicious people are capable of that, proceeds in three rounds; alternately uncle and nephew speak six times.[41] But now the

[40] B. Jacob translates: "... und setzte die Führer der Tiere zu ...".

[41] In Gen. 29: Laban (v. 15) – Jacob (18) – Laban (19);
Jacob (21) – Jacob (25) – Laban (26).
In Gen. 30: Jacob (25f.) – Laban (27f) – Jacob (29f) – Laban (31) –
Jacob (31-33) – Laban (34).

tables have been turned! Jacob takes advantage of Laban – forewarned is forearmed.

In ch. 29 Laban was the helmsman of the conversation, coming directly to the crucial point, i.e., assuring himself of Jacob's service for fourteen years. Now the positions are reversed. Jacob takes the initiative, leading the transactions to the stage at which he can make a well-considered proposal, one convenient to him. And when Laban accepts the terms we see him manage these affairs with the same steady hand and the same inner certainty of purpose (= v. 43).

Laban sets (v. 36) a great distance between himself, with his "abnormally" coloured cattle, and Jacob, so that not one speckled goat may wander, gratis, to Jacob's property. But precisely this distance is an indispensable condition for his defeat, for Jacob wants very much to devote himself to his very special stock-breeding, without being disturbed...

Jacob's actions, from v. 37 onward, betray a steady hand. The story conveys a strong impression of certainty and firmness of purpose, but at the same time it does not yet reveal the source of this certitude. Matter-of-fact-ly it reports the amazing actions of vv. 37-39 (and 41f.), confining itself strictly to facts. But this is exactly why the narrative raises with us, its audience, the burning question as to the source of Jacob's steadfastness: How is it that he goes his own way so certainly? Certainly, it has everything to do with Jacob's enormous cunning; he has lost none of his buoyancy yet. And we surmise that his great success (*m^{e}'od m^{e}'od*) has been made possible by the blessing; that the promise made at Bethel has found its first provisional realization here is confirmed by the key-word *pāraṣ* of v. 30 which appears again in v. 43.

Whether or not our surmise is correct this story will not divulge to us. But it cloaks a secret from which we can learn the source of the invincible power of Jacob's stratagem. With a striking and ironical pun the narrator discloses to us the secret of Jacob's success. His breeding-method makes us think of magic, for a while, but the real magic is revealed by a pun simple in itself.

To borrow the pun, Jacob is not guilty of black magic but uses *white* magic, His uncle is called "*lābān*" – which is Hebrew for white. In verse 35 the story begins to manipulate this word. As quickly as possible, in three words, the sheep are dispatched, whereas thirteen words are spent on the goats. The first seven or eight words specify he-goats and she-goats, of the "abnormally" coloured kind, and then there is a remarkable summary, *kol 'ašer lābān bō*, "in short, everything that shows *white* on it". Laban, this first part of the pun says, takes all those animals that answer best to his nature; the "White Man" takes the white animals – that is simple logic.

The pun is prolonged in v. 37. Jacob takes the branches of the *libnę̄* (a kind of poplar), so according to its name "Whitey", and of the *lūz* (a very heathen tree? – perhaps this is an allusion to Luz in Gen. 28, who knows?) and he peels them in such a way that there are white stripes on them (*p^eṣālōt l^ebānōt*). An emphatic adjunct to his action follows in v. 37b: *maḥsōf hallābān*, "exposure of the white on the branches". Having been bred with such white the goats bring forth young with white on them, "*'ašer lābān bō*", and in this way we may repeat the words of v. 35.

This is the technical, literary explanation of the fact that the explicit terms of v. 39b can only refer to the goats and that the sheep in v. 40a are a loose end, and are mentioned perfunctorily and then quickly forgotten. The objective, extra-literary problem for this story is that the colours that are most or least common with the sheep are exactly the opposite of those with the goats; in other words they are not useful in a text which wants to exploit the white against Laban. As a result of this problem the narrator drives the sheep out of our visual field as much as he can, we notice. It strikes us that not only in 40a but also in 35 the sheep are dispatched as quickly as possible and that in v. 32 it is the "goat-words" *kol sę̄ nāqod w^eṭālū* that begin the verse as a summary. He who tries to deal congenially with this unruly text in this way has no need of the theory that the story is no more than a patchwork review of several breeding-methods.

So what has Jacob done? He fights Laban with Laban, and the goats with *lābān* on them are rightfully his. Just as an expert *judoka* can defeat his adversary without too much effort by "taking him over" when he exerts force on him, Jacob takes over Laban; Jacob causes white to appear on the branches of "the Whitey", the branches pass the white on to the young of the flock, and Jacob becomes very rich. Thus Jacob fights Laban with his own weapons and defeats him.

Jacob exploits his perception of his uncle's nature which has been revealed by his name, in exactly the same way as in Gen. 25. Here everything we see is white, there it was red. There Jacob lifted his adversary, the *'admōnī*, from his archimedean position with the help of *'ādom*, and so Esau became the ancestor of Edom.

To this technique of "taking over" Laban has no retort; once thrown off his balance he is easily floored. It is the final stage in this story:

Gen. 27 Jacob is a deceiver
Gen. 29 Laban is a deceiver of a deceiver
Gen. 30 Jacob is a deceiver of a deceiver of a deceiver

What this repeating "fraction" shows is: whenever people like Jacob and Laban mix with each other, there is no end to it. How is this to go on? Will the two take to an escalation of deceit, will they continue *ad infinitum*? What a prospect!

§ 9 Scene 9: *Jacob's speech to his wives and their flight,* Gen. 31.1-21.

The construction of this scene is easy to grasp:
- introduction vv. 1-3
- Jacob's speech to his wives vv. 4-13
- their answer vv. 14-16
- flight vv. 17-21

Introduction. The beginnings of v. 1 and v. 2 run parallel:

v. 1 wayyišmaʿ 'et dibrē bᵉnē Lābān
v. 2 wayyar 'et pᵉnē Lābān

This makes their difference even more distinct. Laban's sons fret at Jacob's wealth, and Jacob hears them, indirectly, as yet, in verse 1. But then, v. 2, Jacob notices very directly that thunder-clouds are gathering. His own eyes tell him that the game with Laban is now over. Laban is no longer *kitmōl šilšōm* towards him.

These two words are the slender central pillar of a bridge stretching from 30.36 to 31.22. The distance of three days' journey (*šᵉlōšet yāmīm*) was the scene behind which Jacob could practise his white magic, and this distance, as the subtle punning on the root of "three"[42] tells us, has now also become a distance in time, which makes the alienation complete. The development of total estrangement is irreversible.

The ending of the preceding story – Jacob's acquisition of wealth –

[42] And in a sense even on "day": the adverb of time *šlšm* is derived from *šlš* + *yōm*; perhaps it is a calque of the akkadian "*ina šalši ūmi*" (already old-babylonian: *šalšūmi*), or perhaps even a loan-word. See BL, p. 504k and Joüon, § 102b.

at once provides the fuel for the conflict of Gen. 31. Laban is not going to readily accept the fact, that for seasons on end succeeding generations of flocks "go over", as it were, to Jacob. Disaster is threatening Jacob, which is not to be stemmed by human ingenuity. Then God intervenes; in the relation Jacob – Laban it is the first time we hear of his intervention. The darkest hour is before the dawn.

God sends out a warning, and by his words he immediately shows Jacob (and the narrator shows us) that he wants to keep the promise given at Bethel. "Return to the land of your fathers" links closely with the promise in Gen. 28.15, "I will bring you back to this land" and with the vow in 28:21, "if I come again to the house of my father". Yahweh assures Jacob shortly and warmly, "I will be with you" just as at Bethel (28.15).

The two powers around Jacob have been placed with that one preposition, but how far apart! Laban is by no means "with him" (31.2), but fortunately Yahweh is then "with him" (v. 3).

Jacob's speech. We have come to the moment of rhetorical fireworks, for the first time in Gen. 25-35. Jacob summons his wives and gives a view of the past six years that seems to be at great variance with what the narrator has told us in Gen. 30. Therefore, it is an important task for the interpreter to determine the relation between 30.34/6-43 and 31.7-12 and to find out if these texts are compatible. We shall first follow the text closely.

In v. 5 Jacob starts by entering into the current situation. Of the two experiences narrated in v. 1 and 2 he chooses to relate the most immediate (v. 5a). At once he brings his ally into the picture: God is with him; in this way 5b has resumed the heart of v. 3, the warm final word. Thus the speech turns out to relate well with the introduction to this story.

There is one difference between v. 2 and 5a which demands fuller explanation. Jacob saw that Laban was *'ēnennū 'immō* and now he says, using a different preposition, *'ēnennū 'elay*. In my opinion this is not just a variant, but, on the contrary, something that reveals the change in Jacob's situation. Once Jacob has discovered that the one party Laban is not "with him" any longer, the other party, God, assures him: "but now I am with you!" Instead of the warm *'im* Jacob chooses in v. 5 the neutral *'elay* "towards me" with respect to Laban, as a contrast to what follows presently, "but the God of my father is (thank God, genuinely) with me." Characteristic of Laban is that he wants *l*^{e}*hāra‘ ‘immādī* (v. 7 ending), that he wants "to harm me".

In v. 6 Jacob pleads for his cause, pointing with cogency to his loyal work for his uncle. The same terms he used to Laban in Gen. 30.26//29, he now uses to his wives. In v. 6 he defends his own part, in v. 7 he takes the offensive: Laban has deceived me. We notice that Jacob does not use the word *mirmā/rimmā* (verb) anymore (as in 29.25), a word which has worked like a boomerang, but that he chooses another word.. The chiasmus of the dénouement shows how much Laban acts contrary to what his faithful servant had a right to expect; in place of fair wages maltreatment:

with all my strength
I served ⟶ **your father**
your father ⟶ **has cheated me and changed..**

The charge against Laban is that he has changed the wages (*mskrt*) ten times. Again we see the two great key-words *service* and *wages* (*‘bd* and *skr*) in each other's company as characteristic of Jacob's stay at Haran, and again, they occur after the first (29.15-30) and the second wage-disputes (30.25-34). With that this story aligns itself with the previous scenes.

Laban has cheated. Here it is confirmed that Laban was noncommittal in his "approval" of 30.34. From v. 8 we now understand what Laban intended to do when, more than five years previously, he soon observed that with Jacob, the blessed one, the flock brought forth many young animals which by virtue of their "abnormal" colour were his, Jacob's, wages. Laban took refuge in shifting, or twisting, "No, Jacob, we had agreed that the speckled animals should be yours" and a season later, "but, Jacob, you must be mistaken! I said the striped animals..."

Laban turned, "fate" turned too! The strict parallel in v. 8 where a and b, but for one consonant, are equal owing to the careful choice of the adjectives *‘qd* and *nqd*, has, stylistically, much to offer:

" 'im kō yōmar: n^{e}quddīm yihyẹ s^{e}kārekā w^{e}yāl^{e}dū kol haṣṣōn n^{e}quddīm"
"w^{e}'im kō yōmar: ‘^{a}quddīm yihyẹ s^{e}kārekā w^{e}yāl^{e}dū kol haṣṣōn ‘^{a}quddīm".

The irony of this verse must be painful to Laban. No matter how he changes his arrangements,[43] the flock changes too, accurately and completely – frustrating enough to make someone gnash his teeth in rage. But we listen, too, with the wives: this verse describes a miracle and at this moment they surmise that perhaps it must have something to do with the blessing given to Jacob, but – in spite of that surmise – the mirroring reactions of nature remain amazing. What is the mysterious power to which the animals are so unconditionally obedient?

Before telling his audience more Jacob finishes with his uncle in one stroke: "thus God has taken away the flock of your father and given them to me", and without much ado and with the forceful *nāṣal* "snatch away" he points to the real agent: God. With that v. 9 has, temporarily and briefly, identified the mysterious helmsman of nature in v. 8.

Let us take one more glance at v. 7f. In 7 Laban's trickery is contrasted with God's protection. These two "factors" are also found in v. 8, Laban's trickery explicitly so, God's protection implicitly. Here the real agent of the "white magic" stays behind the scenes. The function of v. 8 is to offer two concrete examples illustrating v. 7.

V. 9 concludes the first half of Jacob's speech. The entire passage is dominated by the "influences", which affect Jacob so much that he himself, although mentioned in vv. 1-3, is absent there as an agent and is entirely absent in vv. 7-12. The structure, which fits the introduction exactly, shows this:

v. 1f. Laban angry ⟶ (J) ⟵ v. 3 God: *'immāk*

5a Laban angry ⟶ (J) ⟵ 5b God *'immādī*

(v. 6 you – I – your father)

7a Laban cheats ⟶ (J) ⟵ 7b God protects; *'immādī*

two examples illustrate this:

8a Laban turns ⟶ (J) ⟵ 8a "Fate" turns, too

8b Laban turns ⟶ (J) ⟵ 8b "Fate" turns, too

explanation:

v. 9 your father's stock God has taken

and given it to me

[43] The imperfects *yōmar* + perfect tenses *yālᵉdū* taken in iterative sense.

The diagram shows two blocks: Jacob is the issue of a conflict between two parties. God wins. "Therefore" Laban does not occur in the rest of the passage. The speech is extended from a threatening beginning (Laban wants to harm me, v. 5) to a relieved ending (God delivers, v. 9 and 13b).

The second half of the speech no longer describes a duel, but a dialogue, which ensues between Jacob and God, now that Laban has beeen discarded. This second half, too, goes from one to the other quite regularly:

v. 10 Jacob's dream
v. 11 God speaks
v. 12 Jacob's dream interpreted
v. 13 God reveals himself, and orders Jacob to return.

In his speech Jacob has gone *ad fontes*. Piercing through the phenomenon (Laban's face, v. 5) and the events (Laban's deceit, the young of the flock) he takes his wives to the source: a dream of divine origin. So we see Jacob, chronologically, reverse his steps in his speech. Starting from the present (v. 5) he digs through the phase of six years of work (vv. 6-9) and ends up with the revelation-in-dream-form at the beginning of that period (vv. 10-13).

In this speech by Jacob, too, the narrator confines himself to mentioning the goats, with descriptive adjectives (vv. 10//12). Naturally so, for this sample of rhetoric would suffer serious loss of tempo, and so of persuasive power, if he, conscientiously but monotonously, had mentioned the sheep and their attributes, too. We have already seen how, in Gen. 30, he de-emphasized them because of the extra-literary problem of their reverse colour. This confirms our interpretation of the reason the sheep are mentioned less frequently in Gen. 30: in 31.10, 12 the goats are entirely *pars pro toto* (= *ṣōn*, v. 10//12). Here, too, this handling promotes the euphony: again there is a perfect set of three, *ʿaquddīm, nequddīm uberuddīm*, variating slightly on 30.29 and the assonant *ʿattudīm* seems to have been chosen in order to anticipate this.

Vv. 10-12: Jacob has a) a dream, b) in which he sees things and c) meets a "messenger from God", an angel. These three elements make us think of Gen. 28, and yes, as at Bethel, this dream brings a revelation. Jacob sees that the he-goats have acquired the colour that the animals assigned to him were to have. He understands that the he-goats will transmit this desired colour to their progeny when they breed, and he wonders: does this mean that I am to be rich? Then a messenger from God, so an authoritative interpreter, appears and he uses the same words as Jacob did in his description, v. 10. This means: you were right, Jacob; yes, you will be rich and Laban's cheating will be of no avail to him. God's last sentence, v. 12b, contains the words of deliverance, which are often used when people are in distress or are suppressed, and which indicate God's mercy, as in Gen. 16.13f; Ex. 2.25, 3.7, 9, 16 (where, again, "Israel", this time the people, is in a house of bondage); Gen. 29.32, 31.42.

The similarities between this event and the revelation at Bethel turn out to be not accidental. God himself reveals himself to be the God who at Bethel promised Jacob support on his way going and on his return, v. 13. In the dream it must certainly have come at the beginning, just as in Gen. 28.13: the beginning is the place for the formula of *Selbstvorstellung.* But in this speech Jacob puts the revelation at the back in order to attain a powerful, convincing ending. The power lies especially in this, that the speech is concluded by a cogent order: arise, go forth ... return! In this way Jacob exerts great influence, pressure on his wives. By quoting God's order the narrator/Jacob enframes the speech. V. 13b refers to 5b and especially to v. 3b.

It is the first time, since Bethel, that Jacob has been in distress, but God is at his side at once. The connection with the scene at Bethel has been carefully made: the heart of the matter in Gen. 28 was conveyed twice by the words "be with you", (*hāyā*) *ʿim*, spoken once by God and once by Jacob. Exactly twice is it used in Gen. 31, again once by God (v. 3b) and repeated by Jacob (v. 5b). Exactly twice Gen. 28 mentioned the ultimate purpose, "return" (*wahᵃšibōtīkā* ... *wᵉšabtī*), exactly twice is the verb found, too, in Gen. 31, "return" (v. 3) and "return" (v. 13).

Then, of course, there is the explicit reference in 31.13a. The narrator has Jacob say and in the story Jacob has God say:

"... Bethel, (a) where you anointed a pillar,
(b) where you made a vow to me."

A reference like this is an exegesis in itself. The exegesis of Gen. 28.10-22, here contained in 31.13, has been given by 1) God, 2) Jacob and 3) the narrator. God's words are heard in the review of Jacob's speech and we owe this to the narrator. The explanation, we find, brings out the heart of the Bethel-scene: a) the hard, actual core, the vision seen (ladder *muṣṣāb,* God *niṣṣāb*), now immortalized in a hallowed, anointed *maṣṣebā*, b) the vow which determines Jacob's life, he is to be a "Yahwist".

It is remarkable that God (no, Jacob; no, the narrator) should summarize the event at Bethel in the sentences (a) and (b) on the basis of the mirroring half 28.16ff.; in other words God does not say, on the basis of the first half: "... Bethel, where I was *niṣṣāb* with you, and where I made a promise to you." God tackles him on his actions (mirroring, grateful, full of awe) and points out Jacob's responsibility to him by quoting Jacob's part. "If you want to keep your vow, you, Jacob, must now proceed to action."

The forceful appeal God makes to Jacob is, in Jacob's speech, his forceful appeal to his wives, three short, snappy imperatives, *qūm*... *ṣē* ... *šūb*, urging them to show their colours.

Are we surprised that his wives support him completely? Jacob has been very convincing. He has effaced his role in the event; God is behind him, inspires him and has already defeated Laban.

The words of Laban's daughters resemble those of Laban's sons very closely, but they mean the opposite, as appears in comparing them with Jacob's summary of the event:

sons, lāqaḥ Yaʿ^{a}qob	'et kol ^{a}šer l^{e}'ābīnū
v. 1 ume'^{a}šer l^{e}'ābīnū	ʿāsā 'et kol hakkābod hazzę̄
daughters, (a) kī kol haʿošer	(b) ^{a}šer hiṣṣīl '^{e}lōhīm me'ābīnū
v. 16	(c) *lānū hū*
cf. Jacob, (a) wayyaṣṣel '^{e}lōhīm	(b) 'et miqnē '^{a}bīkem
v. 9	(c) wayyitten *lī*

The sons think, Jacob has pinched everything; no, Jacob says, God himself has taken it away from Laban and given it to me. That is true, the daughters say, God himself has taken it away from Laban, it belongs to *us* by right. Rachel and Leah are entirely in agreement with Jacob's version, that God is the main agent of his wealth. They feel very aggrieved themselves because they have never received a dowry or wedding-presents (15b), they also consider Laban an exploiter and feel disowned (15a). They in turn incite Jacob with an imperative.

Now that this dialogue has been concluded, we look at the story once more, retrospectively, in order to assess its relation to Gen. 30. Ultimately it is a question which can only be solved adequately by understanding the scope of the two texts, but right now it is possible for the two texts to be brought into line with each other, on the level of information only. The reconstruction of the facts is not, in my opinion, extremely difficult and is as follows:

1. When the last period of six years begins, Jacob and Laban agree that Jacob, beginning with normally coloured animals, shall have all "abnormal" animals, i.e., black/brown sheep and "everything that shows white" among the goats.

2. With his great experience and clever breeding-methods, with his "white magic", Jacob sees to it that with the strong animals all the young that are born have "white on them" (30.39).

3) The white colour is manifested in three or four ways on the goats: by stripes, spots and speckles.

4. Laban, not having committed himself, is going to take advantage of this, for in the course of the six years he sees the young of the strong animals "going over" to Jacob's property, because of their "abnormal" colour. Driven into a corner, he starts temporizing and twisting in a subtle way. He continually asserts that the agreement was different, and he chooses a different variant of "*lābān bō*". Verse 31.8 illustrates this well.

5. Jacob's cleverness is of no avail to him. Laban manages to circumvent the earlier agreement. But this in turn does not avail Laban either. A third figure interferes, Providence, adapting itself exactly to Laban's new agreements (31.8). Surprisingly enough, Jacob's profits remain as large as they were earlier (v. 30.39).

This reconstruction is confirmed and made possible by the very different scopes of Gen. 30.36-43 and 31.5-13. Gen. 30.36-43 assumes a special position in the whole of the Story of Jacob: it is the only story in which not a word is spoken, neither by Jacob, nor by anyone else. From a to z it is a report by the narrator, concerned only with Jacob's unchecked acquisition of his wealth.[44] It proceeds along the single line of Jacob's actions so that we (primarily the narrator's audience, thus Israelites, thus descendants of Jacob!) can fully enjoy the deceit and defeat of the deceiver of our patriarch. The impression, hereby created, that Jacob, from a to z the agent, now becomes conqueror under his own steam or by his own ingenuity, is now demolished by a

[44] Eising, p. 197, on Gen. 30.25ff: "Wie auch sonst, zeigt uns hier der letzte Vers des Stückes die Tendenz des Ganzen. Er spricht vom Besitz, den Jakob sich zu verschaffen wusste. In der Tatsache des Besitzes liegt also das eigentliche Ziel des Erzählungsabschnittes."

highly authoritative witness, ... Jacob himself. In the second text (now, truly, from a to z the words of Jacob's) Jacob himself has eliminated himself completely as an agent. Jacob testifies that the six years had not passed without problems, but that, on the contrary, he had had to contend with Laban's full-fledged opposition which mere human cunning could not have countered. Into this Jacob weaves a grateful testimony to God in his providence, the sole agent, the creator of all his wealth, and pictures himself as innocent observer, full of surprise (v. 10//12). Jacob's words are a speech to his wives meant to convince and rally support for his plan of escape.[45] This is also why he denies his role as agent and presents himself as the one deceived and manipulated by Laban and protected and blessed by God.

The set of three in 30.39 and 31.10, 12 sums up the colour variants as alternative possibilities, the distinction of which does not become important until Laban starts switching his arrangement from one variant to another. In Gen. 30 this endless shifting is not important to the narrator: at one stroke (37-40a and 41f) he wants to go through the six years[46] as a "horizontal" event. He can afford this because in Gen. 31 he can make Jacob himself show the reverse side of the medal perfectly. There, too, is the right place to tell us that by Laban's evasions the colour variants become relevant, and that Jacob can follow all of Laban's evasions only because he is guided and initiated by Providence. The "vertical" event is decisive.

The scope of Jacob's speech is the precise complement of the scope of the report in Gen. 30. That is why the two texts are corresponding descriptions of the outside and the kernel of one and the same event.

Now the moment has come to, expressly and for the second time, pose the question of the moral responsibility. The balance-sheet of

[45] Ibid., p. 205: "Seine Rede ist ein Meisterstück an Eindringlichkeit und Zartgefühl. Jakob kehrt stark das Moment der Gotteshilfe hervor, die ihm zuteil wurde, indem er sie sowohl als Mittel zur Rechtfertigung wie auch als Anlass zur Abreise erwähnt, ohne Laban durch seine Darlegungen ausdrücklich blosszustellen. So ist Jakobs Rede nach der Meinung des Verfassers unwiderstehlich." P. 209: "Eine Rede braucht das Geschehen nicht nur berichtend und ohne Tendenz darzustellen. (...) man muss die Verse 10-12 als Redeteile in Redeabsicht auffassen."

[46] Ibid., p. 199: "Um Jakobs Klugheit darzustellen, genügte es, einmal von seinem Mittel zu erzählen. Davon abgesehen, hätte unser Erzähler auch eine Zehnzahl ähnlicher Handlungen nicht gestalten können. Eine solche Darstellung würde ohne jede literarische Wirkung geblieben sein."

a twenty years' stay at Haran can be drawn up, for Jacob's flight does not bring anything that is really new (not even a theft of *terafim* by his party, though Laban thinks it does!).

Regarding the first fourteen years Jacob obviously has nothing to reproach himself with, while his uncle has all the more to feel guilty about. His uncle has put him under such compulsion that after seven years there was nothing for Jacob but to serve another seven years. And he has just done that, without fail, "with all his strength" (31.6) he has done his duty as a shepherd and he longs for recognition. In his repeated plea to Laban and his daughters, "you know how I have served you(r father)" (30.26, 29//31.6), he authentically asks for recognition. The reader who fails to see this as yet will find out later (31.36-42) when Jacob gives Laban a piece of his mind.

But where do the responsibilities lie for the last period of six years? Laban's riches have flown to Jacob and Laban feels cheated, as can easily be understood. But has he been cheated? We cannot dismiss the question lightly by saying simply "no" and by pointing out that Jacob has acquired his property within the bounds of legality. Formally speaking this is true, as it is true that Laban acted "properly" within the bounds of usage when he married off Leah to his nephew first. But morally speaking Laban was a deceiver, viz. because for seven years he consciously left Jacob under the impression that his reward for those seven years would be marriage to Rachel. Laban was ambiguous: his real intentions, to give Leah, were different from what he pretended. Similarly in Gen. 30.31f Jacob's real intention, to get rich by means of "white magic", is very different from what he makes Laban believe; he leads Laban to think that his wages will be low, according to the statistical fact that goats "with white on them" and dark sheep are uncommon. Therefore we may conclude, at least for the time being that Laban has been cheated.

But now the balance is tipped to the other side because Laban starts cheating again as soon as he sustains another loss: he starts tampering with the contract, more than once (his self-interest is so obviously at stake that we have little difficulty in understanding his motives; that is not the point). His ever-changing arrangement of Jacob's wages cannot be followed any longer, not even by the cleverest breeder, even if he is a "Ya'ᵃqob", thus an arrant cheat.

When, finally, Laban appears to be the victim, it is only because of the miraculous "correction" of the flock by Providence. And if we should like to regard Laban as one deceived (instead of, for example, as one punished) then one thing is certain: it is no longer Jacob who deceived him but God himself; Jacob was only the instrument, the executer, through which God made the blessing flow to the patriarch.

In short, by nature Jacob was a deceiver and Laban his victim. This relationship Laban tries to reverse every year, but in vain. Now it can be said of him, chickens come home to roost. God himself controlled his manipulations with the wage-agreements and eliminated Laban. God remains the only effective "factor" in the attack-counter-attack of the two sly men, which does not come to an end by itself and which can only end in force by Laban.

This interpretation stands or falls with the truth of the version Jacob gives to his wives. But as he persuades his wives out of his own self-interest, would we not be too generous to so readily believe the "Heeltaker"? Is his modesty, by which he eliminates himself as an agent from the event, not questionable? In short, who is Jacob, what image of Jacob is presented in this story?

It is possible to start from an image of Jacob formed *a priori*, assuming he will always be motivated by ulterior motives. On the basis of this opinion it is possible to understand Gen. 31 as a form of *pia fraus* which Jacob commits in order to throw dust in his wives' eyes. Such a skeptical interpretation has serious consequences. After all the entire story, including Jacob's speech in Gen. 31, derives from the author. He would have cast Jacob's speech in deceitful, quasi-pious tones, having him of his own accord place his last years with Laban in the perspective of God's promise at Bethel. But there is no evidence in the text for such an interpretation, and he who favours it is, like any other exegete, obliged to show the basis for it in the story; the burden of proof resting with him seems unbearable to me in this case.

A correct literary analysis is not interested in a preconceived portrait of Jacob, but wants to elicit the image of Jacob from the story itself, line by line.

Negatively seen, it seems a hazardous undertaking to me to assume that in Gen. 30 the narrator conveys a very partial message only to add a hypocritical complement in Gen. 31, without subsequent criticism. To me it seems untenable to suppose that Jacob would, of his own accord, make a connection with Bethel (which would conflict with 31.3!) and justify his action, i.e. deceit, by means of "white magic" by sheltering behind the authority of Providence.

However, seen from a more positive viewpoint, the wonder that has been presented with two concrete examples in 31.8 has been experienced by the wives themselves. Jacob is not making them believe surprising events that have not taken place; he points to things that are as perceptible to Rachel and Leah as to Laban. The only thing he reveals (to the wives and so to us) is that God had made him see them before in a vision, a fact which he, and thus by inference the narrator, apparently found ill-suited in terms of timing for revealing earlier. His speech is a thoroughly bona fide testimony of gratitude, an interpretation which, piercing through the outside (Gen. 30), lays open the heart of his history (Gen. 31).

In this speech the narrator presents a Jacob who is the pious and grateful interpreter of his own history and who, pointing away from himself, confesses that God is the only decisive factor in his life when he is in distress. On his journey to Haran Jacob had met this God at Bethel, and via massebe and vow he had articulated a correct religious attitude. Now God keeps the promise made there and again Jacob is the keen observer and genuine believer and grateful proclaimer of God's help; his interpretation is profound and authoritative. Frey's opinion that "*tām*" in 25.27 means "ein Gott hingegebener" is easy to defend with 28.10ff and 31.5-13. Where God enters Jacob's life, Jacob has a *sound* relationship to him.

The flight, 31.17-21

Jacob now clears out, on the authority of God. His wives are completely behind him. In their first sentence (v. 14) they had radically dissociated themselves from their father. In the form of a rhetorical question they perform an action which in the (real) world of seminomads and in the (literary, of the genre) world of the saga is most serious: they break with their family and their father. The rupture appears from the fact that they use a set formula which in other places we find as the expression of or a summons to rebellion and secession from lawful authority (e.g. the king's): II Sam. 20.1, I Kings 12.16.

In v. 18 there is, just for once, a hint of the narrator's own opinion that Jacob's riches are legitimate. In his turn he uses a formula that strikes one as being official: "all his cattle, all his live-stock which he had gained, the cattle in his possession which he had acquired in Paddan-Aram." They are turns of a chronicler's, such as appear in verses about important journeys in Genesis (and nowhere else in the O.T.) like 12.5, 36,6 and 46.6,[47] and (as regards *miqnē qinyānō*) of

[47] *R*ᵉ*kūš* only in 13.6, 14.11, 12, 16, 21 and 15.14.

deeds of sale, as Gen. 23.17f. This use of language indicates that this journey of Jacob's is as definite and important as Abraham's journey in 12.5 (which likewise derives from divine command!), and he takes all his rightful possessions with him.

Jacob "arises (v. 17, 21) and flies" (v. 21). The first period of his life he had concluded in the same way, the repetition of words draws attention to that. Then he went on the initiative of his mother (27.43: "listen to my advice, my son, arise and flee!" – *qūm ubᵉraḥ*). Now he concludes the second period of his life with a flight, too, again from an *'āḥ* (= h.l. "relative", 29.15). This time his flight is not the consequence of high-handed deceit but the consequence of God's own play with Laban and done on God's initiative ("*qūm* ... *ṣē*... *šūb*").

The decisive moment of the event is in v. 21, "he crossed the River" (sc. the Euphrates). With this he has left Haran behind him and is looking forward to reaching Yahweh's crown-land which begins in Gilead. Only there will he feel secure. "Cross the river", quite an undertaking as it is, encumbered by many young children and flocks with sucklings, is not only an outward event, but has an inner meaning as well. This appears from the four words, *qūm, pānīm, nāhār* and *'ābar*, which 31.21 has in common with the famous Jabbok-scene and which are all key-words there. Here they are used to explain that Jacob is crossing his Rubicon.

V. 19f. "Rachel stole Laban's *terafim*" and "Jacob stole Laban's heart", an intriguing repetition of the root, which implies again that Rachel is a true Jacoba, related by nature to Jacob. This is expressed in parallel thefts. Only after this word about Jacob do we hear that in his case it refers to the flight.

We are clear about Jacob's case; this "deceit" is nothing new in so far as the flight *eo ipso* rules out Laban's knowledge of it. But Rachel's theft is something new and serious. This action of hers has risky consequences: what Jacob is hoping for, viz., that Laban will resign himself to Jacob's flight, is now out of the question. Laban's *terafim*, i.e. his patron-gods, have disappeared with Jacob and of course Laban relates the two. The Israelite listener, conscious of the fact that he will never make any graven or cast image of his God (the second commandment, which is so characteristic of "Yahwism"), realizes that someone like Laban, who does possess graven images of gods, must be very much attached, indeed a slave to (the presence of) those images. Why has Rachel done this? We may assume that, as a compensation for Laban's exploitation of her (v. 15), she wants to seize her father's patron-gods, and that she hopes to derive prosperity and "blessing" from them.[48]

Jacob's departure takes place under the most unfavourable of auspices. He is suspected of a capital crime, for that is what stealing someone's penates amounts to (in 31.32a Jacob expresses the same opinion!).

§ 10 Scene 10: *the disputes between Laban and Jacob, and parting,* Gen. 31.22-32.1.

Scene 9 was composed around a speech. So is scene 10. These two stories are nicely linked, for scene 9 ended with a report of five verses on Jacob's flight and scene 10 continues the story, and tells us how Laban, informed of his flight, launches a pursuit.

The composition of scene 10 is as follows:

- vv. 22-25 pursuit by Laban
- vv. 26-35 *rīb* I and house-search
- vv. 36-43 *rīb* II
- vv. 44-54 making of a covenant
- 32.1 leave-takings

A. *Jacob overtaken*: *first confrontation*: vv. 22-35.

We are almost as surprised as Laban when, in v. 22, we hear of "the third day": Jacob has taken advantage of the distance between himself and Laban which Laban had thought to be necessary (30.36). At one blow Laban's advantage – not to suffer losses thanks to this separation – has turned into a great disadvantage.

Jacob's train, however, proceeds so slowly that after ten days Jacob is confronted with Laban's tents opposite his own. In a long series of words the tense atmosphere of threatening war is wafted to us. Jacob had "fled", now he has been "overtaken" in a "pursuit"; angrily and resolutely Laban's men pitch their tents. *Tāqa'*, used instead of

[48] Speiser, ad loc.: "According to the Nuzi documents, which have been found to reflect time and again the social customs of Haran (...), possession of the house gods could signify legal title to a given estate, particularly in cases out of the ordinary, involving daughters, sons-in-law, or adopted sons (see Anne E. Draffkorn, Journal of Biblical Literature 76, (1957) 219ff.)" Much more tentative, and rightly so, about possible borrowings of the O.T. from Nuzi: R. Frankena, the Semitic Background of Genesis xxix-xxxi, in OTS xvii (1972) pp. 54-57.

the normal word *nāṭā*,[49] sounds their aggressiveness. There are "women carried off as prisoners by the sword"; there are allusions to "do you harm" and someone is "afraid" of "being robbed" (v. 31)! We shake our heads, when we think of Gen. 24 and consider the peaceful, almost enthusiastic departure of Abraham's servant, who took Rebekah with him as a bride for Isaac, accompanied by the blessings of ... Laban and his people. What contrast to see Rebekah's son pursued and cornered by the same Laban!

The connection with Gen. 24 has been made explicitly, perhaps, but in any case it is revealing in the words of v. 24, where God warns Laban that he must not "say a word to Jacob, either good or bad". When Abraham's servant has shown by his story (24.34-49) how Providence had brought him into contact with Rebekah and when he expressed the wish to leave with her, Laban and his people reacted adequately with: "this comes from Yahweh! We cannot speak to you "bad or good"." This was a set phrase expressing the idea, it is not for us to judge of this, God has arranged this affair.[50] What Laban saw in Gen. 24 willingly and of his own accord, must now be impressed upon him threateningly by God. Jacob's marriage and departure, too, are irrevocable and God-pleasing. Laban should have seen, "this comes from Yahweh", and now he is ordered, "do not speak good or bad"! And because with the Hebrew *dbr* word and action blend into each other, it implies a prohibition to Laban "to treat Jacob in a harsh (inimical) way, to do things against him."[51]

[49] Nāṭā in connection with tents: explicit in Gen. 12.8 and 33.19, II Sam. 6.17, cf. Dan. 11.45 with *nāṭā*, and Jer. 43.10 (tent of state?); *nṭh* short for *nāṭā 'ohel*: Jer. 14.8. Implicit via the comparison "God stretches out the heavens like a tent", Job 9.8, *passim* in Deut.-Is., Jer. 10.12, 51.15; Zach. 12.1; *with* the point of contact "like a tent" Ps. 104.2 (cf. Is. 40.22). *Tq'*, however, only here and in Jer. 6,3, where it is used also out of "literary necessity", i.e., two fine connections with "Teqoa" and the blast on horns (= *tq'*)!

[50] "Good-and-bad" are often used as a merismus; the complements denote a totality, so that, for example, "the knowledge of good and bad" (Gen. 2f!) means "complete insight". This is easy to demonstrate by means of the parallel between vv. 17 and 20 in II Sam. 14: "the king is like the angel of God (*bis*), by hearing good and bad = by knowing everything in the country". See on this subject J. Hoftijzer, p. 441 note 3 of his article "David and the Tekoite Woman", VT 20 (1970) pp. 419-444.

[51] Quotation from J. Hoftijzer, Absalom and Tamar: a Case of Fratriarchy?, pp. 56-61 in "Schrift en Uitleg", (Festschrift W. H. Gispen), Kampen, 1970. See p. 55f.; he discusses Gen. 31 and 24 in connection with II Sam. 13.22. His explanation of 24.50, "we cannot do anything against you" seems a little

How far Jacob and Laban have diverged we notice from a detail of v. 24. In a cool and detached way it says that "Laban the Aramean" is being addressed. Laban has, as it were, become a stranger now that we have arrived in territory where the God of Israel is pre-eminently Lord. Thus Laban's slyness and his exploiter's practices have brought about the evolution from "Laban 'aḥī 'immō" (mentioned three times in 29:10), denoting a relative, one of whom clan-solidarity towards Jacob might be expected, to the stranger, Laban hā'arammī.

Jacob's testimony of God, 31.7, "God did not permit Laban to harm me", was true. God intervenes and reveals himself to Laban, again by means of a dream. God is truly behind Jacob. It is striking that v. 24 is repeated quite literally in v. 29. The narrator makes Laban himself (there is no authority more unimpeachable) tell Jacob about the warning he had had in a dream.[52] The narrator puts this sentence immediately next to the most hostile sentence of Laban's first dispute, next to the words, "do you harm", which in themselves call to mind 31.7, and with it repeats once more the "two-blocks-structure" which we discovered in Jacob's speech to his wives (above p. 154). This structural detail is of no small importance, for with it the narrator makes Laban himself admit that Jacob spoke the truth in describing himself as the object of Laban's opposition and God's protection. Laban himself – there is no authority more unimpeachable.

Psychologically Laban is now completely trapped. He wants to punish and have his rights (and have back the *terafim*!). He fumes with rage – but he may not fume: God has corked the bottle of his aggressiveness. The frustration of his state, the control he must exert to check his stymied emotions, has been expressed in vv. 26-30. This speech is a psychological portrait of thirteen sentences, in which rage and resignation, castigation and sweetness contend for mastery and eventually achieve an unstable equilibrium. Honest indignation here enframes the whole, v. 26 (first two words) and 30b. But as early as v. 26a it passes into feigned indignation, which is more like anger at having been taken in (26b, 27a). Laban continues with pure hypocrisy: he

too negative to me – there is a difference in tone between this text and Gen. 31 and II Sam. 13, perhaps expressed by the slightly different *miṭṭōb weʿad raʿ*, whereas other places have *ṭōb weʾ/ʾō raʿ*. Hence, probably, Buber's translation "reden vom Guten weg zum Bösen hin".

[52] A similar confirmation by means of a strict parallel, this time in reversed direction, in 31.10 (man) – 31.12 (God); here, too, it concerns a dream which has come from God.

would have loved to have given him a festive send-off with music, etc. (just as in Gen. 24), 27b. In v. 28a he mixes these sweet words with a reproach that would have been sincere from a genuine father, "I could not kiss Rachel and Leah farewell". Then, with a shake of his head, he comes to a denunciation ("you have done foolishly", v. 28b), which inclines towards anger: v. 29a is a threat which is undermined in the nick of time by a report (29b) on the Mighty One of Jacob, who calls things to a halt. Laban tries to resign himself to it and forces himself (30a) for the first and last time to "understanding"; he "tries to realize" Jacob's position...! Then he stops short[53] with the perplexed reproach: "why have you stolen my gods?" The accusation is genuine; that he is addressing the wrong person Laban cannot possibly know.

The inner contradiction of this speech can be indicated quite precisely on two points. It is demonstrated by the reversal of sounds in Laban's third and fourth sentences: ḥ-r-b becomes b-r-ḥ. First Jacob is accused of pursuing his own ends with the sword, and then he appears to be a fugitive! The combination is absurd!

This is proved simultaneously a second indication of the inner contradiction in Laban's position, one of which *ḥrb* is a part. Laban accuses Jacob of carrying away "my daughters" (not "your wives" of course!) as prisoners by the sword (they are *kišbūyōt ḥareb*). But if anyone, it was Laban himself who detained Leah and Rachel, as well as Jacob (29.25!), who kept them for another six years and made jealousy and hatred wreak their devastating effect upon their family-life. What Leah and Rachel think of this they have said unambiguously in 31.14-16; and in v. 31 Jacob returns the ball. In short, Laban commits what might be termed a Freudian Fehlleistung, accusing Jacob of that which he himself would love to, but is restricted from doing.

That which really worries Laban has been indicated in three instances by a key-word, *gnb*, which enframes the speech. First Laban mentions (26a, 27a) the "theft" (c.q. delusion), of which we were told in v. 20, but then he discovers a different theft, that of v. 19, which perplexes and shocks him most of all as seen in his last words of v. 30. This frame indicates the main point, that from beginning to end he is

[53] The emotional value of the transition from v. 30a to b is conveyed very well by Buber: "Nun denn, deinen Gang gehn musstest du wohl, weil du dich sehntest, sehntest nach dem Haus deines Vaters, – aber warum hast du meine Götter gestohlen?"

addressing a thief. Although his anger of 29a is checked by an order in 29b that "makes him see" Jacob's longing (29b), at this one point he does deal him a blow.

The word *gnb* is important because Jacob had used it himself in 30.33, in order to maintain his truthfulness and sincerity (*ṣ*^{e}*dāqā*) against it. In a final settlement theft would be the very last thing that Laban could impute to him; he had provided against that (30.33b). Therefore Laban now touches upon a tender cord in 31.26f, 31 which continues to vibrate for a long time. Presently Jacob will use *gnb* to defend his *ṣ*^{e}*dāqā* again (v. 39).

What strikes us is that Laban does not use "steal" in the same sense (viz. steal goats and sheep) as Jacob did at the time. This makes us realize that Laban is not making a final settlement at all, although we might expect this on the basis of Gen. 30. He says not a word about goats or sheep, avoiding mention of Jacob's work as a shepherd. That, too, is significant. Apparently he cannot reproach Jacob with his record of service. Otherwise he would certainly have done so, but Jacob has anticipated this by giving proper service. In other words, Laban's silence on Jacob's work as a shepherd confirms Jacob's version that he has legitimate possessions only; from 31.6-13 nothing can be detracted.

Just as Jacob used law-terms in the arrangement of 30.33 Laban has now expressed his words in legal form. He begins a *rīb*, as is said in Hebrew; modern scholarship accurately defines this, a *"vorgerichtliche Beschuldigungsrede"*. Hans Jochen Boecker[54] wrote a correct analysis in an excursus on this *rīb* and the next. In an accusation such questions as "what have you done", "why have you ... stolen" are rhetorical; they are the set phrase for a reproach or an accusation. V. 28b is to be regarded as the conclusion in the summation.

What follows this conclusion are important words (29b), the full sense of which has not yet been recognized, not even in Boecker's monograph. The following interpretation provides us with a better understanding: if the charge of theft can be proved and Jacob's guilt has been established, then this does not imply that there is an independent tribunal with servants of its own to execute the sentence. Laban will have to do it himself and that is what he means in v. 29a. What should now be discussed in a study of the *Redeformen des Rechts-*

[54] Boecker, Redeformen des Rechtslebens im AT, Neukirchen, 1964, (the excursus on Gen. 31:) pp. 41-45.

lebens, is this. The words "*yeš le'el yādī*" seem to be an idiomatic expression, which in the world of law has a set value. The places in the O.T. in which this idiom occurs all refer to the execution of legal power, annulment of an unlawful situation and the power to do this.[55] Therefore I favour this rendering of Gen. 31.29a, paraphrased as follows:

"it is in my power, and I am entitled to do you harm" (meaning, to punish, lawfully), or:
"I am qualified now ...", etc.

In his defence Jacob tries to exculpate himself by explaining his motives, v. 31, "*vorgerichtliche Beschwichtigung*". It is even more obvious that we are in the domain of law in v. 32a, for the sentence we find there fits perfectly into the casuistic laws of the O.T. Jacob agrees on a death-penalty, also mentions explicitly of whom the tribunal is comprised, under these circumstances "our relatives", and asks Laban for a legal debate, the legal correctness of which is supervised by the tribunal.

The accusation of vv. 26-28 does not recur; it has been satisfactorily answered in v. 31 by an explanation by Jacob of his behaviour. But the accusation of v. 30b remains. Jacob does not, however, avow to the deed – for he does not know of Rachel's part – but denies the charge and is prepared "die Sache in einem ordentlichen Prozess prüfen zu lassen. Deshalb verlässt er den Bereich der privaten Auseinandersetzung, wird zum Kläger und erhebt offiziell Anklage gegen Unbekannt, den Dieb des Gottes: V. 32."[56]

We know who the true thief is, and we are seized with terror as we see Jacob, in a fit of honest indignation, fix a death-penalty for the one found guilty. The fool, little does he know that he signs the death-sentence of his favourite wife!

[55] a) Deut. 28.32 b) Mic. 2.1 c) Prov. 3.27 d) Neh 5.5. In a) a punishment is described, the judgement by the highest legal authority, God himself; "you" have not any legal power anymore, to turn it back. Micah 2.1f. is the accusation of a GV and mentions all varieties of violations of the law, for they (v. 1b) think they can use their power for that without being punished. Prov. 3.27-31 describes cases of keeping from a person something that is (rightfully, but especially morally) his. Neh. 5 begins with complaints that are comparable with the beginning of Micah 2; the man with the greatest legal power intervenes, the governor Nehemiah himself. For origin and meaning of the word *'el* see Frankena, OTS 17 (1972) p. 60f.

[56] Boecker in the excursus on Gen. 31.

Thus with v. 32 the first level of suspense, heretofore unequaled in most of the preceding stories, has been reached. A story essentially dependent on mere suspense we had found only in Gen. 27. It even strikes us that its counterpart, 29.15ff., consciously refrains from creating suspense.[57]

The narrator is master of his trade. Quickly he has increased the tension with the statement, "Jacob did not know that Rachel had stolen them" nor does he let the suspense fade away. On the contrary, he adeptly lets it grow, by gaining time and delaying the solution as long as he can. With v. 33a he carries suspense to extremes: first he has Laban examine all those tents in which we know the terafim will not be found, so that subsequently the fatal discovery seems inevitable. Trying our nerves the narrator says threateningly, "then he entered Rachel's tent". He has avoided telling us until the last possible moment, that Rachel had made a provision against discovery. Now, v. 34a, he can delay no longer. Suspense turns into malicious pleasure at the deadly fun made of the *terafim*: they are only to be "saved" by a menstruation. This means that they are as unclean as can be, in this new position they come near functioning as ... sanitary towels.

What Laban does is "feel all things, one by one". An effective choice of words, this iterative *pi'el* of *mšš* (vv. 34, 37), because the verb had already been used in Gen. 27. There Jacob's father was trying to learn the truth about his son by ... feeling, but in vain because of a trick of Jacob's. Thus Jacob received the blessing; it could not be taken from him anymore. Here Jacob's uncle is retrieving his own "truth", feeling, frisking, house-searching, and now a trick of Jacoba's renders this search vain. Thus Jacob can retain the blessing and leave with his most precious "asset".

Laban is the great loser, for he cuts a foolish figure. His rage[58] seems ridiculous, now that his only dangerous accusation "seems" to be utterly unfounded. Laban is perplexed, he "is nowhere". The text

[57] a) There is no suspense in the seven years because of the enormous leap of 29.20b; and especially b) Jacob's discovery "behold, it is Leah!" (v. 25) is not new to the reader; it had been let out by the narrator in v. 23. Usually a bible story lets us join in the discovery when it uses *hinnē*, at the very moment when the main character "lifts up his eyes and sees".

[58] The expression *'al yiḥar bᵉʿēnē* must be a contamination of *yaḥᵃrę̄ 'af* and *yeraʿ bᵉʿēnē*...

indicates that with a three-fold *lō māṣā*, (v. 33a, 34b and as a conclusion in v. 35b:) *lō māṣā 'et hattᵉrāfīm.*

B. *Second confrontation: Jacob's rīb,* vv. 36-43.

If we may call this great confrontation between Laban and Jacob a fight and ourselves the referee, then our judgment is soon passed: the first round is won by Jacob, for Laban's straight right missed the mark and he may not use his left hook (29b). Jacob is fresh when entering the second round, whereas Laban is still gasping for breath.

We have now come to the rhetorical climax of the Story of Jacob and even of the whole of Genesis: Jacob's dispute. And because his *rīb,*[59] vv. 36-42, is the heart of this story, we can from this vantage point also understand the function of the scene with the *terafim.* To use another image, vv. 25-34 are the trigger which explodes the bomb of 36ff. For Laban's house-searching, which puts him in an impossible position, is the last straw for Jacob – again a metaphor – and gives Jacob the strongest starting position conceivable. The tables are now turned. Laban, the prosecutor, becomes the accused and Jacob leaves the defensive to take the offensive, a final, frontal, massive attack.

The preceding part, vv. 22-35, is easy to understand as a (relatively) independent scene. The passage has a conflict of its own – although no solution as yet – and rising and falling suspense. But the connection with vv. 36ff. is near-perfect. What we now hear is enacted in the same place, at the same time, is a part of the same final event and presents the same protagonists as opposed to each other, vis-à-vis.

The oratorical art we are here going to deal with is felt as the story imposes its own rhythmical discipline upon the words. Vv. 36-42 are a perfect example of metrical "*Kunstprosa*". I scan them as follows[60]:

[59] Cf. B. Gemser, The rīb- or controversy-pattern in Hebrew mentality, SVT III (1955), pp. 120-137.

[60] Scanning O.T. texts remains a venture, which will always bear the stamp of provisionality. It is a matter of showing one's colours from syllable to syllable and therefore an easy target for criticism.

I have not pursued a precise reconstruction of pre-masoretic Hebrew; such fundamental efforts, which still remain theoretical, are great but fairly profitless. The following (my p. 172) is only an approximation, an impression only roughly correct. I have dropped the anaptyctic and *ḥāteph*-vowels.

The following alternatives are also quite acceptable: the lines 11f. and 13f.

1 (A) מה פשעי   מה חטאתי
2 כי דלקת אחרי   כי משׁשת את כל כלי
3 מה מצאת מכל כלי ביתך   שים כה נגד אחי ואחיך   ויוכיחו בין שנינו

4 (B) זה עשרים שנה אנכי עמך
5 רחליך ועזיך לא שכלו   ואילי צאנך לא אכלתי
6 טרפה לא הבאתי אליך
7 אנכי אחטנה   מידי תבקשנה
8 גנבתי יום   וגנבתי לילה
9 (הייתי) ביום אכלני חרב   וקרח בלילה   ותדד שנתי מעיני

10 (C) זה לי עשרים שנה בביתך
11 עבדתיך ארבע עשרה שנה בשתי בנתיך ושׁשׁ שנים בצאנך
12 ותחלף את משכרתי עשרה מנים
13 לולי אלהי אבי אלהי אברהם ופחד יצחק היה לי
14 כי עתה ריקם שלחתני
15 את עניי ואת יגיע כפי ראה אלהים ויוכח אמש

(now from left to right:)

A. ó oó // ó ooó   2 + 2
o oóo ooó // o oóo oó oó   2 + 3
ó oóo oó oó oóo / oó o oó oooo / oooo o oóo

B. o oó oó ooó oó
oooo oooo o oóo // ooó ooó oooo   3 + 3
ooó o oóo oóo
ooó oooo // ooó oooo   2 + 2
oooó ó // ooooó óo   2 + 2
oó oooo ó // oó oóo // ooó ooó ooó   3 + 2 + 3

C. oó oó oó oooo
oooo oó oó oó oó oooo / oó oó oooo /
ooó oooó oó oó
oó ooó oó – ooó ooó oó oó – oó o /
o oó oó oooo
ooó oooó oó / oó ooó / ooó ó

are parallel and, being anti-poles, they deserve the same metrical position, as follows:

11f. oooo oó oó oó oó oooo / oó oó oooo - ooó oooó oó oó

13f. oó ooó oó (ooó ooó oó oó) oó o - ooó oó oooo

At least six out of these fifteen lines are pure poetry[61] and therefore this text refuses to be classified unequivocally as "*Kunstprosa*" or poetry.

This division into A, B and C will have to be corroborated by analysis. It is, however, clearly marked by two repetitions. The vv. 38-40 and 41-42 begin with similar sentences, the beginnings of B and C; and A and C both end in "pass the right sentence", *hōkīaḥ*.

A = vv. 36-37. One glance at the contents is enough to know what distinguishes A as the first part. With these seven sentences Jacob draws attention to recent events, in the first place, for example, the affair with the *terafim*. First he must blow off steam over the humiliating house-search imposed upon him, and he must recover his self-confidence with the satisfied statement that Laban is not able to produce any evidence of the alleged theft.

Jacob makes short work of Laban, as is shown by the taut beginning, which applies such poetic means as anaphora and rhyme with elementary force:

ma piš'ī
ma ḥaṭṭātī

kī dālaqtā 'aḥaray
kī miššaštā 'et kol kelay

After two rhymes with the suffix for "my" there are two sentences ending in "your": ... *bēteḵā* ... *'aḥēḵā*. Sentence seven (v. 37b) concludes by joining "me and you": "us two".

Jacob is agitated and indignant, he does not use one affirmative, indicative sentence. He starts with a "two-stroke" question "*ma* ... *ma* ..." which ends in a "two-stroke" reproach "*kī* ... *kī* ...". Again he asks for evidence in line 3. In v. 32 this was still phrased as, "find your gods"; now in v. 37 Jacob speaks of "what have you found of all your household goods". Is that a covert polemic against the *terafim*? His tone sounds wounded, defiant: he repays Laban for his utterly unfounded accusation. Triumphantly he demands Laban to prove the unprovable by using a command (imperative) plus final clause.

Laban had formulated his accusation in terms of law. So does Jacob: he asks what his crime is, and he asks for a *corpus delicti* as a piece of evidence. Again he mentions the judges and asks for a correct

[61] Viz. the lines 1, 2, 5, 7, 8, 9. Caesura indicated by //.

judgment, though rhetorically, for the case has been settled already.

The sixth sentence resumes, with a chiasmus, the proposal he had made in v. 32, unaware of any injustice:

v. 32	neged 'aḥēnū	hakker-l^{e}kā ma 'immādī
v. 37	ma māṣātā sīm kō	neged 'aḥay w^{e}'aḥēkā

This chiasmus suggests how radically things have changed after the house-search. Jacob does not want to use the words "our kinsmen" (v. 32) any longer. He no longer has anything in common with this uncle, so he divides "our kinsmen" into "my kinsmen and your kinsmen" to indicate the definite separation of the two parties, in accordance with the wedge which the sentence will drive "between us two", *bēn š^{e}nēnū.*

B = vv. 38-40.

The middle part, too, is easy to distinguish. All the time its subject is "I", my shepherd's role during twenty years. If, for once, the subject is Laban (middle of v. 39), then, quite characteristically, he is the master who incessantly demands compensation. But all the time, even in that sentence, only one thing is under discussion: the hard, rough reality of the shepherd's life that Jacob has led.

Jacob is marked by cold and heat, by thirst and weariness. The never-ending cycle of night and day is represented in the chiasmus of v. 40:

bayyōm	('^{a}kālanī)	ḥoreb
qeraḥ		ballaylā

Their inconveniences are characterized with two rasping, snappy words: **ḥurb* and **qarḥ*. For twenty *šānā* (years) *šenā* (sleep) fled from Jacob, thus lines 4 and 9 enframe this ego-document.

Parallel to the night and day, but not chiastically, is v. 39b. What does not change, but remains the same twenty-four hours per natural day is the risk of robbery. Guarding against this is more than necessary because Laban, relentless employer, does not wish to distinguish between theft of flock by day and theft by night. This is hardly flexible, to put it mildly, although strictly speaking, perhaps, it is a tenable position. But with "*treife*" Jacob could not bother his uncle either, and how heartless that is may appear from Ex. 22.12 where O.T. law discharges the shepherds on this point.[62]

How much Laban is obsessed by property we gather from Jacob's second, third and fourth sentences (v. 38 and 39a). Heavy and emphatic are the nouns in their frontal position, an obvious inversion of the usual sequence of verbal sentences. Item by item Jacob goes through his list; item by item he displays his punctuality:
"Your ewes and your she-goats? – They have not miscarried!
"The rams of your flocks? – I have not eaten them!
"Animals torn by wild beasts? – A poor excuse to bother you with."
Here we hear speak the faithful servant, who has become embittered at long years waiting in vain for recognition and who now gives free play to his pent-up indignation in moving, resolute sentences.

How cheated Jacob feels, appears in his resumption of the *gnb*-thread. In A, omitting the word completely, he has nothing to do with a theft of Laban's *terafim*, if there ever was any; his innocence of that has been proved to the hilt. But the word had lodged in his throat like a fish-bone: Laban had accused him of one more theft and used the word *gnb* so emphatically that Jacob now seizes the opportunity to make it clear, once and for all, that things are quite different. There has been only one victim of theft and I am that man, Jacob says in v. 39. For whether I was robbed by night or by day, you never suffered the loss; I always made it up. Thus Jacob proves his integrity, the *ṣ^edāqā* of 30.33 at the final settlement. It is also juridically proved by the use of such technical terms as *ṭ^erefā* and the words *g^enūb^etī yōm/laylā*, with the fine archaic case-ending -ī seemingly unaltered from time immemorial, a law-term rooted in and arising from pastoral life of old.

Not only is v. 40 with its chiasmus pure poetry, but so especially is v. 39. It contains a quartet of half-verses, as strictly organized as the beginning of the speech, by means of sound-devices and repetition of words:

'ānōkī 'ᵃḥaṭṭennā
miyyādī t^ebaqšennā

g^enūb^etī yōm
ug^enūb^etī laylā

[62] Gen. 31 links up quite well. There, too, the term *ṭ^erefā* and the hiph. *hebī* with respect to the evidence. In Babylonia, too, "*treife*" was overlooked: Codex Hammurabi § 266 (cf. § 267), see Frankena, OTS 1972 p. 57f.

The parallelism in sound and metre of the first two sentences is so striking and their meaning ("I compensate" versus "you demand") so precisely complementary, that they must be regarded as the two half-verses of a poetic line which belong together[63] – a fact with which most translations are in conflict. They display a sentence-arrangement which disturbs the poetry, and which the Masoretes (the *'atnāḥ*!) did not think right either. The English Version of the *Bible de Jérusalem*, for example, reads, "As for those mauled by wild beasts, I have never brought them back to you, but have borne the loss myself; you claimed them from me, whether I was robbed by day or by night." I advocate the following as the correct translation of v. 39: "torn animals (*treife*) I did not bring to you; I always made good what you always demanded from me – whether it had been stolen by day or by night."

Apart from the correct sentence-arrangement, the two *pi'el*-forms constitute a ὕστερον πρωτερον, interrelated as they are by complementary meaning, assonance, the same suffix and the same iterative function; "I made good / you demanded it from my hand". This sequence shows how accurately Jacob did his work. Even before Laban had put in a claim all losses had been made good.

C = vv. 41-42.
The third part seems to begin like B, but the difference is revealing and it divulges a great deal about Jacob's intention as to the conclusion of his dispute. In B he described the facts briefly and forcefully and in the beginning he said, "For twenty years I was with you", with the unmistakable connotation of "I was on your side", committing myself loyally. However the beginning of C, where Jacob, no longer able to make the word *'im* pass his lips, says, with held breath, "for 20 years I was at your house", reveals the truth about his stay at Haran: I was your servant, *'ᵃbadtīkā*. This, in itself, need not have negative

[63] The great problem (what does the object-suffix in *-ennā* refer to?) is not unequivocally solvable, linguistically: such a suffix may refer to a preceding feminine (so h.l. *ṭᵉrefā*) but it may also be proleptic (so h.l. refer to the fem. *gᵉnūbat*). If *-ennā* is made to refer to *ṭᵉrefā*, then one lands in a blind alley, semantically speaking: what comes after *tbqšnh* is then an explicating apposition to *ṭᵉrefā*. In the first place, it is not a very satisfactory solution and, secondly, O.T. law distinguishes clearly between *ṭrf* and *gnb* as two (different) kinds of accidents. So *gnwbt* (2 times) indicates a special (law-)case. That, however, does not imply that *-ennā* refers to it by anticipation. Perhaps it refers neither backward nor forward! In that case the stiche with *ḥt'*//*bqš* is a self-contained sentence, "neutral" in the middle.

connotations, thus immediately the famous key-word *skr* is placed next to it, ***maskoret***: "You managed to change my wages at least ten times; so those are your thanks for my loyal service!"

We soon understand that in C Jacob is going to evaluate his time of service, the hard facts of which had been first mentioned in B. The dispute closes with an interpretation. Jacob has come to the final account – an account, indeed, for the balance-sheet of service and wages is drawn up with the help of four numbers.

What Jacob had already told his wives (31.7a) he now hurls at Laban straightaway: your tenfold evasiveness. And again he puts it quite emphatically: only God could do something against it and has done it. Again he makes it clear, in the fruitless secret-and-open struggle for power between you and me the decision has been made by God; only his intervention has resolved it.

Jacob now analyses, incisively revealing the kernel of the story. No wonder that he has passed from fierce poetry, contracting and releasing emotions, to long prose sentences, v. 41 and 42a. The latter, as a carefully extended period, may be called the kernel of C; it also contains the climax, the solution to a twenty years' conflict.

And of course it is not accidental that v. 42a is the stylistic junction of Gen. 31. It forms part of no less than four chiastic contexts, especially by use of those words that form Jacob's serious charge against Laban, "surely you would have sent me away empty-handed!"

(a) A not very striking chiasmus is formed by 42a and v. 29:

it is in my power to do you harm	but the God of your father has warned me
if the God of my father had not been with me	surely now you would have sent me away empty-handed

This chiasmus explains of what the so-called lawful "harm-doing" of Laban consists. Jacob unmasks him. Laban would have taken all his lawful wages from him. But God's effective intervention undermines Laban's threat and even uses it against him, in the form of an accusation. What the chiasmus makes visible is this, that now the tables have been radically turned, the accuser of a moment ago (Laban, v. 29) is now on trial as the accused, and has already been judged by God (42b).

(b) Together with 41a, 42a forms a chiasmus in respect to 30.25, in which the key-words *šlḥ* and *ʿbd* are combined for the first time:

30.25f. do send me away	for you know the service which I have given you
for 20 years I've served you	empty-handed you would have sent me away

What Jacob connects, loyal service and permission to go, Laban tries to keep widely separated. By ignoring Jacob's careful service and by withholding the recognition due him, Laban thinks he can send him away as lonely as he came. This appears even more clearly from the following:

(c) V. 42a forms a very effective chiasmus with v. 27, in which Laban himself talks of sending Jacob away:

I might have sent you away, *wā'^{a}šalleḥakā*	with mirth and songs, with tambourine and lyre
rēqām, empty-handed	you would have sent me away, *šillaḥtānī*

This cross-construction effectively unmasks the diametrical contrast between Laban's hypocritical sweetness and the stern truth which Jacob lays bare by this reversal. All the fine attributes in v. 27 are reduced to one word, bare and harsh, the adverb *rēqām*. And finally, violent is the contrast between the two irreales: *wā'^{a}šalleḥakā*, uttered in grumbling, false self-pity by an impotent Laban, versus *šillaḥtānī*, spoken by Jacob in sincere anger, but relief, protected as he is by God.

The use of the irrealis and the adverb *rēqām* as its spear-point are very important in v. 42a:

(d) Verses 41b and 42a also form an effective and subtle chiasmus with 29.15:

29.15	h^{a}kī 'aḥī 'attā wa'^{a}badtanī ḥinnām?	haggīdā lī ma maskurtekā
	wattaḥ^{a}lef 'et maskurtī 10 mōnīm	kī 'attā rēqām šillaḥtānī

Are we justified in making such a far(-fetched) connection, as far back as 29.15? Certainly, if we consider the following observations:
– in the outer parts of this four-leaf clover irreales occur; elsewhere[64]

[64] Only the one of chiasmus c, from v. 27 (the same verb!).

in Gen. 25-35 there is hardly any other irrealis. Both irreales are perfect tenses rhyming because of the same object-suffix.
– in both cases there is an adverb next to them with the uncommon adverbial ending *-ām* (which does not occur anywhere else in Gen. 25-35[65]).
– there is nearly maximum equality of sounds in *kī... 'attā* and *kī... 'attā.*
– although the root *skr* occurs twelve times as a key-word in the Story of Jacob (yes, twelve ...) the form *maskoret* is found only here and in the parallel 31.7; in the rest of the O.T. the word occurs only once (Ruth 2.12), versus twenty-two occurrences of *sākār*.

The best evidence, however, for justifying this connection must, in fact, appear from the explication itself.

Here, too, the bubble of Laban's false claim is pricked, as Jacob pulls down the façade furiously. The linking of 31.41f. with 29.15 produces to begin with the chiastic situation of Laban to Jacob – Jacob to Laban. Its implications we can best follow by considering the primary indicators of meaning:
– "wages". The seemingly generous Laban asks Jacob to determine the wages himself (29.15 and 30.28), whereas actually Laban manipulated them, devaluated them tenfold.
– "serve for nothing". Laban refused to accept uncompensated service from Jacob. But now Jacob holds it against him that he would have happily sent him away empty-handed. This means that Laban wants sole possession of the fruits of the blessing on Jacob. He wants Jacob's wages to find their way back to himself. Within the members 1 and 4 of the chiasmus the important verbs plus adverb themselves form another chiasmus: *'ᵃbadtanī ḥinnām* × *rēqām šillaḥtānī*. This reversal underlines, once more, Laban's deceit, – "because you are my brother". If anyone has denied the solidarity towards his relatives (nephew and daughters), then it is Laban. We have already seen in v. 37 how this led to a separation of "our kinsmen" (v. 32) into two parties.
The critical factor, which fortunately turns Jacob's fear of being sent away "empty"[-handed] into an irrealis, is invisible in the chiasmus, but is mentioned between the last two members: in 42aα he is there, as the saver of Jacob, for the first time with all his antedecents ("God of Abraham and the Fear of Isaac"). He has filled up the vacant place

[65] Except for *'ūlām* in 28.19.

beside Jacob as it becomes apparent that Laban is no longer "with him". The title "Fear of Isaac" is well placed here: last night God called Laban to a halt; he went to meet him terrifyingly, as a *mysterium tremendum*, in order to sound a note of warning.[66]

Once more Jacob gives two nouns a heavy and emphatic frontal position by inversion, in a verbal sentence, v. 42b. He evaluates the hard facts of B (vv. 38-40) definitively: misery and "labour of my hands" was my existence here. But God saw it and "rebuked you last night."

The words "last night" are a conscious quotation from Laban's own message, v. 29, to make it clear to him that God's intervention is significant for his entire stay at Haran and that it decisively concludes the conflict to Jacob's advantage in spite of Laban's tricks and traps. The words "he has done justice" bring about an instructive connection with the ending of A ("they must do justice") and v. 32. What Jacob says is: of the recent (accusation of) theft (viz. of the *terafim*) our kinsmen must judge (vv. 32, 37b). In v. 37 this became a cutting summons after Laban's failure with the house-searching.[67] But most of all I should like to discuss my whole time of service (B + C) here, and upon that God himself sits in judgment. Yes, he has already done justice, to my advantage; the matter has already been decided.

V. 42b forms a chiasmus together with v. 12b, where Jacob spoke to his wives and quoted God:

[66] Gunkel, op.cit., p. 349: "Der Name "Schrecken Isaaks" ist geschickt in die Erzählung eingefügt. Es ist der Gott, der als Gott des Vaters Jakobs erschienen ist (29) und der Laban so sehr bedroht hat (24)."
Eising, p. 221: "eine rechte Beziehung dieses Namens zur Scene ist aber nur soweit herzustellen, als Gott vielleicht deswegen Pahad Jiṣḥāq genannt wird, weil er die Vertragsverletzung bestrafen wird" – especially in connection with the ending of Gen. 31. *Nur soweit* – is this not amply sufficient?

[67] Boecker, in the excursus mentioned above: Jacob "will die Beschuldigung nicht unbeantwortet auf sich sitzenlassen. Er will sein Recht haben. Deshalb appelliert er an richterliche Entscheidung: wajjōkīḥū bēn šᵉnēnū" und sie sollen zwischen uns beiden die Rechtsentscheidung treffen" (V. 37b). Diese Worte sind entscheidend für die Charakterisierung der hier vorliegenden Rede. Es wird mit ihnen die richterliche Entscheidung angerufen. Die Initiative dazu geht vom Beschuldigten aus. Wir haben hier die von Begrich herausgestellte "Appellationsrede des Angeschuldigten" vor uns. Das Charakteristikum dieser Redeform liegt in der ausdrücklichen Appellation an das Gericht, nachdem vorher die als haltlos empfundenen Beschuldigungen des Gegners ins Visier genommen waren."

(God:) I have seen	all that Laban is doing to you
my affliction and labour	God has seen

It is most revealing that materially the object is the same, but in v. 12 it refers to Laban and in 42 to Jacob. In his speech to Leah and Rachel Jacob had hardly accorded himself a position in the conflict, interpreting his service as the struggle (for him) between the scheming Laban and the saving God. This led to a "two-blocks-structure" in his speech (seen on a smaller scale in verse 12). This duel-structure now recurs in his speech to Laban, 41b (Laban) × 42aα (God) × 42aβ (Laban) × 42b (God).[68]

Whereas in v. 12b he would not and could not mention himself he now describes "all that Laban is doing" as "my affliction and labour". In this dispute he cannot leave himself aside; on the contrary, he is describing his relation to Laban and his loyal service. He wants to put himself right with the unfair employer and therefore he points out that God has put him right. He has seen "him in his affliction", exactly as he saw Leah (29.32 *rā'ā Yhwh b^{e}'onyī*) and Rachel (*dānanī* 30.6 comparable with *hōkī^{a}ḥ* 31.42). The verses 41 and 42 draw the entire triangle Jacob (v. 41a) – Laban (41b, 42aβ) – God (42aα, 42b), in which God triumphs as the most important partner. With this the scope of C has become a fine variant of the speech in 31.5-13. Besides, the parallelism[68] of the speeches clearly shows another difference: the vv. 8-12a, in the middle of Jacob's speech to his wives, do not find their equal in the dispute with Laban. Jacob will by no means allow Laban a peep behind the scenes into the workshop of Providence. It would be wasted on this uncle.

Jacob's last words remind us of the *"Redeformen des Rechtslebens"*, and now we see the importance of the ending. Jacob is so emboldened by the judgement which has already been passed that in the latter

[68] The parallels of the two speeches are these:

v. 6	b^{e}kol kōḥī 'ābadtī 'et '^{a}bīken	41	'^{a}badtīkā 14 šānā w^{e}šeš šānīm
7	wa'^{a}bīken hetel bī		
	w^{e}heḥ^{e}līf 'et maskurtī 10 mōnīm		wattaḥ^{a}lef 'et maskurtī 10 mōnīm
	w^{e}lō n^{e}tānō '^{e}lōhīm l^{e}hāra' 'immādī	42	lūlē '^{e}lōhē 'ābī... hāyā lī
12b	rā'ītī 'et kol '^{a}šer lābān 'ōsē lāk		'et 'onyī w^{e}'et y^{e}gī^{a}' kappay rā'ā '^{e}lōhīm
13	('ānōkī hā'el ... ṣē šūb, in a dream)		wayyōkaḥ 'ameš (by means of a dream)

part of his speech, in C, he has gone from making a plea (= B!) to demanding a sentence. He has developed into Laban's prosecutor. God's judgement comes in the end – in itself a good conclusion – and with it Jacob has come back to the current situation. The past has debouched into the present.

Everything that has been discussed in Jacob's dispute can be pictured as follows, by way of summary:

criterion	A vv. 36-37	B vv. 38-40	C vv. 41-42
time	present	past (20 years)	past (20 years)
subject	house-searching	shepherd's life, labour	reward withheld – given
person	you × me	I	I × you – God
law – form	demand for evidence	plea	demand for sentence
law – J's part	accused	counsel	prosecutor
tone, character[69]	emotional outburst	report of facts	evaluation

Laban's reply, v. 43f.

Laban has nothing much to say, he has been outwitted. Besides, he is in chains because God has denied him the only means of power that remained to him, force. His impotence is to be read in 43b. Before that he speaks two sentences, the claims of which are so sweeping, so exaggerated that Laban loses his remaining credibility in this dispute. The first sentence contains precisely the three main points of Jacob's story, in neat chronological order:

a) habbānōt b^{e}nōtay / w^{e}habbānīm bānay / w^{e}haṣṣōn ṣōnī – three short, clipped, nominal sentences, which display a contentious spite in Laban and an almost childish obstinacy. Then:

b) "in short,[70] all that you see is mine". This sentence is almost grotesque considering the opinion uttered by Jacob (31.9) and Leah

[69] The characterizations according to this criterion shade off into one another. B and C are emotional, too, especially B; the "facts" of B are, as "faits vécus", already aimed at the evaluation of C, etc.

[70] *W^{e}* introduces a summary of the preceding part.

and Rachel (31.16); the parallelism with 31.16 especially catches the eye:

16 kol hā'ošer 'ᵃšer hiṣṣīl 'ᵉlōhīm me'abīnū lānū hū
43 kol 'ᵃšer 'attā rō'ẹ lī hū

It seems that Laban tries to save face by suggesting in his reply that he had always been under the impression that Jacob had contracted a *ṣadīqa*-marriage at Haran. In this alternative marriage model[71] it is the man who is considered to belong to his wife's clan, instead of the reverse. But this statement of Laban's is quite untenable, as he himself knows. Jacob had come to Haran with the same intentions of marriage as (on behalf of Isaac) Abraham's servant; Laban knew that the destiny of Leah and Rachel was to be like that of his sister Rebekah. In 29.18 and 27 the preposition *bᵉ* is used in such a way that it seems to be a reflection of the so-called *bēt pretii*, which defines the bridal price.[72] It is beyond dispute that Jacob's labour and achieve-

[71] Also mentioned in the commentaries by, among others, O. Procksch (Leipzig, 1913), p. 335; G. von Rad (ATD Göttingen, 1953), p. 271; J. de Fraine (Roermond, 1963), pp. 214, 228. See J. Wellhausen, Die Ehe bei den Arabern, pp. 465ff. (Nachrichten von der Göttinger Gesellschaft der Wissenschaften, 1893, pp. 431-480), and p. 434; and W. Robertson Smith, Kinship and Marriage in Early Arabia (London, 1903, 2nd ed.) pp. 75ff. A critical comment on this marriage in historic times is in Th. W. Juynboll, Handleiding tot de kennis van de Mohammedaansche Wet ... (3rd ed. 1925; 4th ed. 1930) p. 180, especially note 1 on this page. – The *ṣadīqa*-alliance discussed in connection with Jacob (and Jud. 8.31, 14.8f., 15.1f.) by R. de Vaux (see note 74 below). The Assyriologist Frankena, too, does not consider it possible to see in Jacob's marriage the *errebūtu*-type, OTS 17 (1972) pp. 54-56.

[72] Strictly speaking, *bᵉ* does not denote the price but the "merchandise"! This is the reading of B. Jacob, p. 589, who, therefore, considers a *bēt pretii* impossible here; but that is a little over-ingenious: although one cannot mix up price and merchandise purchase judicially and materially, linguistically it need not be perceptible in matters that are interchangeable, or approximately equivalent. I consider the *bēt* in 29.10 to be "inspired" by and a kind of reversal (shift from price to merchandise) of the *bēt pretii*, which normally occurs when the *mohar* is concerned. See II Sam. 3.14 (before which comes I Sam. 18 with the word *mhr* in v. 25) and Gen. 34.15 (and *mhr* in v. 12). – That in both cases the *mohar* itself is exceptional (100 foreskins / circumcision of the people of Sichem) detracts nothing from the linguistic fact that the *bēt pretii* has been put with the *mohar*.
The preposition is still plainly called a *bēt pretii* by Procksch, op. cit. (p. 335) and H. Holzinger, Genesis (Freiburg, 1898), p. 194 in 29.18,27, referring to Gesenius-Kautzsch (28th ed.) § 119p. Cf. also Hos. 12.13.

ments during those seven years were meant as a substitute for the *mohar*, a way of payment, work for the girl's father, known even in twentieth century Palestine.[73] Whereas a good father gives part of the *mohar* to his daughter the covetous Laban has given Leah and Rachel neither dowry nor presents. That is what they complain of in 31.15[74]; but it is especially their testimony "for we are regarded as foreigners"[75] that destroys the underpinnings of Laban's juridical fiction in 31.43: like Jacob, Laban himself had long regarded the women as *beʿūlōt baʿal*, as the term is (Gen. 20.3), thus as "property" of Jacob's. It is true that he had carefully avoided a specific agreement in black and white – he loves being non-committal – but here, at last, he has fallen a victim to his own two-facedness. He is caught in his own trap.

Retrospective view of the great dispute

The rest of Laban's words (v. 44) can be discussed later; with v. 43 the *rīb* proper has ended and this is the right moment to reflect on it in retrospect.

In the final chapter of the Haran-period three rounds of debates have been completed; for many reasons the last one is the highlight, among other things because it is the end of, the solution to the protracted conflict, because it is a rhetorical climax using many poetic means and because it contains the only complete sketch of the three-cornered affair Jacob-Laban-God from the mouth of the main character himself. The three rounds are:

1) Jacob to Leah + Rachel (long) vv. 5-13; Leah + Rachel to Jacob (short) vv. 14b-16
2) Laban to Jacob (long) vv. 26-30; Jacob to Laban (short) vv. 31-32.
3) Jacob to Laban (long) vv. 36b-42; Laban to Jacob (short) vv. 43(44).

[73] See Granqvist, Vol. I p. 108f. And in the O.T. itself, de Fraine, p. 217, remarks (in Dutch): "service-marriages (...) still occur in Jos. 15.16f., I Sam. 17.25, 18.17, 25, II Sam. 3.14."

[74] The matters of marriage and *mohar* in Gen. 29-31 (as final phase of the tradition) are dealt with correctly by R. de Vaux, les Institutions de l'Ancien Testament, Paris, 1959, cap. II B 2.

[75] *ḥšb* (here *niph.*): "considered" is a little over-"contemplative": *ḥšb* often includes action, like words such as *dbr*. See J. Hoftijzer in his interpretation mentioned above of II Sam. 14, in VT 20 (1970), p. 435.

Briefly, their relationship is as follows:
1) plan to flight 2) *rīb* on recent events 3) *rīb* on Jacob's whole time of service. To his wives Jacob confined himself to an interpretation of the final phase of his service; now he has described and evaluated the whole of his stay.

Thus the last dispute has become the crown of the narrator's work, it is the heart of the final scene. No wonder that in this passage many threads meet definitively. We have only to think of the chiastic connections which we have explained and nearly all of which contain the great key-words of Gen. 29-31. In Gen. 31.41f. lines come together from among others 29.15, 29.32 and 30.6, 30.25f., 31.7a, 12b, thus from different scenes. We number them[76] and visualize this one aspect of the narrator's labour of composition:

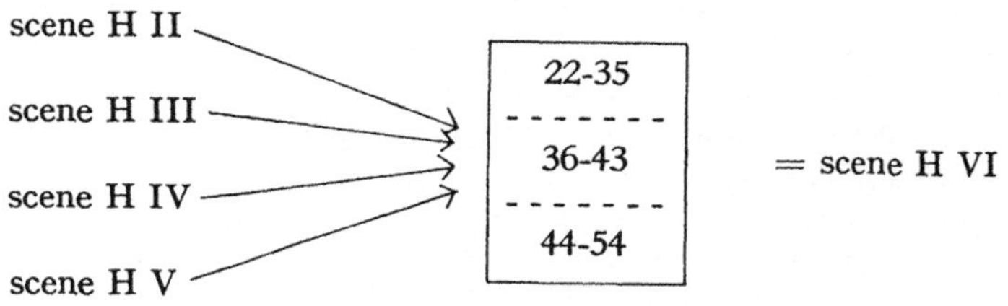

Only scene I neither enlightens nor is enlightened by the final dispute; this is because in scene I the conflict has not yet developed; to the contrary, it must serve as the harmonious background against which the difficulties increase from 29.15 onwards. All the other scenes, however, including the first part of scene H VI (vv. 22-35), are worked into vv. 36-43, which now manifests itself as final reckoning qua composition too.

Bringing together these threads the narrator casts off his work. As keystone – another metaphor – the middle part of scene VI has great integrating power.

When seen externally the narrator lays the keystone; he is the first and the last man responsible for the composition of this narrative, and we are grateful to him. But let us realize how things happen inside the story. The vv. 36-43 are words by Jacob; this means that Jacob is the one through whose hands the threads of the composition run, and he brings them together. Jacob lays the keystone so that the structure will be solid and can accommodate living beings.

[76] The scenes 5-10 of the entire Story of Jacob we here call scene H(aran) I-VI.

In the first speech (to his wives, 31.5ff) and in his final speech Jacob is the first interpreter of his own history – by the grace of the narrative. His observations are profound and in looking at Gen. 29-31 in retrospect (§ 11) we would do well to sit down at the feet of this authority on exegesis.

Now that the conflict between Jacob and Laban has been settled by Providence and only its effect will engage our attention, we can speculate upon the reputation Jacob will carry with him when he leaves. What moral judgment does this story (not explicitly but implicitly) attach to his attitude in the second period of his life? A good starting-point is God's intervention (v. 24/29, described in) "last night he passed judgment", between the two parties of the present lawsuit. It is quite easy for us to formulate the judgment in correct classical Hebrew, which perhaps does not mention Laban, but which is, however, an "*Urteilszuspruch der Schuldlosigkeit*" in respect to Jacob, "you are (in your) right, and Laban is not".[77]

In other words, God's *hōkīaḥ*, his passing judgment consists anyway in God's *haṣdīq* of Jacob, as the O.T. legal term states. Jacob has been declared innocent, and he has anticipated this in 30.33 where he, using legal terms himself, maintained his *ṣ^edāqā*.

But Jacob is called Jacob. In Gen. 25 and 27 he was the Heel-catcher who really deceived his fellow-men; in Gen. 30 he was, at least by nature, potentially, the deceiver. Jacob is not *ṣaddīq* of himself; Jacob cannot be called *Justus*, rather *impius*. But God, who has blessed him, just keeps him from deceit, in Gen. 30, by protecting him against Laban's deceit, influencing the course of events with Laban's revision of Jacob's wages, and in this way he keeps him *ṣaddīq*. To God alone Jacob owes his integrity, God's *haṣdīq* only is the source of his *ṣ^edāqā*. Jacob, *impius* of himself, may be called *justificatus*.

C. *Covenant and parting*, 31.44-32.1.

Laban is frightened in his heart: will the blessing which accompanies Jacob and renders him invulnerable work against him? Forewarned is forearmed, and thus Laban arrives at a creative proposal, the maximum synthesis possible for the two fighting-cocks after Laban's

[77] This on the ground of passages such as Gen. 38.26 and I Sam. 24.18 with privative *min*. See Boecker, op. cit., part C I,1; cf. II Kings 10.9, Ex. 9.27.

thesis of 26ff. and Jacob's antithesis of 36ff, "the making of a covenant".

The text says: "let us cut a *b^{e}rīt*". In this text "to cut a *b^{e}rīt*" means – and this is based on the context of vv. 44-54, and by no means on quite different situations such as Jos. 24 or the covenant on the Sinai! – that by swearing an oath two men enter into a mutual obligation to fulfil a certain pledge, in a ceremony accompanied by a solemn sacrificial repast, and under the supervision of their deity. Most probably the oath mentions sanctions, punishment[78] for the offender in the agreement in the form of a curse upon oneself; this punishment may have been derived from and demonstrated in the special rite which is the origin of the term "cut a *b^{e}rīt*" and which is described in Gen. 15 and Jer. 34.18-21.[79]

This concept of *krt b^{e}rīt* is also true of other texts about the patriarchs, e.g., Gen. 21.22-32 and 26.26-33; it also applies to Gen. 15 in which it is not a man, but God, who binds himself to Abraham with an oath (vv. 18ff).[80] The monograph on this text, recently written by Lohfink and worth quoting,[81] points this out and leads to the conclusion that *b^{e}rīt* deserves to be rendered by "oath".

Laban made the proposal and it is Laban who controls the initiative in the words and actions concerning the "covenant": he is the first to name the heap of stones in Aramaic; it is he who shows the massebe

[78] This is also assumed in the well-known elliptic oath-formulas, as in vv. 50, 52.

[79] J. Henninger, Was bedeutet die rituelle Teilung eines Tieres in zwei Hälften? Zur Deutung von Gen. 15.9ff. Biblica 34 (1953) pp. 344-353.

[80] An oath: *šb'* in Gen. 21.23, 31, 26.31, 31.53.

[81] N. Lohfink, Die Landverheissung als Eid, Stuttgarter Bibelstudien 28 (1967). On *b^{e}rīt* esp. ch. 10. Lohfink follows an "analytisch-synthetisches Konvergenzverfahren" to determine the right concept; this is briefly a combination of gathering the meaning from the context concerned only and in that context supplying what is the average meaning in other contexts. P. 105f.: Die meist eidliche Selbst- oder Fremdverpflichtung kann dazu dienen, dass ein Vertragsverhältnis entsteht, sie kann aber auch andere Zwecke haben. P. 107 summarizes "dass sich krt berīt nicht vom Grundsinn her, sondern erst in gegebenem Zusammenhang als "Bund schliessen" (nämlich "Bund durch Eidablegung schliessen") verstehen lässt. Die eigentliche Bedeutung ist die der Selbst- onder Fremdverpflichtung, meistens durch Eid – in dem Fall, von dem der Ausdruck hergenommen ist, durch Eid unter Setzung des Selbstverfluchungssymbols der zu durchschreitenden zerteilten Tiere." P. 105: krt ist oft gleichbedeutend mit "einen Eid leisten", ... – Note 12 on p. 105 mentions the parallels with *š^{e}bū'ā*, *'ālā*; *šb' niph.* and *hiph.* Es handelt sich bei *krt b^{e}rīt* stets um einen promissorischen Eid. Also see E. Kutsch, Der Begriff b^{e}rīt in vordeuteronomischer Zeit pp. 133-143 of Festschrift L. Rost = BZAW 105 (1967).

and the heap of stones their positions as witnesses; it is he who gives the place another name (v. 49) and it is he who formulates the content of the contract. First there is a familiar clause concerning unmixed endogamy (for which Isaac, too, showed great concern), v. 50. Then follows a clause which shows us Laban and Jacob as the patriarchs of the nations of Israel and Aram, which waged war for ages, esp. in... Gilead. V. 52 fixes the boundary there, for the covenant is also a non-aggression pact. Friends, of course, will never need such a compact to define their relationship, but Jacob and Laban are no friends.

Let us pay attention to Jacob's behaviour. After v. 44 we do not hear him agree to Laban's proposal. The action of v. 45 is not necessary at all to the making of a covenant; it is out of place in that ceremony. What strikes us is that v. 46 also does not explicitly pertain to the "covenant". In v. 47 Jacob only imitates Laban with some translation-work, and for the rest he is silent. He does not formulate clauses, and we do not exactly hear him say amen to Laban's words. Not until v. 53b do we see him take the desired oath, apparently without enthusiasm, and in 54 he takes part in the sacrificial repast belonging to the oath; thus v. 54 enforces the probability that v. 46 described another sort of repast.

In short, Jacob hardly speaks a word in the passage vv. 44-54, and that makes this (sub-)scene practically [82] unique. These facts require close attention; only then can an interpretation be correct. The only actions Jacob takes of his own accord (vv. 45, 46) – the massebe, the heap of stones, the repast – serve purposes entirely of their own and deserve an explanation of their own, to be discussed later. But for the rest Jacob does nothing, whereas Laban is ardently constructing a pact.

The explanation of this difference is rather simple. For Jacob a phase of his life has come to an end, clearly rounded-off with a judgment by God. He does not even want to return to Haran, nor is this a feature of his destiny (28.13f!). He is fed up with uncle Laban, but no longer fears him. As God's protégé he goes away, a victor; he is unassailable and he knows it. For him a pact is needless, he can shelter under God's wings and be safe. But Laban feels "the out-stretched arm" with which God has led Jacob from the house of bondage resting heavy on his shoulder. His tricks have been of no avail to him, he is left a robbed man and he feels threatened: "the fear of the

[82] In 30.35-43, too, there was a special reason for Jacob's silence; and in the birth-scene, of course, he was not yet able to speak – but his behaviour did.

Lord has been put into him". And, what irony! He, the master of ambiguity, who has expressed himself so non-committally twenty different times, now urgently demands the security, the certainty of an accurate, specific agreement, sealed by an oath.

Jacob is the blessed man, Laban is simply inferior; and so Laban wants to ensure his security by means of a pact. This situation is essentially the same as in Gen. 21.22ff. and 26.26 ff. , which is one more reason to mention these texts as parallels for this case of *b^erīt* as *Eidleistung*. There, too, the representatives of a foreign people come to a *b^erūk Yhwh*, with their tails between their legs; there, too, only the adversary of a patriarch has need of a pact; a small difference is that they want to reap (cf. Gen. 26.12–reap..) the fruits of the blessing, whereas Laban has already lost that chance (cf. 30.27, 30) and has been driven into a much more unfavourable position.

God's intervention is the crucial difference between Laban's and Jacob's negotiating positions as the text just points out in v. 53b. Jacob does take the oath desired by Laban; however, he does not swear to God in his capacity as "God of Abraham", but he deliberately calls his patron by the title of *Paḥad Yiṣḥāq*, "Fear of Isaac". Thus he effectively points out to Laban that Yhwh as *mysterium tremendum* has blocked his way (31.24, 29). Thus, once more, after the final words of his speech in v. 42, he puts the *paḥad* (fear) of God into him, the same God (for Isaac is of Laban's generation) who was effective as saver and giver of blessing in Laban's days.[83]

With the stones that Jacob handles, Laban sets to work. Of the massebe, which Jacob sets up (v. 45) and of the heap of stones which he collects (v. 46a) Laban presently says that it was he who raised (51)! Is this not a contradiction?

[83] The title *pḥd Yṣḥq* only occurs in Gen. 31.42,53 and so it is virtually impossible to explain it and deal with it religio-historically. But the word *pḥd* is so common in Hebrew, as a verb, too, that a) it is artificial to understand it as "relative" with the aid of the Arab and Palmyrean-Aramean cognate, and b) the obvious explanation is Fear of Isaac. This then would mean: in the first place (gen. subj.): the God whom Isaac fears, Isaacs numen; in the second place (gen. obj.) the God who inspires fear of Isaac, viz. by leading and protecting him in war (c.q. holy war) – cf. Gen. 35.5. The evidence: the passages on the *pḥd* sacral in every way, which falls upon Israel's enemies: Ex. 15.16, Deut. 2.25, 11.25, Is. 19.16, Ps.105.38, I Chron. 14.17, II Chron. 14.13, 17.10, 20.27; and in Israel itself I Sam. 11.7, Hos. 3.5, Micah 7.17, Job 13.11. Cf. Is. 2.10, 19, 21, Jer. 49.5, Ps. 53.6, Job 4.14, II Chron. 19.7 and the late echo Esther 8.17, 9.2f.
There is also another parallel: *mōrā'*, Deut. 4.34, 11.25, 26.8, 34.12, Is. 8.13, Mal. 1.6, 2.5, Jer. 32.21, to say nothing of *yr'* at Bethel!

It is not unwise to view Laban's words with some skepticism, for what he claimed in v. 43 was not reliable either, but it was quite typical of his character. That is also the case in v. 51. The heap of stones and the massebe have a distinctly "Jacobite" meaning, but Laban is blind to that. Right from the start he saw that they would be of great use for the covenant and now, naming them in v. 47 and interpreting them in 51f., he designates their function exclusively in the frame-work of the treaty: these monuments are to be evidence of a covenant convenient to him. *En passant* he "usurps" – as is typical of his character – the erection of the massebe and the heap of stones, too.

Jacob does not mind. He does not care for the treaty, but it does him no harm, so why not carry on? Laban's interpretation draws no protest from him, for it detracts nothing from his intentions with the stones. But what, exactly, are his intentions?

"Jacob took a stone and set it up as a massebe". But it is not the first time! At Bethel he had erected one, which, with a unique kind of literalness, continues (*maṣṣebā*) the presence of the stairs from heaven (*muṣṣāb*) and God himself (*niṣṣāb*). The massebe which is now set up at Gilead also works *"pro Deo"*, as does the heap of stones:

50b see, God is witness between you and me
52a this heap is a witness and the pillar is a witness.

God as a witness, as guarantor of this treaty, is concretized and symbolically retained by stone witnesses. That is Laban's view and it is he who speaks the two sentences quoted above, which, when joined in a series, convey a weighty message.

What Laban, however, has missed, as Jacob has not, is the "Jacobite" meaning of the massebe. To Laban it symbolizes God's patronage of the non-aggression pact; to Jacob the massebe means much more, a symbolization of the God of Bethel, of the Yahweh who intervenes actively and who saves him. This is the thought behind Jacob's actions in v. 45; this is what he wants to express, grateful as he is, by setting up the massebe. This monument is the everlasting confession in stone of a man released from servitude. Laban is bent on the negative: via an alliteration he equates *maṣṣebā* with *miṣpā* "watchpost", God must be a watchman (v. 49) against something he is afraid of "in case we are hidden [again a negative word] from each other". Jacob has thoughts of his own on the massebe, he is bent on the positive: "God saw my affliction and has done me justice".

We saw that, in terms of composition, Jacob's final speech (vv. 36-42) was the keystone of the six scenes at Haran Gen. 29-31. But Jacob would not be Jacob if he did not place a real keystone himself. The end of the first period of his life he marked with a massebe at Bethel, which was a sign of hope. Now he marks the end of the second period of his life again with a massebe, which now is primarily a sign of thanks.

As a sign of thanks the massebe is also the seal on a series of connections with Bethel, which will lead us to the keystone of our interpretation of Gen. 29-31. What follows had happened at Bethel, had been mentioned in God's promise (and repeated precisely in the long preamble to Jacob's vow) and has had its effect in Haran in this way:

BETHEL	HARAN
– dream, angels	31.10-12
– God reveals himself, massebe + vow	31.13
– "I am with you" (*'im* 2×)	31.3b, 5b
– "I shall keep you"	31.24, 29
– "return to" Canaan	31.3, 13
– "bread to eat"	31.54
– Yhwh will be God to me (*hāyā lī*)	31.42

We have already noticed a number of threads. But there are three others that require an evaluation.

a) I will "keep" you, wherever you go, God had promised Jacob. Jacob went round behind the flocks and kept them faithfully (*šmr* 30.31), but he was exploited by Laban. Against that danger God helped him, finally, and the reverse side of "keep Jacob" became "Laban, keep from doing him harm".

b) While Jacob takes part in a solemn, well-supplied meal "on the mountain" (v. 54), he thankfully remembers how, once, when he was a lonely fugitive, God had given him hopes of "eating bread" again. These hopes have been realized unexpectedly, Jacob has become a blessed man in spite of oppression.

c) The most important point on which the Story of Jacob either revolves or gets stuck is, will the God of Abraham and Isaac also be the God of Jacob? At Bethel it is promised to him, and Jacob attunes his vow to the realization of that promise. At Haran the God of Abraham and Isaac shows that he will also be the God of Jacob, by helping him in a wonderful way for six years and by protecting him against Laban's revenge. This is what all the mapped connections convey and what is also shown by the formula itself:

Bethel	: w^e*hāyā* Yhwh *lī lelōhīm*	28.21
during the *rīb*, at Haran:	*'elōhē* 'abrāhām ufaḥad Yiṣḥāq *hāyā lī*	31.42

With this the decisive vertical dimension has been revealed. At the feet of Jacob, the master-interpreter of his own history, we hear in Gen. 29-31, the story of servitude with Laban, a story of deliverance by God. He had already worded that in a speech to his wives and in the dispute with Laban, now we must also use our eyes: now Jacob fixes and immortalizes this story in stone, in an action needing no more words – the narrator relies on the wise.

But does all this leave an independent function to the heap of stones, the *Gal'ed* which lends depth to the name of Gilead? Jacob is a magician who cannot only perform "white magic" with peeled rods, but can also juggle with stones. The word for heap of stones, *gal* (**gallu*) is derived from the root *gll*, and as a verb this root has been used three times right in ... the beginning of the Haran-period. The only scene that seemed out of place on p. 185 is connected with the end in 31.45ff. The man who immediately left his card at Haran by rolling away (*gll*) an obstacle which was too heavy for four men, shows his skill in working with stones; at his departure he is rolling stones again and making a *"gal"*.[84] Now the heap of stones marks the end of a period of life which in 29.1ff. opened with the 'dis-covery' of a well of living water.

Just as the stone, the heavy obstacle, is returned to its place (29.3 w^ehešībū ... limqōmāh), so the troublesome Laban must return to his place (wayyāšob ... limqōmō), Jacob has "lifted" him, too.

Laban kisses his children and grand-children and blesses (sic!) them, Jacob he does not kiss, much less bless. With that the last contrast with the beginning has been described; we recall Laban's enthusiasm when he heard the tidings of the strong Jacob: 29.13 "he ran to meet him" (cf. Rebekah 24.18, 20 and Laban himself 24.29), "and he embraced him and he kissed him" (waynaššeq). The same iterative tense occurs here in 32.1 (in transl. 31.55), but it is not meant for Jacob!

[84] Compare the sacral nature of *"Gilgāl"*, reduplication of the same root, "circle of stones".

§ 11 *Retrospective view of the period with Laban*

Having focused on the scenes separately we shall try to understand them as parts of the great whole, Gen. 29-31. The structure of the stories 5-10 is as follows:

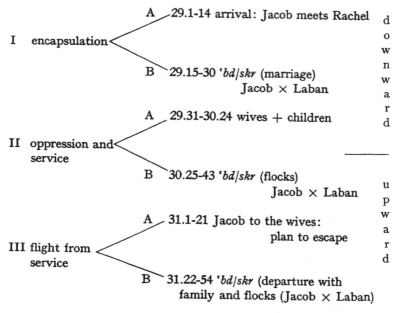

I encapsulation	A	29.1-14 arrival: Jacob meets Rachel	downward
	B	29.15-30 *'bd/skr* (marriage) Jacob × Laban	
II oppression and service	A	29.31-30.24 wives + children	
	B	30.25-43 *'bd/skr* (flocks) Jacob × Laban	upward
III flight from service	A	31.1-21 Jacob to the wives: plan to escape	
	B	31.22-54 *'bd/skr* (departure with family and flocks (Jacob × Laban)	

Now we see that the Haran-period has been described in three parts, with three fighting-rounds between Jacob and Laban (IB - IIB - IIIB). In the first round Jacob is totally knocked off his feet by the deceiver Laban and bound to a fourteen year tenure of hard work. In the second round, precisely in the middle of this period, after Joseph's birth, the reversal takes place: Jacob makes proposals which introduce Laban's fall. Only after the event (in the speech of IIIA) does it appear that Providence has brought about that fall in spite of Laban's devilish, corrupt practices. In the third round it seems for a while that Laban is going to gain ground (his *terafim* had been stolen), but failing to produce evidence and checked by the God of Abraham and Isaac, he becomes the loser. Jacob leaves, untouched, a blessed man. In short, the slant of the B-scenes is – what applies to Israel applies to its patriarch –:

Ex. 1-12 wᵉka'ᵃšer yᵉʿannū'ōtō, ken yırbę̄ wᵉken yifroṣ.

The more he is oppressed the more he expands!

In the A-scenes Laban is absent.[85] In I A Jacob meets with his favourite wife and shows her how he removes obstacles; in II A we get into the serpents' pit of a family-life poisoned under the auspices of Laban; the plan of escape unites Jacob and his people.

A precedes B. But when we render this not very sensational statement into a question which is useful at this point, we ask: what is the meaning of the fact that the A-scenes precede the B-scenes? Apparently the meaning is that Jacob had come to Haran to find a wife, to raise a family, and that, as far as he was concerned the matter could have stopped at *šālōm* (characteristic of I A). But a B always follows, signifying that the difficulties and complications stem from Laban. Line A, the family-life, is hampered and frustrated by line B, the struggle for life of the "man of wages". IB especially is a revelation: Laban does not shrink from subordinating the family-line entirely to his wages policy of line B. The consequences for the family-line are disastrous, giving rise to heart-rending situations in IIA. Laban may be called the White Man, his sins are scarlet.

Composing a series of stories according to a scheme I A+B II A+B III A+B implies the risk of putting away vital history into a lifeless system. But this has not happened in this case. The pattern is not obtrusive, partly thanks to the fact that the six stories are joined perfectly:

– I A ends with "stay with Laban"; I B opens with the continuation of that stay.

– When, finally, in I B Rachel has come side by side with Leah in one family, the beginning of II A tells of their position in the marriage and its consequences.

– II A ends with the birth of a long desired son from the favourite wife; this birth is the occasion and reason for Jacob's asking leave to depart (beginning of II B).

– II B ends with the great results of Jacob's breeding method. The consequence is supplied by the beginning of III A, a great threat from Laban's family which oppresses Jacob, and God's order to leave.

– The flight at the end of III A and esp. the theft of the penates call forth a pursuit (beginning of III B).

[85] Only at the end of the opening scene he is present as a host.

It is fascinating to weigh the narrated time against the narrative time[86]:

narrative time (in vv.)		*narrated time*
I A	15	1 day (+ 1 month v. 14b)
B	16	7 years[87]
II A	29	7 years
B	19	6 years
III A	21	1 hour[88] (+ 3 days v. 21)
B	33	2 days[89]

There is but one scene which gives a strong impression of an extended length of time: II A strings together the births of eleven, no twelve children in a fairly uniform rhythm and that takes time. That is why II A with twenty-nine verses stands out, especially when we set aside III B, the end, for a moment. It is remarkable that the other four scenes are all so short (15-16-19-21).

The end, thirty-three verses, is by far the longest scene, and we remember at once the importance of the story with its two disputes and the making of a covenant: the two decades were entirely described and interpreted in it. For our convenience we may reduce the narrated time of III B to one day. The one verse 32.1 (with a morning) and 31.24 (the night with the warning dream) might just as well be separated, for III B pivots round the conflict, experienced twice (vv. 26-43) and the "dénouement" in a treaty (44-54).

In any case we see three scenes cover three long periods, which include Jacob's acquisition of 1. wives (I B), 2. children (II A) and 3. flocks (II B) and strongly contrasted to it are three scenes covering a short period. The story is framed by instantaneous snapshots: one in the beginning (to describe the atmosphere), two complementary ones (for both are interpretations of the twenty years) at the end. All of round III, with no less than fifty-four verses, consists of two instantaneous snapshots. But in them the whole period is concentrated. Once more we observe that Jacob's own interpretation is very im-

[86] The measure used for the narrative time, the "biblical verse", is, of course, fundamentally a strange measure; but practically, to make a rough comparison, we are justified in using it.

[87] V. 30b need not be included here.

[88] = speech; I just make a random guess.

[89] Night (dream) + a day's quarrel; departure the next morning; exclusive of the introductory v. 23 (seven days).

portant; only (anti-)salvation–history, interpreted and experienced, is history here.

Jacob's destiny was "to be lord over his relatives"; "let peoples serve you" (27.29). At Haran he gets farther from his ideal than ever. For his high-handed manipulation of Isaac by means of a change of persons he is paid back equally well by Laban's manipulations. By means of a change of persons he keeps the Jacoba of the two sisters from reaching the first place. Jacob gets hopelessly entangled in servitude to his relative, the opposite of 27.29.

But at the same time God's blessing works. Many sons are born to him and during the last six years he acquires an enormous wealth in flocks. At the moment when all this is in danger of being taken away from him God intervenes between Laban and Jacob and protects him.

When Jacob has reached the lowest point of his servitude, the imminent capture of the fugitive, God turns everything for the better, and starts Jacob anew on his way to his destiny. The end of the Haran period means a fresh, God-given start. Maybe Jacob learns from it that autonomous, sinful behaviour will be of no avail, that God's help is his only source of strength, and his only change for true integrity (*tom*).

CHAPTER V

JACOB BACK IN CANAAN, GEN. 32, 33 AND 35

§ 12 Scene 11: *Going to meet Esau, A*: Gen. 32.2-13.

Jacob has been in tight situations – but the tightest is yet to come. He is now going to be confronted with his past. A problem easily repressed in the long period at Haran is now quickly revived. In Canaan Jacob had only caused trouble and now at last he must face the consequences; he cannot avoid them any longer.

He had done just that for a long time, as he admits himself in his message, 32.5b (in transl. 4b)[1] to Esau, "up till now I have lingered, I am late." Using the typical *'ḥr*, "linger, lag", Jacob himself acknowledges the psychological significance of his being a foreigner (ger) at Haran, i.e. the repression of his past – until it can be repressed no longer. Every new phase in a man's life lends further meaning to the preceding phases; such is the case here.

With great directness the text has led us to what is essential, by taking Jacob to this pressing problem, passing over irrelevant details and giving no information. Thus great suspense is quickly built up and the suspense with us, as readers, coincides with the tension growing in Jacob, nourished by his fear of Esau's revenge.

But first a short, most particular prelude: the miniature scene 32.2-3. Verse 2 begins with an inversion, which indicates the change of subject. It proves that the story, without losing a single moment, continues straight after the leave-taking and Laban's departure. It says, Jacob "went on his way". The words "go" and "way" are nowhere together in the story of Jacob, except in ... Jacob's vow at Bethel, 28.20. The connection raises the question: will God sustain Jacob now, too, "on the way that he goes"?

[1] The reader who uses a translation should always subtract *one* from the number of verses in Gen. 32; in Hebrew Ch. 32 starts one verse earlier.

Suddenly angels of God "strike upon him". But *pg'* is also used in Gen. 28 at the beginning of the meeting there (v. 10)! And "angels of God" in the plural, he had seen at Bethel, as heralds of their Lord. Then in a short nominal clause Jacob interprets the essence of this meeting, "this is God's army" – as he had last done at Bethel (28.17b). Then "he called the name of that place" Mahanaim – exactly the same formula used in the name-giving of Bethel, 28.19.

The conclusion is obvious: from beginning to end the Mahanaim-scene refers to and builds on the Bethel-scene (as had the previous scene, for that matter). Therefore we wonder, just as Jacob has, whether his "return to the land of his forefathers"[2] will take place *bᵉšālōm*, as 28.21 has it, will be safe and sound. An encounter with angels on the way back may be said to be an omen, and the previous one at Bethel, on his journey going out, was quite favourable.[3] Has not God sent his host to Jacob, our patriarch, to welcome him and accompany him when entering the Promised Land? We are tempted to think so; let us keep this possibility open, considering the words in our hearts.

The text of the prelude itself does not say much. Jacob himself sticks to the facts in v. 3 and does not commit himself to an unambiguous interpretation. And yet, "an army of God" does make one think of fighting. Not long ago Jacob had experienced a near-threat of war, unmistakably, and only God's intervention, in the nick of time, had turned the tables in Jacob's favour (see p. 165). Does he consider another struggle? Does he have premonitions of war? He can hardly avoid such forebodings, now that he is going to meet his brother, the essence of whose nature he has ignored – no, worse, usurped, raising himself to *bᵉkōr*. When Jacob strikes upon "an army" it must be an omen... His uneasy conscience makes him regard the meeting with the angels as something negative, we presume; we will not be sure for a long time. The question is open: is his eye more perceptive or more negative in this tense situation?

Thus this prelude, as an ominous meeting, is a mystery; as a sample of narrative art it is a core full of ambiguity and suspense. Ambiguity because here two diametrically opposed possibilities, each with a very emotional outcome, are kept together. This is expressed in the name

[2] The line šūb 'el 'ereṣ mōladtō of 30.25-31.3, 13 is rooted in the *šūb* of 28.15//21.
[3] The words "Jacob sent messengers before him" in 32.4 remind us of 24.7, God "will send his angel before you"; the previous generation, too, received an escort which was to be interpreted favourably.

which is ambiguity itself become word, both in meaning and in form: Mahanaim, "Double-army" is a dualis![4]

A source of suspense is this moment, because we feel at once that the coming events will be unique, of great "historical" moment. Before anything has happened, the vertical dimension has already been opened over the figures in the future encounters. What is going to happen will gather meaning by this surprising meeting; and vice versa, what is going to happen will shed light on the significance of the meeting and – we presume – make an unambiguous explanation possible. But this certitude will come only after the event. The Mahanaim-scene is so "full of suspense" (creating suspense in the story) because the many premonitions that command our attention are so ambivalent themselves and make us long for a result which will solve our tension: we do not know whether we are to entertain hope or fear after these two verses. The tension is heightened because it is rooted in ambiguity.

For what must "Mahanaim" be taken to mean? Does Jacob see his "camp"[5] opposite or side by side with the host of God (and who, indeed, is the Lord of hosts here), or does he still think of Laban's party as opposite his? Or does he foresee Esau's front opposite his troops? Legitimate questions all of them, to be asked and ... left unanswered. For a solution it is yet too early; we should not force it here.

In Jacob's unsettled conscience an idea is soon ripening, suggested to him by his meeting with the messengers of God: he himself will send messengers to Esau. With winning, humble words he will try to mitigate the shock of the approaching meeting as much as possible, so as to decrease the chance of violent, unpredictable scenes.

The messengers go "to the land of Seʿīr, the country of Edom." These names are found in a linguistic work of art, we come across them primarily in the framework of a literary text. As such they have a literary function in the whole and deserve a literary evaluation.[6]

[4] To avoid misunderstanding: this is not a linguistic or etymological statement. It is a literary statement, valid for this text, with evidence below. The ending *-ayim* may be no more of a real dualis than the one in Miṣrayim, Jerūšālayim.

[5] From 32.11 and 35.8 it appears that his train can be called *maḥªnē* in Hebrew.

[6] With respect to the Song of Songs this is always done by L. Krinetzki, Das Hohe Lied, Düsseldorf, 1964. Most place-names in this lyric poetry function in the first place literarily, connotatively: Jerusalem, Tirza,, Lebanon, Gilead, Karmel, and... Mahanaim. Also Kedar, Salomo, etc.

A good example of the literary valuation of geographical names is found in

Edom is, then, a direct reminder of that occasion on which the *'admōnī* fell for *'ādom*; now he lives in the country of Edom as fits him. But what was the other quality, the only one known about Esau right from the start? He was hairy: *sā'īr*. That is what the name of Se'ir plays upon. Thus the so-called topographical names of v. 4 have, in the first place, a literary effect. We wonder in concern if another conflict will be growing between the now fore-warned, rough, hairy Red-beard and the smooth Heel-catcher.

Jacob, however, tries hard to forestall this. Very precisely and officially the story uses two formal links before the message itself is sounded; first there is the commission to the messengers, then the official formula for messengers, made famous by the prophets, follows perfectly. Thus Jacob organizes this mission so formally and solemnly because now it is all-important to him that the first impression made on Esau should be as correct as possible.

And what is correct? The text is unambiguous on this point. What counts is the title used for Esau in the message and its correlative, Jacob's description of himself:

"thus you shall say to *my lord*, Esau:
thus says *your servant*, Jacob: ..."

But the elder was to serve the younger! From these titles it appears quite clearly that the tables have been radically turned. Here Jacob admits that his actions have brought him in diametrical contrast to his destiny. It is obvious that here we are not dealing with a meaningless use of complimentary phrases. The end of the message removes any

F. M. Th. de Liagre Böhl, Wortspiele im AT, = pp. 11-25 of his Opera Minora, Groningen/Djakarta 1953 (originally in JPOS 1926). Böhl on p. 18f.: "Dieses se'ir war der (im Altertum bewaldete) Teil des edomitischen Berglandes, welcher südlich von Beerseba gelegen ist, wo unsere Erzählung spielt (sc. Gen. 27). Hier, in diesen "rauhen" Waldungen, ist somit der Jäger Esau zuhause. Zwischen diesem Gebiet und der Stadt Beerseba lag nun aber – noch in Palestina selbst, dessen südlichste Grenze es bildete – nach Jos. 11,17 und 12,1 das "glatte" oder kahle Gebirge hahar heḥālāq "das gen Seïr aufsteigt" (...). Hier, in diesen fruchtbaren Weidegründen bei Beerseba, ist der Hirt zuhause. Die Grenze des gelobten Landes läuft somit genau zwischen dem "haarigen" und den "glatten" Gebirge (dem har se'īr und dem har ḥālāq) hindurch. Somit ist bereits auf Grund hiervon alles deutlich: der "glatte" Berg, mit der Stadt Beerseba, dem Schauplatz der Erzählung, und mit dem ganzen gelobten Land nördlich davon gehört dem "glatten" Hirten Jakob, während der "haarige" Esau wie ein bockgestaltiger Satyr s'yr in den Wäldern draussen bleiben muss."

such thought. V. 6b is even more meaningful and is the best definition of the "correct impression" Jacob wants to make on Esau. He hopes to *find favour* in his sight. In fact, that is the only possible thing left to restore the relationship Esau – Jacob: that Esau should forgive his cheating brother, that he should be merciful, for the deceit itself cannot be retrieved. Encampment opposite each other (*ḥānā*) is of no use to Jacob, but mercy (*ḥen, ḥānan*) is.

His hopes seem to be dashed to the ground, when the messengers return: "Esau is coming to meet you, and four hundred men with him." What use are four hundred men, Jacob thinks, if not to wage war? And this explanation seems most plausible. Nevertheless, it is difficult to fix an unequivocal explanation for v. 7, for the verse is a dry, factual and ambiguous report. That Jacob fears for the worst is no wonder; but the reader, not weighed down by so bad a conscience, compares the ambivalence of v. 7 with vv. 2-3. If Esau were out for revenge and destruction of the house of Jacob, would he have let the messengers go back in peace to report the results of their espionage? In that case Jacob would be entirely forewarned and he, Esau, could no longer initiate a surprise attack (e.g., a pincer movement or an attack in the night). It is not quite certain that he is planning war!

And what must we think of the fact that Esau has let the messengers return in peace? Does he feel, and is he justified in feeling, so militarily superior and so sure of victory that he wants to create a cat-and-mouse-situation via the messengers, so that later he will be able to enjoy Jacob's intimidation before giving the death-blow? Compare the besieger Nahash, the Ammonite, who granted respite to Jabesh in I Sam. 11. Or does Esau mean to bring about the effect which, actually, is now produced in Jacob: remorse, fear? Compare the vice-roy Joseph who goes so far as to disguise himself and set a trap, Gen. 44, thus producing great remorse within his brothers.

The test leaves it undecided – and rightly: we are meant to feel the same doubt, to weigh the pros and cons in suspense, just as Jacob does. In this way the narrator keeps his audience in fascinated attention.

Vv. 8f. In his distress Jacob takes a measure which is no more than an emergency dressing. It is a poor stratagem: one half of the troop is to be jeopardized for the salvation of the other. There is the degrading dividing, selecting of the troop: you there I could do without, but you will "cut off" (*plṭ*, v. 9 ending) together with me. It is easy to guess where Leah has been assigned and where Rachel.

There is a division into "two armies", *lišnē maḥ^{a}nōt.* With that this event and the Mahanaim-scene explain each other explicitly for the first time. What we could not surmise as early as v. 3 and had not mentioned among the possible interpretations of "Double-army" is that the two camps would arise with Jacob – a painful and revealing picture of the deplorable situation which has now arisen. The idea for the division may have originated in Jacob from the recently created name, and because of the division the name can now, in the first instance, be interpreted as unfavourably as possible. By his actions Jacob has been a divisive influence in the parents' family, splitting them in two camps; now, as a result, his own family and "house" *(bayit, familia)* is split in two.

The scene concludes with the words of a man in agony, vv. 10-13; they, too, pivot upon the words "two camps", which are in the middle, like a spindle. The simple structure of the whole is as follows, and confirms that the Mahanaim-pıelude works and is integrated backwards towards Bethel, and forwards:

the prelude		vv. 4-13		
mal'ākīm	→	mal'ākīm	send and receive	4-7
mah^{a}nayim	→	2 maḥ^{a}nōt	measure	8f.
			prayer	10-13

The prayer is the perfectly composed climax of this scene. In agony the praying man wants to make as forceful an appeal to God's help as possible. Therefore he solemnly starts with two complete titles; only prefaced by their careful symmetry does he dare to speak the holy proper name, "O God of my father Abraham // God of my father Isaac // Yahweh!" The force of this appeal lies in the responsibility placed on God, the reminder to God of his promises. He works upon God's sense of honour: If you have made such promises, I will now hold you to them. Vv. 10b and 13 start with the same verb – Jacob quotes God! – and then display a framing chiasmus:

hā'ōmer 'elay: return to your country, your kindred	w^{e}'ēṭībā 'immāk
w^{e}'attā 'āmartā: hēṭeb 'ēṭīb 'immāk	promise of numerous progeny

Jacob looks to God for "all that is good" (two occurrences of *yṭb*), viz. the realization of two promises made at Bethel: one of land (here mentioned in the form of a commandment) and one of progeny. Here the promises complete each other crosswise. At the same time vv. 10b and 13 lay the foundations of Jacob's right to call upon God.

Within this framework, almost a pair of trammels with which to tie God to his promises!, are two long, moving sentences. A touching acknowledgement (11a) suggests the great contrast between the past, when Jacob left Canaan alone, and the present, when, although threatened, he returns with riches (two camps); a contrast indicated by reference to the place, "this Jordan here". The words of thanks pave the way for the heart of the matter: the cry of distress *haṣṣīlenī*, with which v. 12 opens, "Deliver me". This one word is the whole prayer. It is followed by a confession of frank directness ("I am afraid") and what Jacob is afraid of is summed up in a fine idiomatic expression, *weʰhikkanī 'em ʿal bānīm.*[7] Thus death is tersely at the end of the cry for help.

What happened? Humbled by agonizing fear of death Jacob looks to God for help and advice for the first time. He who used to arrange his affairs himself so efficiently, preferably at the cost of his fellow-men, is now, for the first time, willing to be little, *qāṭon*, thus not the first man. He used to be the "little" (*qāṭon*, younger) son who could not wait to surpass the "big son" to become the self-made first-born. Now at last he wants really to be little, for now he admits: *qāṭontī*.

Now he also admits, I owe everything to your "steadfast love and faithfulness", O God. Grandeur has not sprung out of myself, from my own labour and exertion. For the first time he calls himself the servant of God. That is the best and only basis on which the God of Abraham and of Isaac can also become the God of Jacob. Frey remarks (ad loc.) with respect to the beginning: noch wagt er nicht, ihn *seinen* Gott zu nennen. And concerning v. 11 he says, Indem er sich so klein vor Gott sieht, darf er sich aber – wunderbare Paradoxie! – zum erstenmal *seinen* Knecht nennen.

A parallelism is developing between Jacob's relationship with his brother, which exemplifies his contact with any fellow-man, and his relationship with God. On one and the same day in his life he asks his brother for mercy, as a servant asks his lord, and he confesses to be dependent on God's *ḥesed* and *'ᵉmet*, as a servant of God.

[7] Also Deut. 22.6, Hos. 10.14; *ʿal* =plus.

His self-confidence has vanished. In the prayer he admits the illusiveness of the measure taken in 8f. There is no way out; the parallel between 9 and 12b makes that clear:

9	'im yābō ... wᵉhikkani wᵉhāyā hammaḥᵃnẹ hanniš'ār lifleṭā
12b	pen yābō wᵉhikkanī 'em ʿal bānīm

Hoping that one half might be saved, was hoping against hope; in 12b this is admitted, in only five syllables (-nī 'em ʿal bānīm) the wholesale destruction is foreseen. Thus, in his prayer, Jacob has given himself completely, and has tried to surrender himself to God. After that he tries to sleep (14a), but fear, tension and remorse haunt him through the night.

It is of the utmost importance to realize how, in a four-part narrative of actions and words, the main character develops, how he grows and how one emotion is piled on top of another. Misgivings after vv. 2-3; humbleness and suspenseful waiting in 4ff; death-agony in 8, leading to a measure of panic in v. 9; and an impressive prayer, in which Jacob, leaning on God's promises, searches for the right attitude of faith and only expresses his fear in the cry of distress "deliver me" after thanking God. Jacob is growing under the immense stress of circumstances, is shedding the "old Adam". And growing is becoming smaller!

§ 13 Scene 11: *Going to meet Esau, B*: Gen. 32.14-22.

An honest prayer may contain the seed of its answer. Jacob's prayer is a pure representation of the triangle Esau-Jacob-God and, psychologically speaking, is a way of coming to terms with the very tense situation. In v. 11f. Jacob sincerely tries to face reality by putting it into plain words. Through this effort he has already come to realize and accept the futility of a stratagem.

Now, after the prayer, the development continues for a whole phase. By verbalizing and thus facing his fear, by humbling himself before Yahweh, Jacob makes important progress towards humanization. He matures enough to see a solution more real and worthy of a human being, reconciliation with Esau. Jacob's prayer contains the seed of its answer. With a profound use of simple key-words, Gen. 32.14-22 carefully outlines the new perspective which becomes gradually clearer to Jacob.

Phase A (vv. 2-13) can be characterized with an alliteration from the text itself: Jacob is far away from the *ḥen* he is in search of because of his *maḥ^{a}nē̦*-position. Phase B (vv. 14-22) proceeds with the alliterations. It is an important step towards the *ḥen* to use a *minḥā* instead of *maḥ^{a}nē̦*.

This word for "present" is the alpha and omega of Gen. 32.14-22, enclosing this phase as part of a chiastic frame. The other part shows quite clearly that Jacob has entered the longest night in his life and how restless his "lodging" is:[8]

14a	he lodged there that night	b)	he took from what he had with him a *minḥā* for his brother Esau
22	the *minḥā* passed on before him		he himself lodged that night(...)

Darkness surrounds Jacob!

In v. 15f. the narrator becomes Jacob's obliging and most accurate notary. What a row of flocks, what variety of animals! Esau, it appears from this very long enumeration, is going to be snowed under with presents. Jacob intends to have Esau "encircled" by cattle to such an extent that (psychologically speaking) there will be no room left for him to move, much less for him to do Jacob any harm. To that purpose he gives his shepherds accurate instructions as to their places in the procession (v. 17) and as to their behaviour, when meeting Esau (vv. 18-21a).

By determining the position of his shepherds ("before" me: v. 17b, 21b, 22a) Jacob determines his own position, "behind you" (vv. 19b, 21). Therewith, however, Jacob has betrayed his moral and psychological position in a revealing way.

Now that the place has become too hot for him, the man of "I first!" is eager to come last, to shelter behind the work of other people, (who are bringing reconciliation in the shape of a present), who are innocent. He would have loved to crawl into the earth, he, who at the birth wanted to lead the way, who came to his old father before Esau

[8] The framing function of (only) the members 1 and 4 (the lodging *ballaylā*) pointed out by P. A. H. de Boer, p. 15 of his article, Genesis xxxii 23-33, Some Remarks on Composition and Character of the Story, Nederlands Theologisch Tijdschrift 2 (1946/47), pp. 149-163: "In Gen. xxxii the passage vv. 14-22 (Rev. Version vv. 13-21) forms such a closed unity"...

in order to make himself the blessed first-born and who wanted to marry first and only the "Jacoba" of Laban's daughters.

Thus two humble prepositions of place and time, "before" and "after/behind", prove to be an important pair of key-words in the text. This also determines the significance of the words "The first came forth ... and afterward came forth" in the birth-story (25.25f.) and the "going out" (yṣ', twice) in reversed order in Gen. 27.30. We also recall, to give "the younger before the *b*^{e}*kīrā*" in marriage, in 29.26. As far back as these verses of ch. 25 and 29 we found the opposites "before" and "after", *lifnē* + *'aḥ*^{a}*rē*. And suddenly we find how characteristic Jacob's message in 32.5 was, "I have lingered up till now" – again the root *'aḥar*! Now we also fully understand he sent the messengers before him (32.4) in a first attempt at concealment. So in the previous phase, too, the opposition *lifnē -'aḥ*^{a}*rē* was already present, at first latently, retrospectively speaking very efficaciously.

The relinquishing of his frontal position, the modest withdrawal to the rear is realized by the "passing on" (*'br*) of the shepherds who must take the present to Esau, v. 17b, 22a. That, too, is noteworthy: Jacob allows himself to be passed by, for the first time willingly. And with that this scene actually introduces a new key-word, *'br*, which is to be an important stylistic means, with a double function.

From the preposition *lifnê* the narrative now develops, most ingeniously, a key-word of its own. The noun here, the word ***pānīm***, is resuscitated and rises to the rank of the most radiant key-word in the story of Jacob. At once it appears as a daring end-rhyme in a passage important enough as it is, because it contains Jacob's intentions:

v. 21 for he said to himself:

oooó oó	"let me cover up his face	pānāw
ooó ooó ooó	with the present that goes before my face;	pānāy
oooó oó oó	afterwards I shall see his face:	pānāw
oó oó oó	perhaps he will lift up my face."	pānāy
ooó ooó ooó	The present passed on before his face.	pānāw

Jacob labours under the delusion (and the text indicates this delusion by alternating "my" and "his") that in this way he will come face to face with Esau, that he can establish a real dialogue of reconciliation by forgiveness, by sending a present.

Once more, just as in 32.5, he sends a message in which "my lord Esau" is addressed in the name of "your servant Jacob" (v. 19a). But this humiliation, as genuine as in v. 5, is still rooted only in fear and is an attempt to save his life. This is also why the plan of this phase – finding *ḥen* by means of a *minḥā* – is to fall flat. In the final analysis the present is self-seeking; in fact Jacob wants to buy off Esau's wrath with it. He does not yet see that this gift is no solution to the problem of a relationship broken by him. A present is real and authentic only if given with the right intention, altruistically.

Jacob is enmeshed in an inner contradiction, as yet imperceptible to him, but which is clearly indicated by the narrator:

v. 19 l^{e}'abd^{e}kā l^{e}Ya'^{a}qob ... w^{e}hinnē gam hū 'aḥ^{a}rēnū
21 w^{e}gam hinnē 'abd^{e}kā Ya'^{a}qob 'aḥ^{a}rēnū

In both cases the self-humiliation with the title "servant" is at once followed by "behind us he himself is coming", betraying Jacob's fear. How important it is to Jacob to come in the rear is also apparent from this: only a portion of the message ordered in 18f. is repeated in v. 20b (the rest is only referred to), only that part which is vitally important to Jacob: "Jacob himself is coming, too, b e h i n d us" (21a).

Inner contradiction means ambivalence. Thus since "Mahanaim" we have not yet made much progress! In an off-shoot of the motif maḥ^{a}nę̄, at the end of this scene, the story tells us he lodged that night in the army-camp. The sting is in the tail: so the whole approach-by-*minḥā* is framed by, i.e. encircled and enfeebled by "armies", viz. *maḥ^{a}nę̄* of v. 22b and the entire thread of 32.3-11. In fact Jacob has not freed himself from the atmosphere of fighting, fear, suspicion. Indeed does not the word "army-camp" appear to anticipate the fight on the Jabbok, the passage immediately following the *minḥā*-passage? It also strikes us that Jacob forgets to ask for *ḥen* once more in the new message (v. 18f.), as he had clearly done in 32.6. It seems to be another *Fehlleistung*: deep in his heart he does not want to live on mercy, he wants to buy off a conflict with property – for he can afford it.

Phase B, with its *minḥā*-labour and its *maḥ^{a}nę̄*-ending also clarifies the prelude "Mahanaim". It strongly appears that "Double-army" means Esau's camp opposite Jacob's. The light, conversely falling from the prelude on this phase, reveals the above mentioned ambivalence (the inner contradiction within Jacob).

This inner discord is evident in the almost grotesque verse 22. It is highly ironic that in 22a a whole squad of people with a great quantity of live-stock should pass on to appease Esau, whereas the hero himself prefers to go ... to sleep!

Is that the way to "see the face" of one's brother? The narrator has Jacob himself betray the naivety of this plan in an incorrect figure of speech. For Jacob wants to see Esau's face after he himself has covered it up (the Hebrew metaphor for atonement). As we said before, Esau is meant to be overwhelmed by the present. How, then, is he to lift up Jacob's face (= forgive)? If his face is covered up, can Jacob come and see eye to eye with him? Of course not. Such a reconciliation was impossible to begin with.[9]

§ 14 Scene 12: *Meeting a "man" on the Jabbok*, Gen. 32.23-33.

In Gen. 32 and 33 there is a refined play of lines with a set of three key-words, "army-camp – mercy – present".[10] The plan started in phases A and B and in Gen. 33, where at last the meeting with Esau takes place, it is completed. In the last phase before that meeting, however, *ḥn*, *mḥnh* and *mnḥh* are absent. Scene 32.23-33 is indeed an interlude, but one in which a new protagonist brings a decisive depth to the narrative. Scene 12 is by no means a breathing space, by no means an uncommitted dissociaton from the current situation, but the very opposite.

The narrative art of the Bible knows how to put great elementary force into carefully rounded, relatively independent nuclei ("smallest literary units", the"*Kurzerzählung*"). We found excellent examples of this in Gen. 11.1-9 and in scene 4 of this story, Jacob at Bethel. The counterpart of this nucleus, seen before Haran, is scene 12, Jacob at Penuel, which comes after Haran.

In terms of simplicity the plot supporting this story compares well with the perfectly rounded kernel of 25.29-34, which again consists of a conflict, a fight between two men, now even literally a wrestle. The structure of this scene is transparent:

[9] Again, to avoid misunderstanding: of course this interpretation does **not** imply that reconciliation always renders it impossible to see eye to eye with someone because reconciliation "covers up the face"! By no means. With such metaphors the native speaker no longer normally realizes the origin, the special meaning of each part. With *kapper 'et pᵉnē X* he does not think of the literal sense of "cover up" anymore. But in this case the literal sense is resuscitated because the second half of the expression is part of a five-fold rhyme, and thus, taken literally again, friction is brought about between "covering up" and "seeing".
[10] Mentioned, but not understood in terms of their structural significance, by Böhl, art. cit., pp. 15,22f.

- vv. 23f: the preliminaries
- 25-26 : fight, ending in:
- 27-30 : conversation
- 31-32 : Jacob's evaluation and departure
- 33 : an aetiological side-note

Yet this text is, in a way, unapproachable, and this is due to its great profundity. The Jabbok-scene clearly typifies certain characteristics found in much biblical narrative art and mentioned by Erich Auerbach in his judgement of Gen. 22[11]: "Hintergründlichkeit, suggestive Wirkung des Unausgesprochenen, Deutungsbedürftigkeit".

If there is one text in the Story of Jacob which is *"hintergründig"* then it is this one! And therefore is it very *"deutungsbedürftig"*. In this text we feel that only the top of an iceberg in sight, to use a somewhat hackneyed phrase, and it is nearly impossible to fix in a description the line between what is expressed and what is not, between "foreground" and "background". It is easy for the exegete to lose his footing, here, in interpreting a text by which he is so greatly challenged; to lose his footing by spinning out "subjective speculations." We had better insert some methodological reflection.

Although this text successfully resists a sharp dichotomy into things shown and things concealed, a separation of the front and the back of things, for the sake of clarity we are justified in using this opposition when describing the workable method of exegesis. In my opinion it would be a sensible thing for the interpreter to start at the front. First we should draw up as accurate a description as possible of the "facts" of the text, which must be as easy to verify as possible. The stylistic-structural analysis suits our purpose well, because its pursuit enables us to verify our results within the text.

Not until we have given an "objective" outline of the "exterior" are we justified in and capable of gauging the "interior". We would be wise to pick our way carefully from the certain to the uncertain. Using tested observations of style and structure as a guide line we will be able to make statements about that which is not expressed – although we may eventually be halted at the boundary of the inexpressible.

The context is a great help. We would enter the darkness of what is hidden like blind people if we discarded the context into which Gen. 32.23-33 is integrated, first of all this period in Jacob's life, Gen. 32-33,

[11] E. Auerbach, Mimesis, 2nd ed. Bern 1959, Ch. I, p. 26.

and secondly the whole history of Jacob. Gen. 32 and 33 are the x- and y-axes of the system of co-ordinates within which the Jabbok-scene is presented to us, and the lines of a consistent *Leitwortstil* point to the right angle. In the opposite compartment it is possible for the pious exegete to be tortured for ever by chimeras under the command of a river demon.

In the concluding verse, when the action has been completed with Jacob's passage (v. 32), the narrator makes an aside to his audience: we people of this time honour a usage which goes back to Jacob's wrestling with his opponent and eternalizes it. This aetiological note does not affect what follows and hardly affects what precedes, forms no part of the action and may be ignored now that we have another picture of the structure of the scene, this time an even simpler one:

- preparation (vv. 23-24)
  - FIGHT + CONVERSATION (vv. 25-30)
- issue (vv. 31, 32)

The heart of the scene is a confrontation of two persons proceeding in two ways. Jacob meets with "someone who wants to have a private conversation with him". Therefore all that is his must be eliminated, removed from the stage. There is no better way to do it than by sending them across a river (23f.). After the confrontation Jacob could join them again, v. 32. Now for a suitable river and a suitable action. Suitable for "*ya'qob*" that is.

Thus a set of three words articulates the heart of the matter by means of a hard alliteration:

ya'^{a}qob – yabboq – y/he'ābeq

Tripping his fellow-men by the heel (*'qb*) has for Jacob come to its extreme consequence: a wrestling (*'bq*) with a "man" which to Jacob is the most shocking experience of his life, as appears from the fact that thereafter he proceeds through life a man changed of name, and thus of nature, and under that new name he becomes the patriarch of the "Israelites". (This comes out even more strongly in Jacob's own confession in v. 31).

Let Jacob try once more to trip up this adversary. In the wrestling the consequences of his actions must at last be borne by Jacob-alone; they cannot be shunted off, wholly or partly, to shepherds (who are to deliver a present) or to wives whose lives are decisively influenced by the "Jacob-principle" (by which Leah is "hated" and neglected for "Jacoba"). V. 25a describes an indispensable condition for the subsequent confrontation. That Jacob should stay behind alone is the narrator's aim in the verses 23-24. Casting a glance at the craftman's workshop, we have been telling tales out of the school of narrative art. The individual meaning of the motions leading up to v. 25a is, however, not yet accounted for. Moreover, another intriguing question about v. 25a remains: did Jacob himself want to isolate himself, to be alone?

V. 23. Jacob "arose that night", which must at least mean, he could not sleep. He still could not sleep! In 32.14 he had tried to get to sleep in vain, until in his unrest he saw a new opening: not the *maḥ*^{a}*nẹ*-approach but the *minḥā*-approach, bring about reconciliation between himself and Esau. And so he does, vv. 14b-22a. But again he does not find rest. Nor do we wonder at this, for Jacob was still a prey to inner contradiction; his aim, reconciliation (via dialogue face to face) does not harmonize with his intentions or the means used (a *minḥā* behind which he who is responsible takes shelter, out of fear arising from a bad conscience).

V. 23. Jacob cannot sleep because he continues to be conscience-stricken. Here as in 32.14 he feels that he is not *tām* any longer, a man-of-character. As purposeful and efficient as he was as deceiver, so estranged and split has his personality now become; his humanity, his moral stature has been broken by it. He has embraced a false definition of integrity by pursuing his destiny high-handedly. After twenty years at Haran all this comes to light unmercifully on the eve of the confrontation with Esau. Truth will out.

V. 23. As in 32.14 it is this which sets him going. Again he acts, as in 14b. Again he forms a procession, as in 14b. Again "he took" are the opening words. And again the key-word is "pass", now with a different object, the brook. So it is more than obvious that the beginning of the Jabbok-scene, of phase C before the meeting with Esau, runs parallel to the beginning of phase B. This means that Jacob sees a new opening, he has a better insight into his inner dividedness, he clearly has something in mind. In v. 23f. he initiates a new plan. Whereas in v. 17 he made servants "pass on", he now makes his people "pass" a ford in the Jabbok. He has a plan which goes beyond the *minḥā*-plan of 14ff.

What is his plan? We have now reached the limits of what can be verified and must cross them with care, indicating possibilities. If we leave aside the contents of the plan and glance at v. 25 for a while, we observe two possibilities: either Jacob himself intended to pass the rest of the night alone on one bank, e.g. for reflection, or he did not. If he did, then there is a (too) surprising coincidence with the later event. For what is going to happen in v. 25b cannot be anticipated. The unique fight and conversation of 25-30 is beyond any human scheme. V. 25b would lose the quality of surprise, an element which is very popular, particularly in these short stories, where the action consists in a conflict.

The other possibility is more plausible in my opinion: it was not Jacob's intention to arrive at the isolation of 25a. That means that in 25b he (and so we) is surprised by the appearance of a figure whose significance and plans are still a mystery. In this case Jacob is taken by surprise at a moment when, having sent everyone across, he is alone for a while. Seen from his viewpoint the surprise, at this moment, is "accidental" – but we need not believe that yet. The adversary might have known very well what was going to happen.

Defending the interpretation that the operation of 23f. was not a means of removing the others to enable Jacob to be alone (which, in any case, was the narrator's intention), we are obliged to assign an other meaning to the purpose of Jacob's action in 23f. Such a plan is quite conceivable, yet not incompatible with the artist's intention of leading up to "Jacob was left alone" of 25a.

What was his intention? Should we not turn with confidence to the style? The most conspicuous stylistic phenomenon in v. 23f. is a fourfold *'br* (three times the verb; once the noun), but that is a key-word both before and after this scene! Now Jacob makes the actual members of his house "pass on", whereas in the previous phase the servants had to "pass on" so that Jacob and his people might follow safely (!). This can only mean that in the restlessness of his longest night Jacob has woken up to the fact that hanging behind means hiding oneself, shirking one's responsibility. Although we are beyond the limits of verification, I favour the interpretation that in crossing Jacob wants to make amends, that he wants to lead the way himself and wants to go to meet Esau himself. Whether he has become aware of the extent of his blame can no longer be discerned in the text, but on the grounds of the parallelism of the beginnings of phase B and phase C this seems unlikely to me, for in vv. 14-22 he had not yet recognized the two-facedness of the *minḥā*-reconciliation.

This crossing is most significant: now we have come to Jacob's real Rubicon.[12] In sending his people across he also gives up a line of defence, so that further fighting plans have become pointless (the *maḥᵃnẹ*-solution!) and he makes the Jabbok a serious obstacle, not for Esau, but for himself, should he want to flee. The repetition of *ʿbr* also indicates what a toilsome operation this is for Jacob.

We have now come to the heart of the scene. Looking at the structure of vv. 25-30 the mere difference in length indicates that the fight itself is a preamble to the most important part of the scene, the dialogue of 27-30.

The fight is over in four sentences, and starting from wayyē'ābeq 'īš ʿimmō (25b) it is framed by ending in hē'ābᵉqō ʿimmō. Jacob fights with "a man". We can only learn this adversary's identity by judging him by his words and actions, as Jacob does. Purposely a very general, meaningless word has been chosen which suggests a mystery but reveals nothing. This fits with the "man"'s intentions, for in v. 30 he refuses to reveal himself by asking a counter-question. Thus he provokes Jacob to think about and evaluate things himself, and we are also challenged to do so.

They fight "until the breaking of the day". This thread is resumed in the dialogue: in 27a "the man" asks, "let me go, for the day is breaking". Like metaphors, such an indication in a literary work of art can have various meanings, all of which must be applied and we must control our inclination to choose either this one or that.

Darkness surrounds Jacob (the setting of phase B!). Again the night is – as in Bethel – symbolic of Jacob's position. Fear, uncertainty have seized him. But, first of all he does not see himself yet, does not recognize his new identity which can save him, the renewed integrity which is born in the recognition and confession of one's guilt.

Night is also necessary to conceal the adversary's identity. For he emphatically wants to disappear before broad day-light. If he had not launched the attack in the night Jacob would probably have seen that he was a very particular man, a man of a very special authority (v. 29!) and very special identity (v. 30b). Now Jacob only understands this after the event (v. 31). Simply speaking: if Jacob had perceived at once that he was going to have God, as v. 31 says, (or, to be very modest, a messenger of God) to deal with, he would not even have started a fight or, rather, not have continued it with all his might, with that obstinacy peculiar to him.

[12] Cf. p. 163 about Gen. 31.21.

In hindsight (for example in v. 31) we also notice that God has always revealed himself to Jacob only in the night. This aspect, too, makes the Penuel-scene the counter-part to Bethel. Considering that angels are always involved, it is no wonder that Hosea knows the fight on the Jabbok as a fight with an angel (Hos. 12.4).[13]

Vv. 25-26. The fight is long and violent. Characteristic of his enormous commitment, Jacob cannot be overcome. But the adversary must be a doughty fighter, if we remember the force Jacob was able to muster in 29.1-14! The sequel in v. 26 leads to 32b and 33, and is a brief report, to be considered as information, in order to complete the two verses about the actual struggle.[14] Profound interpretation is not called for here; we need only observe that Jacob suffers a dislocated hip. And that is that. The text does not say whether this is the man's last effort or that a tip of the veil of the mystery has been lifted here for a moment. Who knows, perhaps this is a moment at which the adversary from God (v. 31) makes Jacob feel that he has strength at his command far beyond human understanding and resistance. For the text by no means says, "he beat him", but only uses a much lighter word, "he touched him", and we are strongly reminded of a "magical" touch like the one with which Isaiah's lips were touched.[15] The custom described in v. 33, too, is easily understood as the commemoration of a sacred touch; after all it describes a taboo. But now we are again reaching beyond the boundaries of verification.

The narrator, and this is the point, wants to go on, because above all he wants to unfold the confrontation in the form of a dialogue, the dozen sentences of vv. 27-30.

[13] This does not mean that "angel of God" differs from "God" in content, as Hos. 12.3, ending, shows.

[14] Eising, op. cit., p. 130f., wonders why "die Verletzung Jakobs als Beglaubigungszeichen" is so far to the front, "diese scheinbar falsche Stellung". "Die Forderung des Segens durch Jakob in V. 27b verlangt, dass er ein höheres Wesen vor sich weiss. Weil Jakob das aus der Verletzung merken soll, ist sie also vorher berichtet. Ferner beachte man, dass später die Situation des Ringens verlassen ist, weil nur noch von dem neuen Namen und vom Segen gesprochen wird. In V. 26 kann die Verletzung aber ursächlich mit dem Ringen verbunden werden, das in dem gleichen Vers erwähnt wird."

[15] Is. 6.7 uses *ng'* too. The word which describes the result may also be sacred, cultic in meaning: *yq'*. See de Boer, art. cit., p. 158f.: "The *'ish* acknowledges Jacob's clever strength. This acknowledgement consists of the touching of Jacob's thigh (...). The *'el* sacred [?? this is not the only non-English here, JF], consecrated his thigh. The verb *yq'* also has this cultic meaning in the Hiph. in Numb. xxv 4 and 2 Sam. xxi 6 and 9, Hoph. vs. 13."

V. 27. Although lame below the belt Jacob keeps clasping the man in his arms. He does not let him go until he, the adversary, has blessed him. Blessed him! That is Jacob all over! From the most miserable situation he wants to emerge an enriched man. The key-word of the first phase of his life, also found in the Haran-period, here appears in the third period. At Bethel he had, among other things, received the blessing of Abraham, at his departure; now, at his return, he wants to receive a blessing from the mysterious adversary, on the eve of his most difficult moment. Does Jacob already realize this blessing may affect his present awkward situation? Who knows! For that matter, it is not too important, to concern ourselves with the question whether, as far back as v. 27b, Jacob was already aware of the enormous future implications which the blessing will have. For us it is enough to determine that the narrator was aware of them. We may be satisfied with the fact that in v. 27 this narrative has for some time been leading up to 29 and 30. The very observation that Jacob's fierce fight in v. 27 brings about the prerequisites for vv. 28-30 + 31 (which are a high point in his life) is worthwhile.

On the other hand, it is not unlikely, though, again, no longer verifiable, that Jacob makes such an important demand in 27b because in v. 26b he had realized, with a shock (in his hip!), that indeed his adversary has supernatural, even divine, powers at his disposal.

Within the heart of this story, 27-30, v. 27 itself is the prelude to the rest, to a unique conversation with world-historical implications. In its turn the simple game of asking and answering in v. 28 paves the way and leads up to the statement of v. 29. The man asks the patriarch's name and as he replies "Jacob" we realize that the name indicates his nature; here the Heelcatcher is caught. "Er antwortet "Jaakob"; und der biblische Hörer der Erzählung hörte, wie uns die jeremjanische Stelle beweist: "Fersenschleicher". Das eben, das Namensbekenntnis der Schuld, wollte der Mann ausgesprochen bekommen."[16] Back in Canaan he must again direct his attention to his own name; again this name may not become a mere label, a mere jingle-jangle.

Are vv. 27-30 a dialogue? V. 27 is, and so are vv. 28 and 30,which mirror each other. But v. 29 is not! V. 29 is a monologue, a solemn "order of baptism", spoken authoritatively. Here we attend the most

[16] M. Buber, p. 225 of Buber und Rosenzweig, Die Schrift und ihre Verdeutschung, Berlin 1936.

important baptism of the O.T.; it is the more important for being a re-baptism "only". A well-established nature, a long-fixed route of life must be turned back radically. That is quite different from re-naming Abram and Sarai into Abraham and Sarah, for there the continuity is obvious.

The evil and long-awkward name of Jacob is thrown away[17] and exchanged for a beautiful, theophorous name.[18] The original sense of the name of Israel may never be established for certain by scientific research but the "real" sense[19] in this story is equally unimportant. The "folk-etymological" meaning of Israel, relevant to this story, is obviously given by the story itself, in v. 29b. Then the verb *sārā* "fight"[20] is used. So *Yisrā'el* here means, "God fights" (such a translation as Buber's "Fechter Gottes" is impossible). What does this mean?

First we look at v. 29b. The last word is clearly connected with 26a. "You have striven (...) with men" is not too difficult. Even at the prenatal stage Jacob strove with his brother; once he had been born he settled that strife to his (seeming) advantage by acquiring *bekōrā* and *berākā*, and from Laban he disappeared untouched after a twenty years' struggle for, again, the blessing. But then "you have striven with God". So far Jacob's whole life had been dragging the blessing out under all circumstances for his own use, being the blessed one, but under his own steam, and above all high-handedly and by means of deceit. And precisely because this destiny (to become the first man) had been given to him by God even before his birth, he has been constantly in revolt because he wanted to realize this destiny of his own accord and by means of deceit. He was too self-willed and too proud to let the blessing be g i v e n to him.

That obstinate, proud, grim resistance to God is what he now displays on the banks of the Jabbok – and there it is also ... knocked down. Literally. At the same time, however, it is, as it were, countenanced. It is true, the "man" has, just for a while, shown unambiguously that every human effort pales into insignificance as soon as super-

[17] Buber proceeds, ibid.: "Und nun nimmt er diesen Schuldnamen von ihm: ..."
[18] In t h i s story, as in Gen. 27, it does not count that the name of Jacob is the theophorous name *Ja'qob'el* for short.
[19] Supposing for a while that it is different from the interpretation assigned to it by popular etymology, which is not certain.
[20] This *sārā* is to be found in Hos. 12.4, 5 only, but there it is based on Gen. 32. So we must understand the meaning from the context, and fortunately it shows the way clearly.

natural, no divine, power manifests itself; but on the other hand he accepts defeat ("you have prevailed") from that gnarled, irreducible, primeval will of Jacob's, who does not want to pass under any yoke and who wants to be ruler, not servant. He expresses his appreciation and admiration of this undivided will and commitment. He adorns him with the name "Israel" on the ground of (*kī*!) his recognition of Jacob's unique nature. The name "God fights" may then mean: God fights with you, because he is forced to by your stubbornness and pride. And also: henceforth God will fight for you, for he appreciates your absolutely sincere and undivided commitment.

At first v. 30 seems to be the exact reflection of v. 28 in reversed direction, now that one asks the other to reveal himself. This subject in any case provides the frame for v. 29, and therefore it indicates the name-giving as the high point of the confrontation.

But in 30b events are different. The "man" parries Jacob's question with a counter-question, "why do you ask my name?" He refuses to reveal his identity straight away; but at the same time his refusal points to his secret and draws attention to it! It has not failed to work with Jacob. In v. 31 he produces the interpretation provoked by the adversary himself. The question itself has been put somewhat compassionately and jestingly: but Jacob, do you not ask for the sake of asking? (Think and you will know the answer!)

The morning before Jacob's most critical hour turned out to be Jacob's most critical hour. And when he is blessed by his adversary he understands that he has stood the test. He was the blessed one, he remains the blessed one. The line of his life has been confirmed.[21]

[21] Eising, op.cit., is worth quoting once at great length, because he has devoted one of the best analyses of his book to the Penuel-scene. He defends the view that this blessing is the promise of land and offspring, thus the blessing of Abraham, p. 128f.:
Die Spendung des Segens wird in V. 30 der Verleihung des Namens nur angehängt. Dazu steht diese Erwähnung des Segens noch ganz ohne den Wortlaut des Segensspruches. Wenn wir hierzu nach einer Vervollständigung suchen, so ist es angebracht, 35,9-12 heranzuziehen. Dort finden wir den Namen "Israel" von neuem verliehen und mit einem Segensspruch zusammengestellt. Die genannte Stelle bietet den typischen Verheissungssegen, ist aber statt dessen ohne jeden Anklang ätiologischer Art an den Namen Israel und ohne eine Ausdeutung desselben. In unserer Scene haben wir also zwar diesen Namen und seine Erklärung, aber nicht den Text des erwähnten Segens. Die doppelte Beziehung des verheissenden Namens, dass er nämlich aus einer besonderen Erscheinung entsteht und mit dem Verheissungselement verbunden ist, hat der Verfasser nach unserer Meinung in Kap. 32f selbst auch wenigstens anzudeuten

It is easily understood why Jacob asks the other man's name. For the event of v. 29 is exceptional and Jacob feels that here was someone who spoke with full powers.[22] This also means that the "man" is qualified to renew Jacob's identity. And, still more important, this unknown man knows Jacob, he has even got to the bottom of his old identity!

V. 31. Thus Jacob draws his conclusion, that "man" cannot be a mortal being. It now also dawns upon him that the God of Abraham and Isaac is afraid of his Name being taken in vain; that is why Yhwh is cautious in revealing his identity, for giving up the Name means being exposed to magic manipulations with it.[23] That is why in 30b his question was parried.[24]

versucht. Es war beim Namen "Israel" allerdings nicht leicht, beides in einer Scene zu bringen. Bei der Situation des Kampfes, beim Drängen der Begegnung mit Esau hatte in 32,23ff eine eigentliche Verheissung mit vollem Wortlaut keinen Platz. In 35,9ff aber, wo der Verfasser anscheinend den Inhalt der Verheissung nachholen will, ist andererseits die Ätiologie des Namen "Israel" schwierig unterzubringen. Wie hätte der Verfasser dort auch auf einen Kampf kommen können, ohne den nun einmal "Israel" nach der Volksetymologie nicht zu erklären ist. Was der Verfasser also von den innerlich zusammengehörigen Momenten des Verheissungssegens und neuen Namens in einer Scene nicht unterbringen konnte, scheint er in zweien gebracht zu haben, wobei allerdings eine einwandfreie Ergänzung nicht erreicht ist. Wenn auch erst in grösserem Zusammenhang zu untersuchen ist, ob eine der Stellen der Umnennung Jakobs sekundär ist, so haben wir hier zunächst die Erkenntnis gewonnen, dass es innerlich begründet ist, bei der Bitte Jakobs um den Segen in 32,27 und bei seiner Erteilung in V. 30 an den Verheissungssegen zu denken. Wir befinden uns also auch mit dem Jabbokkampf und mit dem neuen Namen "Israel" in heilsgeschichtlichem Milieu. Das entspricht der Tatsache, dass der Jabbokkampf für den Rückweg Jakob ins verheissene Land und für die Darstellung der Errettung seiner Familie und seiner Güter grosse Bedeutung hat.

Since the text itself does not offer any points to justify this interpretation of the blessing, I myself prefer the simpler explanation given by, among others, Wehmeier, op. cit., p. 135: "Auch hier wird nicht gesagt, worin der Segen besteht, doch lässt der Zusammenhang kaum eine andere Deutung zu, als dass der Kämpfende seinem Partner mit dem Segen einen Teil seiner physischen Kraft mitteilen soll."

[22] Eising, op. cit., p. 120: "Es ist (...) zu beachten, dass Umnennungen immer von Höherstehenden an Tieferstehenden vorgenommen werden. Sie erfolgen in Gen. 17,5.15 und 35,9 durch Gott und in Gen. 41,45 durch Pharao."

[23] Paradoxically enough it even appears when the name "*Yhwh*" is revealed in Ex. 3: *'hyh 'šr 'hyh* is also concealment, God wishes to reserve his own manner of being to himself.

[24] Exactly the same situation in Jud. 13, 17, 18. See also note 25.

He also remembers that his grandfather once was visited by "men" who brought a message about a birth humanly impossible long ago, men who also spoke with full powers. They were the shape in which God appeared (Gen. 18). Lot, too, had been visited by such outwardly unrecognizable men (Gen. 19), messengers whose origin could not be recognized as divine until after the event, on the grounds of their words and actions. Lot, too, was visited in the night. "When morning dawned" he had to save his life, and his safe arrival at Zoar was marked by "the rising of the sun" (Gen. 19, 15 and 23).

Jacob tries to find an interpretation and we could be quite satisfied with his view; as it is true within the context of this story we need not go beyond its bounds. But we are able to defend Jacob's interpretation as the correct one because there are two texts in the O.T. which on many points make striking parallels: Jud. 6.11ff. and Jud. 13. They may be considered to prove that Jacob, too, has had a meeting with, a revelation of, God on the Jabbok.[25]

For the third time Jacob immortalizes one of God's revelations to him by means of a name-giving: *Pᵉnī'el.* Just as at Bethel *angels* preceded God's appearance, and God *blessed* him after that, so in this situation angels have appeared first (at Mahanaim) as heralds of God; now God himself goes to meet "Jacob" on the Jabbok in a unique manner and blesses him.

God has come as close to Jacob as possible; he has laid his hands

[25] See Eising, op. cit., pp. 120ff. Among other things he says:
Gideon sagt dann in V. 33 [what is meant is: v. 22, JF], er habe pānīm 'el pānīm den mal'ak Jhwh gesehen. V. 23 zeigt er die gleiche Furcht vor dem erscheinenden Wesen wie Jakob nach dem Jabbokkampf 32,31. Aus Gideons Ausspruch wird ein Altarname hergeleitet, was wir bei unserer Erzählung an späterer Stelle in 33,20 finden. Die Parallele hat also sehr viel inhaltlich Gleiches und nennt im Gegensatz zu unserer Scene 32,23-33 als erscheinende Person deutlich den mal'ak Jhwh. Aber nicht nur diese Bezeichnung wird für ihn gebraucht, sondern statt dessen tritt auch der Name Jhwh allein auf (vgl. Ri 6,14; 6,22f). In der zweiten genannten Parallele (... Jud. 13,3ff), wird der mal'ak in V. 11 sogar wie in 32,25 auch einfach hā'īš genannt, (...)

In der Samsonparallele tritt sogar analog zur Jabbokscene auch die Frage nach dem Namen des erscheinenden Wesens auf (V. 17), (...). Auch dass Manoach und seine Frau Todesfurcht befällt, weil sie den 'ᵉlōhīm gesehen haben, findet sich in dieser Parallele in V. 22 genau so wie in der Erzählung vom Jabbokkampfe.

Eising concludes, p. 124: on these grounds it is possible "auch die Person des geheimnisvollen Kämpfers am Jabbok näher zu bestimmen."

upon him! More immediately than ever Jacob has experienced the *mysterium tremendum ac fascinans.* He bears testimony to this in a verse which is the second high point of this story, v. 31.

Again Jacob is the first and the best interpreter of his own history; again he produces his authoritative interpretation on the spot, and again he arrives at an adequate attitude of faith, as will appear in the sequel (Gen. 33).

That v. 31 (together with v. 29, as a response to the name-giving of 29) is the high point is, again, stylistically absolutely fitting. Almost all Jacob's words, v. 31b, are vital key-words, so that even v. 31 by itself is powerful enough to integrate the Penuel scene firmly into the context, Gen. 32f. Because of the connections brought together here by the *Leitwortstil,* v. 31 has immensely rich implications. But first we shall translate the verse and look at its history within the current situation. "I have seen God face to face, and my life has been delivered."

It is gratifying to put side by side with these words such well-known theophany-passages as Ex. 20.19-21, 24.10, 33.18-23, I Ki. 19.11-13 and Is. 6; but it is also tricky. For, if seeing God (his glory) is fatal to man,[26] we are easily trapped into reading an incorrect contrast in Gen. 32, as for example, "I have seen God (...) and yet [in spite of that] I have been delivered." This would amount to an uncritical transplantation of the essence of the passages mentioned into Gen. 32. Jacob does not say "[and yet] I live" or "I have escaped".[27] The narrator puts into his mouth: my life has been delivered, *wattinnāṣel,* and that is a vital word. It is the same verb as the key verb of Gen. 32.10-13. Jacob had raised the cry of distress "deliver me", viz. in a prayer to God. By now using *nṣl* again he / the narrator tells us: my prayer for deliverance has been answered by God.

That he has been delivered comes home to him when seeing God face to face. Jacob now understands that because he has seen God face to face he will now also see his brother Esau properly, face to face, no longer afraid, and that therefore he has been delivered.[28]

The text had strongly emphasized that it had been Jacob's own intention to meet Esau face to face. But we also noticed that Jacob

[26] Ex. 33.20 "man shall not see me and live".
[27] E.g. *mlṭ* in Gen. 19 or *plṭ* in 32.9, 45.7, II Sam. 15.14 and elsewhere. *Mlṭ* often in the *pi'el* + *nefeš*.
[28] This use of *pānīm* as a key-word and its meaning have been clearly pointed to by Rosenzweig, p. 253 of Buber and Rosenzweig, op. cit.

himself had not yet fulfilled the prerequisite of looking his brother directly in the eye. The selfishness of his *minḥā* approach, his inner division, the desire to hide in the rear were still with him.

Now the Penuel scene transports him to another state of mind, another mentality which enables him to approach Esau in the only correct way, as we shall see in Gen. 33. This is what Jacob now realizes and he thanks God for it with a name-giving which is a consecration.

The passages from Exodus and Isaiah tell us that Jacob has experienced the greatest moment of his life, indeed, a revolution, when seeing God. It was a direct revelation that took place at Penuel,[29] although God did not deliver himself up, did not reveal his Name, and we can now surmise that the darkness of the night had a protective function, to shield Jacob from the blinding (cf. Ex. 24.15f.) radiation of God's glory.[30] In the night God dimmed his lustre to lend it to the sun for this day, v. 32. But in dimming his radiance he manifested himself, even in physical contact.

Jacob has seen. The God of Abraham and Isaac, who at the end of the Haran-period proved himself to be the God of Jacob too, has not failed him in his longest night, his most critical hour. Jacob has now been delivered because his God has sovereignly lent him a new identity, that of "Israel". God has purified him from the high-handed "Jacob" policy which eventually had jeopardized his life, and he has not withheld the blessing from him.

Quickly and with precision this scene ends in a movement. Jacob rejoins his people by passing Penuel. Thus the story is enframed by *'br*. The verses 23 and 24, with their repetition, have prepared us for this perfect conclusion and have justly emphasized the passage. Jacob's passage is decisive – as will appear in Gen. 33.

But there is something more important and therefore his passing is put into a subordinate clause (*ka'ašer* ...). In this way the emphasis is on "the sun shone upon him". The natural happenings have been taken into the service of the "inner" happenings. The sun, which at Haran had been burning, has received the lustre of God's glory and is shining upon him. The cosmos has changed: it smiles at him, promises security and warmth after the almost sinister night, with its frightening setting. The sun symbolizes salvation, deliverance, as in

[29] Not in a dream, for the first time.

[30] Jacob "drew near to the darkness where God was", Ex. 20.21!

Gen. 19.[31] The nights of Bethel and Haran have been replaced by the glorious day of the "Face of God", Penuel.

The text is admirably directed to the essential (29, 31). We note this, for example, in the fact that the story chooses not to mention, a) that Jacob lets go (*šlḥ*) of the fighter and b) that or how the adversary disappeared. In this way the line from blessing via *pānīm* and deliverance can lead, without interruption, to shining and passing.

In cauda venenum. Jacob crosses the Jabbok as Israel, but how! With a limp! Once more we shudder, for the struggle has left its traces and Jacob is a marked man.

The ending is most ambiguous: Jacob passes as a delivered man, but is lame. Looking back we see that the entire event has been imbued with ambiguity. The adversary's identity, the issue of the struggle, the "striving" in v. 29, the asking for one another's names: all these elements can be and must be looked at from two sides.

The Penuel scene is a high point in the ambivalences of Gen. 32, but also the final point. At Penuel the die is cast and the balancing between good and evil, light and dark shifts finally towards the positive side:

- from the night to the glorious day,
- from passing (or making others pass) in distress to passing in relief,
- from prayer for deliverance to deliverance,
- from deceit and self-deceit (32.21f.) to the confrontation eye-in-eye
- and from Jacob to Israel.

The old Adam has been shaken off, "Jakob" stays behind on one bank of the river. A new man, steeled and marked, Israel, has developed and he continues the journey on the other bank. The completely renewed, purified relationship with God makes a renewed, authentic relationship with his "brother" possible. In the third, but finally decisive instance light is shed back upon the prelude at Mahanaim: the angels were a favourable omen as heralds of God after all, the two camps were those of God and of Jacob and their opposition has found its synthesis in the permanent confrontation "Israel". Israel will always strive with God, proudly and obstinately as His high-handed first-born, and God will admit defeat and recognize and accept Israel. God will continue fighting for Israel and be the only one to bring about

[31] *Šḥr* does not occur anywhere else in the Torah. Sequence of 19.23 just as in 32.32: first the sun.

deeds of deliverance for them: welōhīm malkī miqqedem, pō'el yešū'ōt beqereb hā'āreṣ (Ps. 74.12).

§ 15 Scene 13: *Jacob meets Esau,* Gen. 33.

Jacob's meeting with Esau has not been accomplished easily or quickly! After the third phase, however, on the Jabbok, the time for this meeting has suddenly come. The situation is ripe for meaningful communication after the purification at Penuel, and the story does not tarry. In Gen. 33.1 the contact follows at once.

For two verses the narrator throws dust in our eyes, by making 33.1-2 run strikingly parallel to 32.7b, 8, 18, 20. Again Jacob forms a procession in which important people come behind less important people. Again there is the distinction between those in the front (*rīšōn*) and those in the rear (*'aḥarōn*). Again Jacob "divides". Has he become afraid? It looks like it! For in v. 1 he confronts the sight that made his knees give way in 32.8, "Esau ... and four hundred men with him" – at that time only a report.

Then, in a surprising way, our fears of Jacob's backsliding are put to an end; the inversion with the subject in v. 3a is striking, *wehū 'ābar lifnēhem,* "but he himself went on before them (their faces)". Jacob has radically changed since he made other people pass on before him (32.17). With this brilliant use of the key-words *'br* and *lifnē* we see that Jacob has accepted his personal responsibility and now goes on before them. These two words draw attention to the fact that in this "outward" action the radical change wrought at Penuel is manifested.

"And he bowed himself to the ground, seven times, when he had come near his brother". Here, too, the *Leitwortstil* teaches us how to take in the full meaning of this action by linking up *hištaḥawā* (and "brother") with the blessing of father Isaac; 27.29 said "be lord over your brothers, and may your mother's sons bow down to you."

Now we understand that readily and of his own free will Jacob acts counter to the blessing, which he had stolen from his brother, deliberately releases his hold on the destiny he had taken from Esau. The lord makes himself a servant by complete (7 × !) subjection, his face down in the dust. On the Jabbok the Jacob-line has been called to a halt; the first evidence of this is given in 33.3.

Esau must have felt that his brother, who is now on his knees and who used to be such a ruthless deceiver, had radically changed. Of Esau's intentions we have quite rightly heard nothing, for precisely in this way, silent and with unknown intentions, he was the factor most active in Gen. 32 – an unfathomable threat in the distance, which brought the highest pressure to bear upon Jacob.

The reality of Gen. 33 turns out to be quite different from the many pictures Jacob had formed in his mind. In Gen. 32, Jacob had, in fact, been purely concerned with a projected image of Esau, for the greater part impressed upon him by his own bad conscience, and he had exhausted himself in thinking of means to deal with the Esau of his image, never suspecting that the projected image might change along with his plans.

33.4ff. The real Esau is not rancorous as Jacob had imagined. He is not eaten up with revengeful feelings as Jacob himself would be, had he been the first-born and had Esau deceived him. It is time Jacob got to know his brother for what he is, this brother whom he had always considered a mere obstacle, an object for manipulations. Esau is completely open and he gives Jacob a hearty welcome which reminds one of Gen. 29.11, 13. Instead of defeating him and slaying one and all (32.12) he embraces and kisses his brother.

33.5-7 is strongly parallel to vv. 1-2, and indicates the meaning of it. The division of the train into groups leads to a solemn procession, the scrupulous organization of which reaches its high-water mark in one row of prostrations after another. The literary composition is shaped as stiffly and militarily as Jacob's direction:

6	wattiggašnā ...	wattištaḥ^{a}wẹnā
7	wattiggaš	wayyištaḥ^{a}wū
8	niggaš	wayyištaḥ^{a}wū

In 7b the positions of Joseph (before the mother!) and Rachel have clearly been presented as a climax.

Thus the plurals of 27.29 show to full advantage in this antipole. Esau is now "lord over his brothers" (i.e., relatives), "his mother's sons bow down before him".

The text shows how the brothers look at each other:

v. 1 wayyissā Ya'^{a}qob 'ēnāw wayyar w^{e}hinnē
v. 5 wayyissā (Esau) 'ēnāw wayyar 'et...

We see Jacob determined and relieved after the experience at Penuel, Esau full of surprise and emotion at the reunion. He asks for an explanation (v. 5), for although the detailed instructions of 32,18f.

have certainly been observed, Esau can hardly believe his eyes and he wants to hear the truth about "the present" from Jacob himself, v.8.

The choice of words in Esau's question in 33.8 is very particular, most calculating and ironic of the narrator. For Esau does not ask, what do you mean by all this *minḥā* of yours? – which would have suited Jacob's plan of 32.14-22 much better. No, he asks, "what is to you / what do you mean by all this *maḥ^{a}nẹ* (sic!) which I met (*pgš*, cf. 32.18!)?"

There is a shock for Jacob! Here for the last time, as an offshoot of Gen. 32.2ff., we find the key-word *mḥnh*; certainly it reverberates in Jacob's conscience, only yesterday a bad conscience. Whether Esau teases him on purpose or is unsuspecting of Jacob's distress in Gen. 32 cannot be ascertained. The story is not interested in the questioner but in the man addressed and in the effect of the question on him (just as in 29.25f!).

As in 32.2-6 Jacob follows up the embarrassing "army" with a request for mercy:

32.6 ... l^{e}haggīd ladōnī limṣō ḥen b^{e}ʿēnẹkā
33.8 limṣō ḥen b^{e}ʿēnẹkā

But what a tremendous difference between the two members of this parallel! "Army" and "Double-army" in Gen. 32 caused fear and distress but now they have disappeared. Via his messengers Jacob asked "to find favour in the sight of his lord", but there was no authentic sense of guilt; it was sheer duplicity. Now the ambivalence has been taken away in the clear light of the face-to-face contact. What Jacob says in 33.5, 8 (I am "your servant" / you are "my lord") and showed in 33.3 is sincere and now, at last, they are his own words. Coming to the front he has put his fate in his brother's hands.

He hopes that Esau, following in the footsteps of God, may be merciful to him. The words *ḥānan*, 33.5b, and *ḥen*, v. 8, are the first explicit connection in this story putting the relationship with Esau on a level with the relationship to God.

The brothers' dialogue (vv. 8-11) takes us to the core of the story. Stylistically we have now come to the core. Almost all the great key-words of the Story of Jacob, esp. those of Gen. 32, follow one another in a chain-reaction set free by those used before, *ʿābar, lifnē, ḥen, maḥ^{a}nẹ,* *hištaḥ^{a}wā*. They appear in a concentric order, and thus we have also come to the core structurally:[32]

A	yeš lī rab 'āḥī; y^{e}hī l^{e}kā '^{a}šer lāk	v. 9
B	'im-nā māṣātī ḥen b^{e}'ēnẹkā	10a
C	w^{e}lāqaḥtā *minḥātī* miyyādī	10a
D	kī 'al ken rā'ītī pānẹkā	10b
D'	kir'ōt p^{e}nē '^{e}lōhīm, wattirṣenī	10b
C'	qaḥ-nā 'et *birkātī*	11aα
B'	kī ḥannanī '^{e}lōhīm	11aα
A'	w^{e}kī yeš lī kol	11aβ

The core of the story is a speech by Jacob (three sentences) containing all the key-words, which reveals the kernel of his history. Esau speaks one sentence; he kindly says that he does not want a present, he has so much already (A). Jacob parries (A') by saying, but I have more, I have everything! He accounts for his wealth of cattle by pointing to God's mercy, B', just as he had said, speaking about his children, "God has dealt graciously with me" (v. 5b).

This structure, too, draws a parallel between the positions of Esau and God. In B Jacob insists on his brother being (remaining, as a continuation of v. 4) merciful to him, and by means of the ring B-B' this structure elucidates: just like God, who has set the example.

The syntactic connection between B and C and between C' and B' indicates that Esau's mercifulness, *ḥen*, must show itself in the acceptance of Jacob's present, *minḥā*. If Esau accepts it then Jacob knows for sure that the reconciliation has been accomplished. But it is not the servant who will decide on this, but his lord, Esau.

We have come close to the gist of the nucleus, D-D'. There is the key-word again which may be called the most shining of them all. There Esau's behaviour is definitively coupled with God's behaviour. The meeting with Esau lies in a single perspective with the meeting with God.

"To see your face is like seeing the face of God – with such favour have you received me." Jacob asks Esau to confirm the forgiveness

[32] In translation: A) I have much, my brother; keep what is yours. B) that I may find favour in your sight: C) accept my present from my hand; D) therefore, because I have seen your face D') like seeing the face of God, and you have received me with favour. C') do accept my blessing, B') for God has dealt graciously with me, A') for I have everything.

implied in v. 4 by accepting his present. V. 10b states the reason why Jacob dares to ask him: now Esau is to him like God. Esau is lord of the servant Jacob, as God is. Esau is the wronged and critical authority which alone, by his mercy, can absolve Jacob's guilt and which can lend a new integrity to Jacob. If he grants this mercy, this will confirm the renewal of Jacob on the Jabbok at Penuel. A purified relationship to God necessarily goes with a purified relationship to his fellow-man; Jacob has spoilt and broken the relationship to God by spoiling the relationship with Esau. He had wanted to achieve the destiny assigned to him by God, but his deception of Esau had impeded this.

By his actions Jacob admits to all this, as has become visible in his seven-fold prostration. He now also admits to this in so many words; the narrator introduces a variant in the strict parallelism C-C′, where *minḥātī* is changed into *birkātī* as if by magic, with a rhyme.[33] Jacob's present is a "blessing"! Jacob, who once stole the blessing from Esau with complete self-assurance, now tries to make up for this, as far as possible, by returning a blessing. Now we understand even better why he does insist on Esau's accepting it.

"I have seen your face (...) and you have been merciful to me" (*wattirṣenī*) shows the same order of testimony plus conclusion-in-one-word as the high point of the previous scene, "I have seen God face to face and my life has been delivered." The parallelism proves that in D-D′ Jacob once more describes his deliverance which is from God-and-Esau in one. In 32.31b he knew that his prayer ("deliver me") has been answered, in 33.10b he knows how the answering has been realized. Quite differently from what he had imagined before the Jabbok-scene, certainly. The four hemistichs of 32.21 are to be characterized in two phases:

– (first)	a) cover up his face b) the present going on before me	reconciliation
– "and afterwards"	a) I shall see his face b) perhaps he will lift up my face	forgiveness

[33] Pointed to but not completely exploited by Buber (op. cit., p. 226) and H. Frey (comm. ad loc.); and de Liagre Böhl, op. cit., p. 25.

Things worked out just the other way around! First Jacob has, by going to the front, seen Esau, and Esau has "lifted up" Jacob's face from the dust, i.e. pardoned him (v. 4). Only after that does the discussion about the present (sent on before) take place. That is to say that free and *sans rancune* Esau has pardoned Jacob already before he has, under great pressure from his brother, received the present. To put this more strongly, while the *maḥ*^{a}*nẹ̄*-line has been broken off and replaced by the *ḥen*-line, the *minḥā*-thread is changed into a *b*^{e}*rākā*-thread by being interwoven with the *ḥen*-line. So Esau does not even receive a present – that would indeed be buying him off – but he receives a blessing, and he has a right to it. Materially this blessing is only small compensation for the damage done to him, but the reason for joy is the change in Jacob, his renunciation of deceit and violence for the sake of the blessing.

After accepting the "blessing" Esau first offers to accompany Jacob himself while later he offers an escort by some of his men. Both offers are turned down by Jacob. Thus two dialogues follow the kernel:

- v. 12 (Esau) + 13, 14 (Jacob)
- v. 15a (Esau) + 15b (Jacob)

The first argument which Jacob uses (vv. 13, 14) is an objective one, easily tested and not to be disproved; for one moment we share the shepherd's anxieties, as v. 13 is taken from life. In 15b instead of arguing he once more appeals to Esau's mercy, and gets his way easily. The lives of a shepherd and a hunter are so different and of such differing tempos; they do not proceed together.

Around the nucleus of the ABCD-DCBA structure there are two more parts, X and X′, the mirror-images of each other. The beginning of v. 3 with its revelation that Jacob goes on ahead, finds a correlative in the dialogue 12-15:

X	w^{e}hū ʿābar	lifnēhem		v.3 beginning
X′	yaʿ^{a}bor-nā ʾ^{a}dōnī	lifnē	ʿabdō	14a

Jacob now wants Esau to go on before him, like a lord before his servant. This is the keystone of the key-words used, and what Jacob asks is to him the keystone of the reconciliation and forgiveness. From Esau's compliance he gathers that he has found real mercy (15b *ḥen b*^{e}*ʿēnē ʾ*^{a}*dōnī*). Yet the question keeps bothering us: why does not Jacob want any escort? He gives the impression of being not quite open with Esau, nor free of fear of him.

The narrator's purpose, however, offers a satisfactory explanation. Jacob is not "Jacob" anymore, but Israel. At the end of ch. 33 the narrator proceeds to his last subject, how the patriarch enters and takes possession of the Promised Land.

Let us imagine the situation: the narrator is an Israelite, the members of his audience are Israelites. They live in the country given to them by God, "Israel", and now, repeating the sacred past together, they are concerned with its origin, the patriarch "Israel". Therefore it is better for Esau and Jacob to separate. For Esau "is" Edom – a neighbouring people, a neighbouring country to the narrator and his audience.

He leaves the stage (v. 16) somewhat as Laban – who was also a source of concern to Jacob – did, and again there is an inversion:

32.1,2a	wayyāšob Lābān limqōmō	w^{e}Ya‘^{a}qob hālak l^{e}darkō
33.16,17a	wayyāšob ‘Esāw l^{e}darkō se‘īrā	w^{e}Ya‘^{a}qob nāsa‘ ...

Two chapters were a function of the meeting with Esau; now they have been rounded off by a clear frame. This frame is significant. In 33.16f. a definite answer is given to the question raised in 32.2a, namely, is this way of Jacob's also the way God and he talked about at Bethel? Is this entry his "return" under God's "guard", is it a "way *b^{e}šālōm*"? Immediately after this question – which had been evoked by other connections with the Bethel-scene – suspense was heightened and everything seemed lost, as for example in 32. 11. In Gen. 33 at last, after much distress, the story makes a turn for the better and the entire ending of 33.16-20 tells us explicitly that the promise of Bethel has now been definitively fulfilled. V. 16 starts with this explicit lesson, by using the words *šūb* and *derek*, just as in 32.1f. This means that there is now no doubt of Jacob's safe "return on his way", now that both Laban and Esau have returned on their ways. V. 17 illustrates Jacob's security in a different way. The protection from "Succoth" is meant for Jacob and his property, and the name-giving of this place, Jacob's fourth, is the antipole of the third one, the numinous, ambivalent "Double-army". In v. 18 another thread, running from Bethel, is cast off most ingeniously:

wayyābō Ya‘^{a}qob šālem ‘īr Š^{e}kem.

At Bethel, when he made the vow, Jacob himself had added the word *b^{e}šālōm* to his quotation of God's promise, 28.21a, ... shall I return in peace? In 33.18 the answer is, yes, in peace he has now arrived at the Cisjordanian!

After the reference of Gen. 33 to 28.20b ("the way that I go") and 28.21a ("I come again in peace") the question is raised, will 28.21b, the important conclusion of Jacob's long protasis, be resumed in Gen. 33? 28.21b was concerned with the question of whether the God of Abraham and Isaac would also make himself the God of Jacob. In 31.42a Jacob had already said: in the first instance, viz. at Haran, whole-heartedly yes! Now, in Canaan, now that all problems have been solved, now that the new Jacob has reconciled himself with his brother and has crossed the river Jordan in peace, he speaks another whole-hearted yes, he puts down an altar and calls it "God/El (is) the God of Israel".

A glorious testimony in which he, a man reborn, uses his new name. A testimony that draws wide circles! With the name "Israel" the narrator makes himself and his audience partners in the hallowing of Israel, and a party to the history of salvation, the first milestone of which has been set up by the patriarch himself. Thus the narrator drags his audience into the story, the text incorporates them. He appeals to them/us to continue this history "Israel-like" ourselves.

Jacob has taken care to found this most "Israelitic" altar on the first really Israelitic ground, by clearing the ground of any possible Canaanite iniquity, Canaanite atmosphere. He has bought the land officially and by that deed made the land of Canaan his own, *pars pro toto*, for it is the Promised Land. In this he follows father Abraham's example, who had acquired the field and the cave of Machpelah as his property.

Just how free he feels the peculiar v. 18b seems to indicate. Is it defiant, what Jacob does? "He camped before the city", *wayyiḥan 'et pᵉnē hā'īr* – in any case a great contrast to the distress of his camp in 32.2ff. Besides the well-known *ḥānā/maḥᵃnę̄* we also find *pānīm* once more. How intriguing! Does this mean that frankly and freely he looks into the eyes of the Canaanites (*in casu* the Hemorites)?

Retrospective view of Gen. 32 and 33.

However much the conclusion, 33.16-20, may integrate the return to Canaan into the whole of the Story of Jacob, it consists of three or four rather stray travel-notes. Now that the tensions have disappeared and the conflict in Jacob's life has come to an end, the narrator loosens his grip; the story loses the almost hermetic perfection which has struck us up till now.

It is worth taking a retrospective view of the Penuel-scene after Gen. 33. Between the preparations (32.1-22) and the meeting itself (Gen. 33) this scene assumes a pivotal position. The *Leitwortstil* integrates the passage both forwards and backwards. In this middle position God comes into the relation Jacob-Esau. Again he is Saviour, but now in an entirely new and special way. In Gen. 29-31, the second period of Jacob's life, he was also Saviour, but quite differently.

In the Haran-period there was a triangle, Jacob-Laban-God. God intervened when the relation Jacob-Laban had been broken. He intervened in behalf of one party, Jacob, by stopping the other one. God made his stand against Laban because he had come to deceive, exploit Jacob. The triangle disappears with the breaking-up of the two men.

In the third period, Gen. 32-33, there is a triangle, Jacob-Esau-God. The relationship between the brothers, however, had been broken as early as the first period, Gen. 25-28, because Jacob had deceived Esau. Now, too, God intervenes. Of course he does not take a stand against Esau, but not quite against Jacob either. He does not eliminate Jacob from the triangle but, to the contrary, God heals the triangle by healing the relation Jacob-Esau. His intervention is salvation. It changes Jacob into Israel; the blessed one predestined to be ruler becomes the servant who returns the blessing. When his inner division (32.21f.) has been purified to integrity, God withdraws. From now on the restoration of a good relationship is Jacob's task and the work of Jacob and Esau together, (Gen. 33). The straight line from Jacob to Esau had become blocked, and Jacob can only find his brother by making a detour in the triangle via God's angle.

§ 16 Scene 14: *Bethel revisited, home-coming*, Gen. 35.1-15.

The Jacobitish drama has emerged with a surprising Israelitic outcome; now that the tensions have disappeared the way to the gratification of God and human dignity lies open. The God of Abraham and Isaac has shown himself to be the God of Jacob, too.

With that God's promise of 28.15 has been fulfilled, and this means that the five-fold condition of Jacob's vow has been fulfilled. Now it is his turn to offer something in return. The main clause of his vow must now be realized. Thus the circle of salvation initiated by God at Bethel will be closed by Jacob in that place, too.

Because the conflicts have disappeared, the *"Deutungsbedürftigkeit"* immediately diminishes to a great extent, and in fact Gen. 35 can be left to tell its own story. Yet many interesting observations remain to be made. We shall touch on them lightly.

Jacob's second visit to Bethel is narrated in two arcs. The first one is to be found in 35.1-7, clearly rounded off with a frame which in v. 7 completes the action ordered in v. 1:

1 ʿ^{a}sē šām mizbe^{a}ḥ lā'el hannir'ẹ 'ēlẹkā b^{e}borḥ^{a}kā mipp^{e}nē ʿEsaw 'āḥīkā
7 wayyiben šām mizbe^{a}ḥ .. 'el .. niglū 'elaw hā'elōhīm b^{e}borḥō mipp^{e}nē 'āḥīw

Again we hear the key-word *pānīm*, and we realize that it could characterize Gen. 27 and 28: Jacob's deceit had made it impossible for him to bear the sight of Esau, he could not look him in the face anymore. At the same time we now observe that in Gen. 27 and 28 (the flight) the phrase, "from the sight of", words that are used in 35, has been avoided. The key-word was to be exclusively ıeserved for the dénouement in Gen. 32f.

This objective reference to the past in v. 1 and 7 is resumed and significantly varied by Jacob in the words to his people, v. 3. After he has strictly taken up "qūm ʿ^{a}lē Bēt-'el" from v. 1 in "nāqūmā w^{e}naʿ^{a}lẹ Bēt-'el" he says:

'eʿ^{e}sẹ šām mizbe^{a}ḥ lā'el hāʿōnẹ 'ōtī b^{e}yōm ṣārātī wayhī ʿimmādī badderek '^{a}šer hālaktī

That is the tone of the thankful believer. The subjective rendering of his past is put in poetry, again in the vocabulary of a penitential psalm ending in a word of thanks to the Saviour: "who answered me in the days of my distress". Then Jacob quotes the identical words from the Bethel-scene of Gen. 28 in order to emphasize the fulfilment: "He has been with me on the way that I have gone". The attention we paid to "way" and "go" in 32.2 and 33.17 proves to be justified.

Jacob does not go to Bethel until God himself has ordered him to go. He reacts with an adequate attitude of faith, for his journey is to be a pilgrimage. Therefore he orders the whole household to "purify yourselves and change your garments", such actions as, for example, the Muslim performs when entering the *ḥaram* of Mekkah as a *ḥadji*.

But in the first place there is the purification of the relationship Jacob-God. Now that this relationship has been settled it may no longer be clouded by the presence of *terafim* and other foreign gods. The household gods from Haran and their like, degraded as they are by Rachel's saving "menstruation", are now definitively humiliated because they must be put under ground. Jacob hides them, conceals them like a miscarriage...; their spontaneous abortion had started as far back as 31.34f.[34]

V. 5: God, functioning as "Fear of Isaac", escorts Jacob. He protects his passage; the surprise of the Canaanites all around at the disturbing stranger with his pretentious claims and their envy of his riches cannot harm Jacob. But their anger is especially kindled by Jacob's complete disrespect for their gods. The real God, the living God, however, paralyzes the opposition.[35] V. 6 is the solemn arrival. Its formality appears from the fact that visitors and place are mentioned in full, with three quarters of this sentence consisting of appositions! In a sacral cry, "'El bēt 'el", Jacob dedicates the place once more and now definitively to its destiny: House of God, not Luz.

The ending of paragraph A reflected the beginning (v. 1b). The beginning of paragraph B (vv. 9-15) runs parallel. On the journey out God had "showed himself"; now that Jacob returns from Paddan-Aram "God shows himself once more." After twenty years the circle is closed. After the first theophany in Gen. 28 the second follows symmetrically in this verse.

The topical part of God's promise, 28.15, has been realized with Jacob's return to Bethel. In this second theophany God confirms the other, less immediate purpose: the promises of land (35.12) and offspring (35.11).[36] In 28.13 and 14 they were in the reverse order.

The *Sternstunde* of Jacob's life, his "rebirth" at Penuel, was the decisive moment in the realization of God's promise to be Jacob's

[34] The verb *ṭmn*, used in 35.4, is actually used in connection with a miscarriage in Job 3.16 (cf. 40.13).

[35] In the Genesis text as final product Gen. 34 also counts: Jacob has to fear the revenge of the Canaanites after the Sichem-Dinah affair.

[36] Eising, p. 128f (quoted by me, supra p. 217f.), is convincing when he maintains that the blessing given by God in 32.30 contained the promises of land and offspring, and that these could not be put down explicitly in the Jabbok-scene. Next to this "Penuel-ratio" we may now add the positive "Bethel-ratio": the explicit promises may only be sounded at their ultimate confirmation, which "may" only take place at Bethel.

protector. The Penuel scene had become the correlative to the Bethel-scene. That is why God first (35.10) confirms the basis on which Jacob's future is to be founded, i.e., to be his new identity, "Israel".

In the first theophany God had made a chiastic link with the blessing of old, the leave-taking of Isaac in 28.3, 4. Now in the second theophany at Bethel he announces the fulfilment of Isaac's wish. Verse 35.11 is linked very closely with 28.3, by a number of connections, including the epitheton El Shadday:

28.3 'el šadday ...	yafr^{e}ka	w^{e}yarbekā	w^{e}hāyītā liqhal	'ammīm
35.11 '^{a}nī 'el šadday:	p^{e}rē	ur^{e}bē	uq^{e}hal gōyīm yihyẹ	mimmekkā

Only this passage confirms that 28.3 is a sentence linking up finally with 28.2, "in order that El Shadday may bless you." The "blessing of Abraham" of 28.4 is picked up by God in 35.12 with the same *casus pendens* as in 28.13.

God's words to Jacob in 28.13ff. had not been called a "blessing". In 32.30 he does give a blessing, but the contents are not mentioned; but now Isaac's wish of 28.3a has been fulfilled explicitly and definitively. What strikes us is what God does not confirm: the blessing to the first-born. The blessing of Isaac has, symbolically, been returned to Esau in 33.11. For Jacob has forfeited his destiny as ruler. It disappears behind the traditional promises of land and offspring.

Jacob completes the symmetry with Gen. 28 by setting up the/a massebe once again, by pouring oil on it and by regauging the place-name of Bethel. A whole sentence recurs as a kind of refrain:

13 then God went up from him in the place where he had spoken with him
14 and Jacob set up a pillar in the place where he had spoken with him
15 so Jacob called the name of the place where God had spoken with him Bethel

Does this three-fold repetition reflect the three distinct oracles of vv. 10, 11 and 12? Anyhow, 13-15 make a monumental conclusion to the last revelation befalling Jacob. This set of three is echoed in Hosea (12.5), where, in his special way, the prophet says what our text, too,signified to the narrator and his audience: the theophany to the patriarch is one of the most significant roots of the history of salvation. "At Bethel He found *us*" – in the patriarch the prophet envisages the people; "at Bethel he spoke with us" – in the patriaıch God also speaks to the people.[37]

§ 17 *Final notes*, Gen. 35.16-29.

The composition of Gen. 35 is no longer compelling. After the extended and well sustained *"Hintergründigkeit"* (up to and including Gen. 33) 35.1-15 strikes us as a trifle too easy, as a somewhat too artificial reference to the Penuel- and Bethel-scenes. Little remains to be guessed; too little is left to the reader's imagination and effort. The Story of Jacob shows a somewhat fragmented ending. Two short notes have been inserted which we might just take for granted, v. 8 and v. 22a.[38]

After the last Bethel-scene there is a short, life-like scene (16-21) which might have been a fitting bead on the string of 29.30-30.24. As it is, this birth-story is, within the whole of the composition, a correlative to Rebekah's troublesome pregnancy in Gen. 25. We now see how real the death-agony of Rachel's mother-in-law was. Here things go wrong: in a complementary part, which strikes us (but not the contemporary audience) as cruel, two etymologies are also connected with the second son of the favourite, as with Joseph. "Ben Oni" is the "son of my sorrow". With an inversion Benjamin is placed opposite this.

"Kings will spring from you", this promise (v. 11b) is first realized already shortly after Bethel. For the narrator's audience was aware of the fact that the first king of united Israel sprang from Benjamin. But he, Saul, too, went down as a "Ben On".

Close to Bethlehem Rachel was buried, so close to the place where the second king came from who was to found a lasting dynasty, David. This sorrowful moment is rounded off by verses about the journey (16a,21) which surround it like a frame. But first Jacob had erected a monument as he alone, a conjurer with stones, could do. After Bethel (positively) and Gilead (neutrally, as an armistice) now the turn has come for Ephratah, as a third point, to receive a massebe - negatively,

[37] The last word of Hos. 12.5 should not be emended. On the contrary, it is a feature of Hos. 12 that the nature and the valuation of the individual Israel and the people blend, as for example in Gen. 25.

[38] V. 8 is overbearing, we do not know what to do with it. Moreover, we feel inclined to change "Rebekah" into "Rachel". V. 22a prepares for the bitter anti-blessing of 49.4.

a sepulchral monument. Rachel is not to enjoy the pleasure of staying in Canaan and meeting Isaac and Rebekah.

23-26. The complete list of the twelve sons is drawn up; genealogies are the pride of many a Semite. Eventually Jacob reaches his starting-point, Hebron. V. 27 presents him as the third generation to live there as "foreigners", and completes the set of three, Abraham-Isaac-Jacob. Abraham's grandson living under the "blessing of Abraham" will rediscover Abraham's son in a real "place of Abraham", for Mamre/Hebron well deserves that name.

Another name for it is *Qiryat Hā'arba'*, "Town of the Four". Drawing associations with it we wonder: is this not the first time that the family-quartet is together after a long time? Just before Isaac's death, but also because of Isaac's death.

27-29. Now Isaac can die in peace, the great rupture in the family has been healed, his principal son has brought a cognate wife. He can die like Abraham in ch. 25, after his son had been united with Rebekah. The brothers Esau and Jacob are on good terms again when they lay him to rest. With Isaac's death Gen. 25-35 is completed in a frame with 25.19f. Around the Story of Jacob a narrow frame has been laid, the father's birth and death.

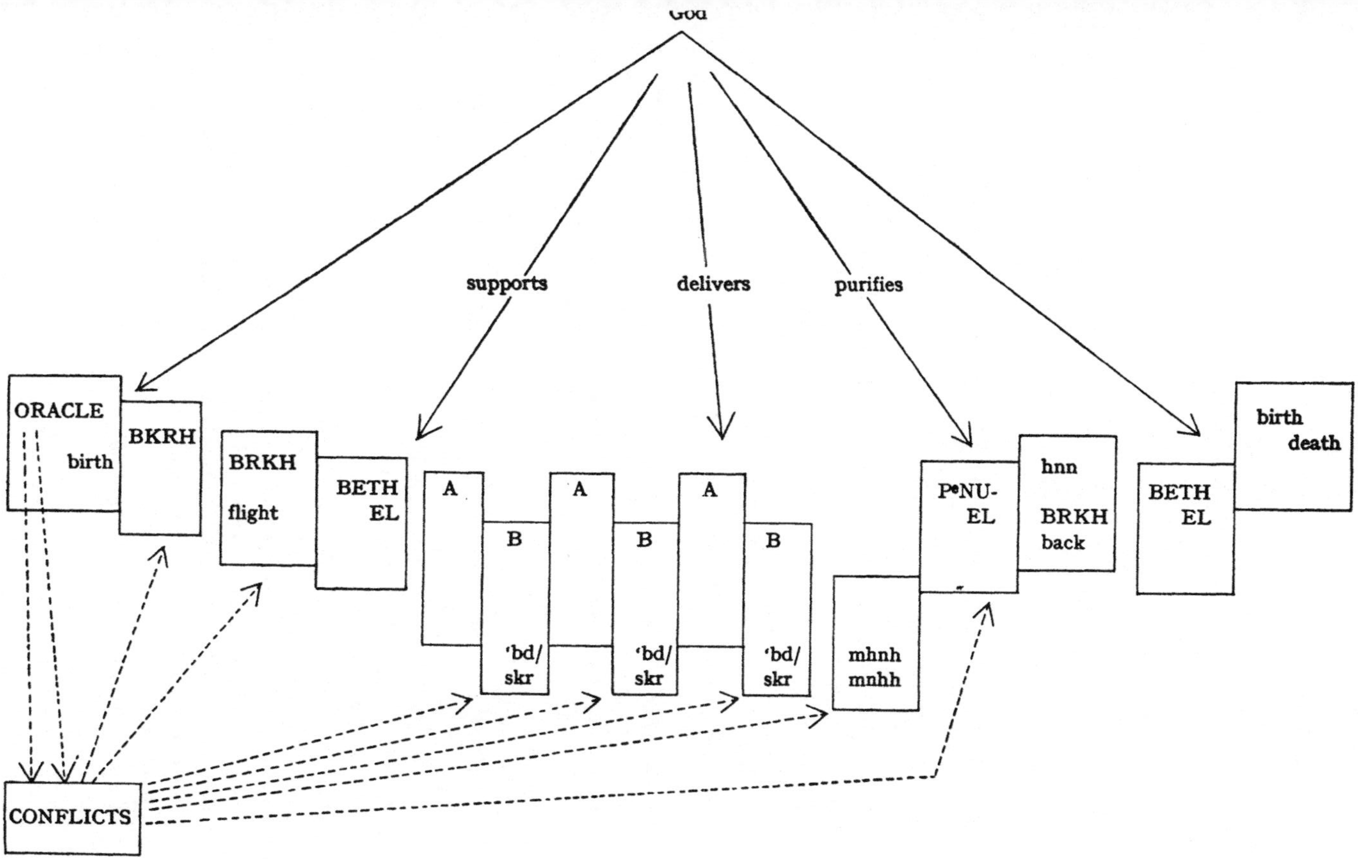
God
supports
delivers
purifies
ORACLE
birth
BKRH
BRKH
flight
BETH
EL
A
B
'bd/
skr
A
B
'bd/
skr
A
B
'bd/
skr
mhnh
mnhh
P•NU-
EL
hnn
BRKH
back
BETH
EL
birth
death
CONFLICTS

CONCLUSION

We have followed fifteen stories which are to be found in Gen. 25-35. The criterion we used to define our field of research was: in which story is Jacob the central character? But this means of selection cannot be used silently, for there is something arbitrary in it, as will have been noticed by the reader who observed that Gen. 26 has been treated summarily and 34 hardly at all, although these passages are well within the bounds of the Story of Jacob.

The absence of Gen. 26 and 34 does not impair the coherence of what has been dealt with, a coherence which has been visualized in the above diagram, but the interpretation of the Jacob-cycle now turns out to be incomplete. Therefore the cycle must be returned to its context, first of all the book of Genesis, and it must be clearly stated in which frameworks the cycle functions; in the scope of the present work these frameworks can only be touched upon but they must be dealt with exhaustively in a structural analysis of the whole of Genesis.

The analysis of "Jacob" has already indicated the direction into which we must now turn our research. At several points we have noticed that Jacob was not pictured as a private character, as an individual interesting in himself, but as a link in a chain; he is a member of the family to which the blessing of God has been given since Abraham. He is – God willing – an heir to that history-making continuity and with him the famous set of three in "the God of Abraham, Isaac and Jacob" is to be accomplished. More than once we pointed out that narrator and audience observe and follow the main character because they realize that he is their patriarch. More than once the character of Jacob displays national aspects, he is a corporate personality. Speaking in terms of genre, we are here dealing with a series of sagas in Genesis. Jolles' definition of the "*einfache Form*" saga is certainly elucidative for O.T. scholarship and has even been adopted unconditionally and gratefully by someone like Claus Westermann.[1] These sagas do not exclude, but include, the concept of history.[2] The stories about the patriarchs, which in ancient Israel no doubt functioned as authoritative texts (their canonization is by no means accidental) on the national history, are evidence of an elementary urge to occupy one's mind with one's own history. That these sagas as religious texts are samples of a most specific interpretation detracts nothing from the basic fact so characteristic of ancient Israel: viz. that, in its own opinion, it is both here and often elsewhere busy verbalizing its own history, transforming it in a religiously authorized way, inventing it, and repeating it.

So a first frame of references, in which the stories about Jacob belong as perfectly as those about Isaac and Dinah with her brothers, is that of Genesis as family-history which at the same time is national history. Thus it is easily understood that Genesis is larded with a kind of text that also answers a basic need (a common Semitic one), *tōledōt* and genealogies. Referring to Gen. 28.6-9 and also to Gen. 36 we may say that Esau is a loose end, but it must absolutely be added that Esau does belong – the texts are there, after all! He may have been counted out in regard to the first place in the family, but still a complete picture of this generation should be handed down to us. Not until then can the *tōledōt* of the next generation be discussed (Gen. 37.2a). So the bounds of the middle part of Genesis can be set more widely from *'ēllę tōlᵉdōt Yiṣḥāq* in 25.19 to *'ēllę tōlᵉdōt Ya'ᵃqob* in 37.2. Then they are made to include Esau, too, for he is and remains one of the "descendants of Isaac".

A second frame of reference in which Gen. 26 and 34 fit as perfectly as the fifteen stories dealt with tells more about the contents of that family-history and about its meaning. It is the blessing of God that sets this history going, starting with Abraham, and it is the blessing that from generation to generation ensures its continuation, so much so, that the "generating process" itself is only possible thanks to the blessing. All the matriarchs are barren and only because God "opens their wombs" *tōlᵉdōt* plural are made possible. Here, too, we mention the genealogies of Genesis, which are, as it were, a notarial act to demonstrate that the genealogical tree is rooted in God-blessed soil and branches richer and richer because of his blessing.

[1] See note 1 of Ch. III above.

[2] At the beginning of the chapters concerned Jolles makes the fundamentally important observation that the nature of myth, saga, legend, etc., can only be misunderstood if first of all it is privatively defined as non-historical.

Berākā is a theme, brought out at once after the so-called primeval history (Gen. 1-11) and with great force in 12.1-3, where Abraham receives his "vocation" from God.[3] Literarily it is strikingly articulated in Genesis because the prose is enriched and tied together by a strand of poetry. The blessing works in many ways (progeny, protection against foreigners and their king, property of cattle, finding wells, etc.), but the main expression of it is to be found in those lines of poetry, the promise to the patriarchs of the land of Canaan and of numerous offspring. In other words, not only in the realm of the denotatives, not only on the semantic level is the blessing important; it is also conspicuous within the signs of language which are subjected to a separate shaping, the discipline of poetic metre and diction.

The religious perspective in which Genesis puts the family-history also implies that the patriarchs may very often be agents in the foreground but that, for all that, God is the decisive agent. Always the decisive point is that *he* sends away, warns, saves and delivers with blessings. And in the matter of the blessing and concerning the decisive agent the cycle of stories about Jacob is part of a much larger whole. The second frame of reference, which enables us to integrate the stories about Jacob into Genesis and, moreover, to integrate Genesis into a still larger context, e.g. the Hexatauch, is that of the history of salvation.

What is, concretely speaking, the position of Gen. 26 and that of 34? Represented as squares they are symmetrically distributed in the diagram as we know it:

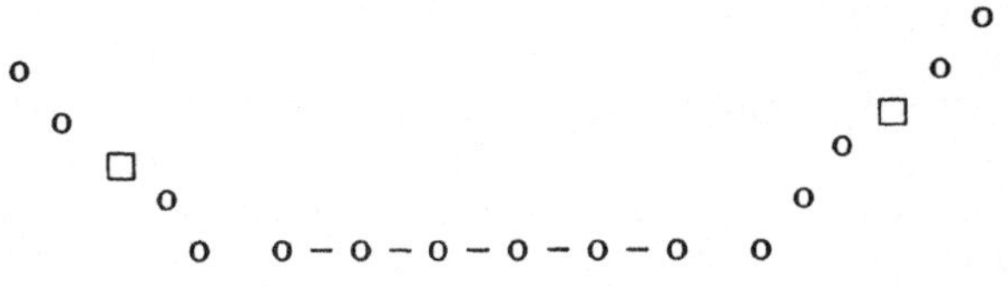

Both are exactly two scenes away from the boundaries! They have a lot in common, for that matter. Firstly, both passages are about people from other generations than Jacob's; in Gen. 26 his father Isaac is the main character (as an object of God's actions), in Gen. 34 his children are protagonists. Thus a precise concatenation of three

[3] H. W. Wolff, Das Kerygma des Jahwisten, 1964; published in Evangelische Theologie 24 pp. 73-98, and in Gesammelte Studien zum AT, pp. 345-373.

generations has come about, a good illustration of the scope of the family-history:

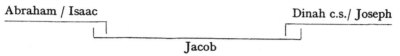

Abraham / Isaac — Dinah c.s./ Joseph

Jacob

Secondly, Gen. 26 and 34 – and they are not alone – make the contents of the "blessing of Abraham", viz. the promised land, thematic and they are similar in that they both show what a source of problems the land of Canaan is in itself, problems which, again, can only be overcome with the aid of God's protection and blessing. The land is by no means empty or ready to be taken over; it is inhabited by all kinds of people such as Philistines and Hemorites. The relations which Jacob and the children of Jacob respectively open with them are at least ambivalent and sometimes definitely unfavourable and threatening.

Near Sichem Jacob erects a stone, for the third time. Now he raises an altar to settle the bond Israel-Yahweh, on land which he had legitimately acquired (Gen. 33 ending; an elaborate parallel is Abraham's acquisition of land in Gen. 23). Precisely there he gets into troubles. The relations with the people of Sichem founders on the extremely important points of sexuality, relationship by marriage, and fertility. It is impossible for this God-blessed family to mix with a group of Canaanites; it would be like combining two chemical elements that do not go together (Gen. 34). God's intervention only can keep the relation to the country unimpaired (35.5). Opposed to the negation near Sichem God puts the positive sign of Bethel and the revelation in that place (Gen. 35). The subsequent consecration by Jacob and the erection of the massebe are final, they are not hit by a negation. Bethel, the gate of heaven, is the true means of entry to acquire the Promised Land.

Following Jacob so closely can easily involve too narrow a range of vision; in tracing the Story of Jacob we have not yet taken in account the broader perspective which is requisite to the integration of the Story of Jacob, together with Gen. 26, 34 and 36, into its context, viz. the book of Genesis as inner circle and the Hexateuch as outer circle. When seen at a distance, thus with a wider range of vision, we see that the texts appear to us in three perspectives; the themes of land and of family-history are a function of the even larger perspective that God's plan of salvation means to a chosen people on its way to a promised land.

CONCISE BIBLIOGRAPHY

This bibliography contains both those titles which I quoted frequently and those which are important from the point of view of literary scholarship. The reader who wishes to have a relatively complete survey of truly literary studies on the O.T. should consult

- the various series of titles, often with reviews, in Alonso, Estudios,
- the bibliographies at the end of Koch, Formgeschichte and Richter, Exegese.

I. *Literary scholarship, general part.*

Auerbach, Erich: Mimesis, dargestellte Wirklichkeit in der abendländischen Literatur, Bern, 1959 (2nd ed.)

Gadamer, H. G.: Wahrheit und Methode, Grundzüge einer philosophischen Hermeneutik, Tübingen, 1965 (2nd ed.)

Jolles, André: Einfache Formen, Tübingen, 1930 (= Darmstadt 1958)

Kayser, Wolfgang: Das sprachliche Kunstwerk, Bern, 1963 (9th ed.)

Lämmert, E.: Bauformen des Erzählens, Stuttgart, 1955.

Staiger, E.: Die Kunst der Interpretation, Zürich, 1955 (2nd ed.)

Todorov, Tzvetan: Grammaire du Décaméron, den Haag, 1969

Wellek, R. & Warren, A.: Theory of Literature, Peregrine Book, London, 1963 (3rd ed.)

II. *Literary Studies on the Old Testament.*

Alonso Schökel, Luis: Estudios de Poética Hebrea, Barcelona, 1963 (a German translation of Part II, Procedimientos, appeared in Köln, 1971)

idem: Erzählkunst im Buche der Richter, Biblica 42 (1961) pp. 143-172

idem: Die stilistische Analyse bei den Propheten, SVT vii (1959), pp. 154-164

idem: Motivos sapienciales y de alianza en Gn 2-3, Biblica 43 (1962) pp. 295-316

Buber, M. & Rosenzweig, Fr.: Die Schrift und ihre Verdeutschung, Berlin, 1936

Koch, Klaus: Was ist Formgeschichte? Neukirchen, 1967 (2nd ed.)

Richter, Wolfgang: Exegese als Literaturwissenschaft, Entwurf einer alttestamentlichen Literaturtheorie und Methodologie, Göttingen, 1971

Strauss, A. L.: בדרכי הספרות, Jerusalem, 1960.

Talmon, S.: דרכי הסיפור במקרא, Jerusalem, 1965 (3rd ed.)

Weiss, Meir: המקרא כדמותו, שיטת מחקר והסתכלות במקרא על פי עיקרי מדע הספרות החדש, Jerusalem, 1962

idem: Einiges über die Bauformen des Erzählens in der Bibel, VT xiii (1963) pp. 460ff.

III. *Other studies on the O.T.*

Boecker, Hans Jochen: Redeformen des Rechtslebens im AT, Neukirchen, 1964

Ehrlich, A. B.: Randglossen zur hebräischen Bibel, vol. I, Leipzig, 1908

Eising, H.: Formgeschichtliche Untersuchung zur Jakobserzählung der Genesis, Emsdetten, 1940

Frey, H.: Das Buch des Kampfes (= his comm. on Gen. 25-35), Stuttgart, 1938

Galbiati, E.: La Struttura letteraria dell'Esodo, Contributo allo studio dei criteri stilistici dell'A.T. e della composizione del Pentateucho, Alba, 1956

Granqvist, Hilma: Marriage Conditions in a Palestinian Village, 2 vols. Helsingfors, 1931/35

Gunkel, H.: Genesis, Handkommentar, 3rd ed. Göttingen, 1910

Jacob, Benno: Genesis, Berlin, 1934

Joüon, Paul: Grammaire de l'Hébreu biblique, Rome, 1947 (2nd ed.)

Lund, N. W.: Chiasmus in the New Testament, a Study in Formgeschichte, Chapel Hill, 1942 (pp. 51-138 deal with the O.T.!)

Pedersen, Johs.: Israel, its life and culture, 2 vols., Kopenhagen, 1926

von Rad, Gerhard: Theologie des AT, 2 vols., München, 1961 (3rd ed.)

idem: Genesis, Göttingen, 1953 (in the series das AT Deutsch); 9th ed. 1972

Speiser, E. A.: Genesis, the Anchor Bible, New York, 1964

Wehmeier, Gerhard: Der Segen im AT, eine semasiologische Untersuchung der Wurzel BRK, Basel, 1970

Westermann, Claus: Arten der Erzählung in der Genesis, = Ch. I of Forschung am AT, Gesammelte Studien, München, 1964.

Abbreviations used:

BL	=	H. Bauer and P. Leander, Historische Grammatik der hebräischen Sprache, Halle, 1922 (= Hildesheim 1965)
KBL	=	L. Köhler and W. Baumgartner, Lexicon in VT libros, 2nd ed. Leiden 1953; 3rd ed. (alef – ṭbḥ) Leiden, 1967
JPOS	=	Journal of the Palestine Oriental Society, Jerusalem
OTS	=	Oudtestamentische Studiën, Leiden
VT	=	Vetus Testamentum, Leiden
SVT	=	Supplements to VT, Leiden
(B)ZAW	=	(Beihefte zur) Zeitschrift für die alttestamentliche Wissenschaft

Concluding Words

What the reader should know is that the interpretations of texts in this book had been completed as early as 1971 and that the manuscript was closed in 1972. Its going to press was delayed mainly by problems of financing.

In the transcription of Hebrew I have not aimed at consistency. Neither layman nor expert would be in need of this.

I here wish to express my best thanks to Corrie; this work could only prosper under her sympathy with my studies.

A great debt of gratitude I owe to Puck Visser-Hagedoorn, who undertook the English translation. Her loyalty has been a great help to me.

J.P.F.

Printed in Great Britain
by Amazon

32146890R00145